# Dynamics of Virtual Work

Series Editors

Technological change has transformed where people work, when and how. Digitisation of information has altered labour processes out of all recognition whilst telecommunications have enabled jobs to be relocated globally. ICTs have also enabled the creation of entirely new types of 'digital' or 'virtual' labour, both paid and unpaid, shifting the borderline between 'play' and 'work' and creating new types of unpaid labour connected with the consumption and co-creation of goods and services. This affects private life as well as transforming the nature of work and people experience the impacts differently depending on their gender, their age, where they live and what work they do. Aspects of these changes have been studied separately by many different academic experts however up till now a cohesive overarching analytical framework has been lacking. Drawing on a major, high-profile COST Action (European Cooperation in Science and Technology) Dynamics of Virtual Work, this series will bring together leading international experts from a wide range of disciplines including political economy, labour sociology, economic geography, communications studies, technology, gender studies, social psychology, organisation studies, industrial relations and development studies to explore the transformation of work and labour in the Internet Age. The series will allow researchers to speak across disciplinary boundaries, national borders, theoretical and political vocabularies, and different languages to understand and make sense of contemporary transformations in work and social life more broadly. The book series will build on and extend this, offering a new, important and intellectually exciting intervention into debates about work and labour, social theory, digital culture, gender, class, globalisation and economic, social and political change.

More information about this series at
http://www.palgrave.com/gp/series/14954

Sabine Pfeiffer · Manuel Nicklich · Stefan Sauer
Editors

# The Agile Imperative

## Teams, Organizations and Society under Reconstruction?

palgrave
macmillan

*Editors*
Sabine Pfeiffer
Nuremberg Campus of Technology (NCT)
Friedrich-Alexander-Universität Erlangen-Nürnberg
Nuremberg, Germany

Manuel Nicklich
Nuremberg Campus of Technology (NCT)
Friedrich-Alexander-Universität Erlangen-Nürnberg
Nuremberg, Germany

Stefan Sauer
Nuremberg Campus of Technology (NCT)
Friedrich-Alexander-Universität Erlangen-Nürnberg
Nuremberg, Germany

Dynamics of Virtual Work
ISBN 978-3-030-73993-5 ISBN 978-3-030-73994-2 (eBook)
https://doi.org/10.1007/978-3-030-73994-2



This Palgrave Macmillan imprint is published by the registered company Springer Nature Switzerland AG
The registered company address is: Gewerbestrasse 11, 6330 Cham, Switzerland

# Acknowledgments

The editors received financial support for this publication in the context of the research project 'diGAP—Decent Agile Project Work in the digitised World' (ref. no. 02L15A306), jointly funded by the German Federal Ministry for Education and Research (BMBF) and the European Social Fund (ESF). Moreover, we would like to thank Romy Blinzler as well as the textworks for their support during the preparation of the manuscript.

# Contents

# Notes on Contributors

**Craig Anslow** is a Senior Lecturer in Software Engineering within the School of Engineering and Computer Science at Victoria University of Wellington, New Zealand, where he co-leads the Human Computer Interaction Research Group. Craig also teaches on the MSc in Software Engineering Programme within the Department of Computer Science at the University of Oxford, UK. Craig's research interests are human aspects of software development, visualization and digital health.

**Robert Biddle** is a Professor at Carleton University in Ottawa, Canada, appointed to both the School of Computer Science and the Institute of Cognitive Science. His research is primarily in human factors in cybersecurity and software design, especially creating and evaluating innovative designs for computer security software and collaborative software development.

**Takahiro Endo** is an Associate Professor of Organizational Analysis at Hitotsubashi University. He earned his Ph.D. at Cardiff Business School (UK). His research interest lies in long-term change and continuity of management practices such as "Japanese Management", which has witnessed a significant change in terms of the "meaning" attached to it, shifting from "best practice" to something else.

**Marion Flécher** is a Ph.D. candidate in Sociology at Paris Dauphine University, France. Based on interviews, observations and statistics, her research aims to study the world of start-up companies in a comparative approach between France and the United States.

**Masatoshi Fujiwara** is an Associate Professor of Strategic Management at Hitotsubashi University. His research interest lies in knowledge transfer and strategic management. One of his research projects includes long-term action research on a large Japanese manufacturer's business model innovation. He recently received the Economist Award for his co-authored book on the long-term evolution of water purification technology.

**Olivier Jegou** is a Ph.D. candidate in political sociology and a teaching assistant at the UCLouvain's School of Labour Studies in Belgium. He is a member of UCLouvain's Interdisciplinary Research Center on Work, State and Society (CIRTES) and the Institute for the Analysis of Change in Contemporary and Historical Societies (IACCHOS). Through workplace ethnographies, he studies the democratic potential of managerial doctrines, policies and practices promoting workers' autonomy.

**Martin Kropp** is a Professor for Software Engineering at the Institute of Mobile and Distributed Systems at the University of Applied Sciences and Arts Northwestern Switzerland. In the research group Efficient Software Development, he aims to develop concepts and tools to make software developers and software development teams more productive. His interests are in build automation, testing, refactoring and methodologies. His current focus is especially on agile methodologies and tools supporting agile teams in their daily work and their collaboration. He is a co-founder of the Swiss Agile Research Network, and a member of the management board of the Software Engineering Network.

**Andreas Meier** is a lecturer and researcher on software engineering at Zurich University of Applied Sciences. He teaches classes on programming and software engineering both on the Bachelor's and the Master's level. Additionally, he is involved in a start-up company in the software industry. His special interests are agile methodologies and their positive influence on innovation, team spirit and software systems. He is a co-founder of the Swiss Agile Research Network and introduced the Swiss Agile Study to deliver independent facts and figures to the interested public.

**Phoebe V. Moore** Associate Professor of the Future of Work, is based at the University of Leicester School of Business and is a Research Fellow at the Weizenbaum Institute, WZB Berlin. Dr. Moore has published three books and many articles on work, labour struggle and digitalization. Moore and her research have appeared in such prestigious outlets as the *Financial Times*, *Computerworld*, *Wired*, *Buzzfeed*, BBC Radio 4, BBC World Service and the *Atlantic*. She has been commissioned as an expert by the European Parliament Science and Technology Office, the European Union Agency for Safety and Health (EU-OSHA) and the International Labour Organization of the United Nations to highlight and identify the risks and benefits in digitalized workplaces today.

**Azuka Mordi** is a research associate at the Department of Information Systems I at the University of Hohenheim in Stuttgart, Germany. His work focuses on agility and information technology in organizations. He is currently working on the interaction between agility and software tools. Azuka received his M.Sc. in Industrial Engineering from the Berlin University of Technology. Prior to his career at the University of Hohenheim, he worked as a management consultant in the technology industry, especially in the field of project management and product development. He is a certified Scrum Master (CSM) and Project Management Professional (PMP), and holds a Six Sigma Green Belt.

**Andrea Müller** Professor for Human Capital Management at the ZHAW Zurich University of Applied Sciences, School of Management and Law, studied Psychology at the TU Dresden, doctorate at the University of Goettingen in social and business psychology, was a research associate at the German University of Administrative Sciences Speyer, after several years as a research consultant for industries. She has worked at the ZHAW since 2008 (main topics: organizational behaviour, leadership, human capital management).

**Gordon Müller-Seitz** is the Chair of Strategy, Innovation and Cooperation at the TU Kaiserslautern, Germany. His inter- and transdisciplinary research activities focus primarily on the interface between theory and practice. His research is underpinned by collaborations with renowned national and international partners. His main topics of research, teaching and consulting are technology and innovation management, in particular open innovation and business model innovations, network and cooperation management, managing the digital transformation and risk management.

**Manuel Nicklich** is a postdoctoral researcher at the Nuremberg Campus of Technology. He is a sociologist with a special focus on new forms of organizing work and questions of professionalization. He wrote his Ph.D. on the establishment of new vocational training schemes in the emerging field of industry-related services and worked on several projects funded by the Hans Böckler Foundation, the German Ministry of Education and Research (BMBF) and the ESF. His research appears in publications such as the *Journal of Professions and Organization*, the *European Journal of Industrial Relations* and the *International Journal of Human Resource Management*.

**Sabine Pfeiffer** as held the Chair of Sociology (Technology—Labour—Society) at the Nuremberg Campus of Technology at the Friedrich Alexander University of Erlangen-Nuremberg since 2018. Since the 1990s, her main research focus has been societal conditions and consequences due to the digital transformation. During her scientific career, Sabine Pfeiffer has successfully conceptualized and managed around 30 third-party-funded projects, funded by the BMBF, the EU, the DFG, the Hans Böckler Foundation and others. She is a member of several scientific advisory boards, e.g. the German platform "Industrie 4.0", or the Federal Institute for Vocational Education and Training (BIBB), and has served on the boards of international scientific conferences like T.A.S.K.S. or Human Computer Interaction.

**Kerstin Pichel** lecturer for Strategic Management at ZHAW Zurich University of Applied Sciences, School of Management and Law, studied Economics and doctorate at the technical university of Berlin. She worked for more than 15 years as a strategy consultant for profit and nonprofit organizations. Since 2008 she works at ZHAW with a research focus on strategy processes.

**Stephanie Porschen-Hueck** has been a sociologist at the Institute for Social Science Research (ISF Munich) for many years. Her main area of interest is sociology of work. She received her doctorate (Dr. rer. pol.) from the Faculty of Economic Sciences at the University of Augsburg. She studied Sociology, Social Psychology and Business Administration at the Ludwig Maximilian University of Munich, prior to which she completed professional training as a bank clerk. She is involved in various research and design projects. Her fields of research include postmodern forms of organization and participation, and good work with regard to innovation, interaction and networking.

**Stefan Sauer** is an academic councillor at the Nuremberg Campus of Technology, Chair of Sociology (Technology—Labour—Society). He works as a sociologist with a special focus on self-organization and self-organizing, sustainability, project-based and team-based work as well as recognition and trust. After studying Sociology, Philosophy and Psychology at the LMU Munich, Warsaw University and Lublin Catholic University, he worked as a research fellow (2009–2015) and as a senior research fellow (2015–2018) at the Institute for Social Science Research (ISF) in Munich. During that time he worked on many projects founded by the German Ministry of Education and Research (BMBF) and the European Social Fund (ESF).

**Fyriel Souayah** holds a Master's degree in Human Resources Management from UCLouvain and works as an HR consultant. Her Master's dissertation investigated the influence of the implementation of Agility on the autonomous motivation of workers. A trained ethnographer, she is interested in new ways of working and the culture of virilism in the workplace.

**Yuki Tsuboyama** is an Associate Professor of Organizational Analysis at Hitotsubashi University. He is currently working on his forthcoming monograph based on more than 150 interviews with fast-stream retired ex-bureaucrats at Japanese National Railways. His monograph will be published by Yuhikaku in 2021.

**Werner Weiss** is a managing partner and co-founder of Insiders Technologies, a spin-off of the German Research Center for Artificial Intelligence (DFKI). The company, located in Kaiserslautern and Berlin, has received awards as one of the most innovative medium-sized applied research companies in Germany for several years in succession. In 2015, Insiders Technologies was named "TOP-Innovator of the Year" and at the same time "Most Innovative Medium-Sized Company in German Medium-Sized Businesses" in the 50–250 employee size category.

# List of Figures

# List of Tables

CHAPTER 1

# The Agile Imperative: A Multi-Level Perspective on Agility as a New Principle of Organizing Work

*Stefan Sauer, Manuel Nicklich, and Sabine Pfeiffer*

Focussing on paradoxes, one might say that "all organization is founded on paradox: on the one hand it contains free, creative, independent human subjects; on the other hand, the relation between these subjects aspires to be one of organization, order and control" (Clegg et al., 2002: 483). The unfolding "project society" (Lundin et al., 2015) and ever-changing environments and customer demands have brought new challenges for organizing and managing work and thus sharpen this paradox. Not least since it is increasingly addressed by the idea of

S. Sauer (✉) · M. Nicklich · S. Pfeiffer
Nuremberg Campus of Technology (NCT), Friedrich-Alexander-Universität Erlangen-Nürnberg, Nuremberg, Germany
e-mail: stefan.sauer@fau.de

M. Nicklich
e-mail: manuel.nicklich@fau.de

S. Pfeiffer
e-mail: sabine.pfeiffer@fau.de



S. Pfeiffer et al. (eds.), *The Agile Imperative*, Dynamics of Virtual Work,
https://doi.org/10.1007/978-3-030-73994-2_1

agility (Prange & Heracleous, 2018; Russo et al., 2013; Vijayasarathy & Turk, 2008). Although the concept originally emerged in the context of software development with a strong critical reference to conventional project management, more and more companies from other industries are adopting agile practices and interpreting agility as a holistic organizational strategy beyond simple project management methods.

From its very beginnings, agile work has claimed to be a radically different approach. Today, the core of agile work is formed by the four values "individuals and interactions over processes and tools", "working software over comprehensive documentation", "customer collaboration over contract negotiation" and "responding to change over following a plan" (Beck et al., 2001). By applying strong customer integration, agile work produces increments and organizations can react flexibly to changing environmental demands. Moreover, agile work emphasizes that the team autonomously plans its work and has the necessary resources at its disposal (Cockburn & Highsmith, 2001; Whitworth & Biddle, 2007). In brief, concerning the ideas of agile work one can say that "agile methodologies represent a 'people' centred approach" (Whitworth & Biddle, 2007), in which "the most important implication to managers working in an agile manner is that it places more emphasis on people factors in the project: amicability, talent, skill, and communication" (Cockburn & Highsmith, 2001: 131). Furthermore, the increasing necessity of customer-orientation enforces new principles for organizing and managing work (Sauer, 2017), and digitalization is seen as a supporting facet of enterprise agility (Overby et al., 2006). Interpreted from a positive perspective, both agilization and digitalization are seen as promising, enabling more self-management on the team level (Grantham, 2000) and thus fostering better working conditions as well as employee participation (Mann & Maurer, 2005), as well as unleashing greater efficiency and higher productivity (Lee & Xia, 2010). Where some scholars thus see a kind of win–win situation, others criticize agile methods as a management fad (Cram & Newell, 2016) and another new form of heightened worker control (Hodgson & Briand, 2013; Moore, 2018; Moore in this volume).

Against the background of the ambiguous state of research we ask why the promises of the agile are often not kept, especially for employees: is it due to implementation processes that were initially done badly? Or are the qualitative, emancipatory goals of agility not compatible with the logic of the market, revenue and accounting and control in the long run?

On the basis of these more empirical questions, and assuming the ideas initially formulated in the Agile Manifesto (Beck et al., 2001) are substantially different in addressing a truly new way of work, this volume will follow two guiding and more principal questions: is it possible to save and foster the benefits of agility in a market- and numbers-driven environment at all? Or are there systematic and immanent reasons opposing this? The agile idea, first formulated by developers for developers, was increasingly appropriated by consultants and change managers—often following quite different goals. While the original core of agile work was oriented towards value of work and aspects of decent work, its deployment in companies increasingly emphasizes effectiveness and productiveness. On the one hand, agility lives from its original core, which on the other hand is being eroded within agile practices. Companies, management and developers have to cope with this immanently paradoxical situation of agile work.

But how do scholars see this situation? Cicmil and Hodgson (2006) explicate with respect to research on projects: "While this introduction of sociological perspectives to the field of projects is clearly welcome, indeed long overdue, the more conservative of current work in this tradition remains strongly wedded to a functionalist viewpoint, focussing upon improving project performance through attention to social (i.e. human) factors" (Cicmil & Hodgson, 2006: 10). Consequently, while the literature on agile work often examines agile instruments from a business perspective, debating the functionality of these methods (Hobbs & Petit, 2017; Overby et al., 2006; Prange & Heracleous, 2018), the present volume contributes to advancing the above-mentioned debate by focussing on agile work from a (more critical) social science perspective. This means focussing on the social issues of agility and not least examining the discrepancy between aspiration and actuality. The pure business angle often has a universal perspective, whereas the social science perspective contextualizes the application of agile work more consistently.

The agile method was substantively developed in the US, which tends to be classified as a liberal market economy (Hall & Soskice, 2001). Nevertheless, other countries also adapt agile practices. Besides the differing adaption rate among countries (West, 2011), one can also see differences in adapting agile work between corporations in various industries and countries (see Endo et al. in this volume). Indeed, a common notion concerning context is the relationship between the institutional environment and the adaption of management practices. And even paradigms of organizational management such as scientific management, which seem to have spread all over the globe, "were variously adapted to national circumstances, including the characteristics of the workforce" (Guillén, 1994: 1). Management paradigms are usually adapted in selective ways among different countries and depend on the specific problems they face. In consequence, it would be oversimplifying matters to assume that the universal notion of the agile method is "out there", regardless of the context. Rather, it needs to be understood by referring to different aspects in order to develop a more specific view of agile work.

In the specific compilation of the selected contributions, the volume aims to achieve a view of agility not only within organizations but also within market contexts and institutional settings. With this broader and more fundamental view, we intend to scrutinize whether agility is just a discursive imperative or an organizational and institutional response enabling companies to deal better with complexity and volatility.

As the answers to these questions can vary at different levels, we examine agility on the level of teams, organizations and societies. Moreover, this book assembles different perspectives on the sustainability and virtue of agile instruments. By bringing together international scholars from different disciplines which bring in different—sometimes controversial—views on agile work, the project aims to stimulate a comparative discussion. Ultimately, we seek to identify similarities and differences among countries and disciplines and classify the different perspectives along the continuum of interpreting agile promises as fact or fiction. Thus our book project deliberately combines researchers from different theoretical backgrounds with an empirical view of the most diverse phenomena of agility in different institutional settings. And equally well-founded perspectives of established researchers are deliberately brought into dialogue with the fresh, critical view of young scholars.

In order to relate the cultural embeddedness of project management to the macro institutional arrangement as well as specific relations in the workplace, we need to look at different levels to capture the full perspective on agile work. As organizations' output of narratives, decisions by management and action on a work level are not necessarily coupled (Brunsson, 1989), it is crucial to investigate the impact of agile methods and their interplay on three levels: the team level, the organizational and/or the managerial level and the societal level. This means "case studies of firms that adopted or attempted to adopt paradigms exemplify how macro institutional factors affected the behavior of particular managers and firms" (Guillén, 1994: 6). While a perspective on the macro-level institutional arrangements provides a useful starting point, it may overlook the dynamics of more micro-level work contexts. That is, the national or industry-specific context may be too macro and more micro-level context such as the actual implementation of agile work on a day-to-day basis may need to be embraced in order to adequately specify the key context for realizing this new principle of organizing work.

Consequently, first, on a team level the contributions pose questions on the actual leeway for self-organization and application on a micro-level. Second, on an organizational and/or managerial level, there are questions as to whether and how well these new instruments support innovation, which problems of up-scaling and implementation arise and what role is played by leadership. And third, contributions focussing on a societal level address the potential interrelations of new management instruments with broader cultural phenomena and their ideological import within specific institutional settings, which act as a precondition for the legitimate and desirable practices.

In line with these notions, the book is structured along the three levels examined (team, organization and society). More precisely, the agile movement, which is based on the agile manifesto, could be seen as a bottom-up-approach for participatory and sustainable software development, but its operation and implementation is quite paradoxical—on a societal, organizational and team-based level. Hence agility could defend qualitative aspects of work like the use value of work and prevent exploitation and organizational separation of developers, but it could (also) increase productivity, workload and demands for flexibility and innovation (societal level). It could set teams free from one-sided bureaucratic demands and hierarchies, but it could (also) increase the marketization of organizations (organizational level). And finally it could (also) frame self-organized and sustainable teams, but it could increase self-control, self-exploitation and peer pressure (team level). These paradoxes—like all paradoxes—cannot not be solved, but must be dealt with—within a capitalistic regime. Therefore, instead of just condemning or obeying agile strategies and frameworks, we advocate critical support, including ongoing verification with agile principles and the manifesto.

## Agility on the Team Level

Similar to the idea of agility emanating from the team, our volume begins with contributions focussing on concrete work in agile teams. More precisely, the chapters deal with the impacts of the agile manifesto and the satisfaction of employees, the use of digital tools within agile approaches and the interplay of self-organization, agile management approaches and organizational change. Especially against the background of agile ideas referring to the question of empowering people and self-organization on the team level, agile work, if it is more than just a consulting and management narrative, materializes on the micro-level of teams in which employees fulfil tasks, cope with customer requirements and use digital artefacts. This is where the ideas of agility thrive and become alive—or fail. This is where the ideas of the *Agile Manifesto* do manifest themselves in everyday work—or do not.

In the first contribution, Manuel Nicklich, Stefan Sauer and Sabine Pfeiffer examine "*Antecedents and Consequences of Agility*" and show that these new concepts such as agile methodology are necessary for revitalizing the discussion concerning employees' participation and the self-organization of teams. According to claims of agile project management, empowerment of teams and individuals within organizations is both the anchor point and the promise of organizing work. However, it seems that scholars have discussed aspects such as employee participation and self-organization in a more or less similar way for decades. Based on these considerations, the text focuses on the relationship between agile work and these pre-existing approaches. By analyzing the historical development of management literature, the contribution illustrates the antecedents and development of these ideas culminating in the ideas of agile work. The text shows that the permanent invocation of self-organization and humane work is a symptom of an underlying paradox. More than ever, global and digital capitalism needs forms of organization and employees that are both capable of self-organization. This is the only way to deal efficiently with complexity. On the other hand, self-organization is a problem for this form of economy, because hierarchy, control and inhuman demands are part of its inherent logic. That is why the debate continues, but under ever-new headings. The text illustrates that agile work needs organizations and employees that are both capable of self-organization but cannot stand self-organization, because control and inhuman demands are part of its inherent logic.

Also examining the issue of self-organization in their text "*Agile Software Development: Practices, Self-Organization, and Satisfaction*", Robert Biddle, Martin Kropp, Andreas Meier and Craig Anslow deal with the *Manifesto*'s essential principle of self-organizing teams. The authors highlight that one of the common themes in previous debates was adoption of agile methods, and resistance to self-management was a common concern. Studying agile teams from these early days on, the authors found that the team bonds were impressively strong, involving cohesion and a sense of identity that lead to self-efficacy. Today, agile software development is no longer new, and the *Agile Manifesto* will soon be 20 years old. In recent work, the authors examine the state of practice using data from a study of software professionals in Switzerland, especially addressing the issue of overall satisfaction. These recent studies look at a range of practices and how they have influenced projects, revealing that the most striking correlation to satisfaction is the level of adoption of self-managing teams. On the other hand, the strongest hindrances to satisfaction are a lack of ability to change the organizational culture and lack of management support. The analysis also shows that both technical and collaborative practices were related to self-organization and satisfaction, but these practices on their own were not enough to explain satisfaction. A combination of both technical and collaborative practices proved a better approach. But even with strong technical and collaborative practices, satisfaction is not always assured and it shows that goals of creating timely and successful products and services matter.

Although looking at the team's daily work and one of the main values within the *Agile Manifesto*, Azuka Mordi takes up a specific perspective on virtual work in his text "*The Use of Software Tools in Agile Projects*". He provides concrete insights into the actual use of software tools in agile projects and its implications for the claims made in the *Agile Manifesto*. The contribution stresses the fact that software tools play an important role in agile projects. Especially against the background of increasing distributed work, software tools become even more relevant to agile contexts. Yet to date, there remains a lack of understanding of how tools are actually used in agile projects. The goal of this chapter is to provide insights into software tool use and its implications. The contribution follows an explorative approach and incorporates semi-structured interviews, video observation and participant observation in the German IT sector. The findings show that tool use is impacted by environmental factors like company standards and policies, data security concerns and personal preferences. The author makes it clear that there is no systematic tool selection process in the projects studied. Based on these findings, two recommendations are made: integration of a tool reflection process and integration of a role Tool Guide. Both elements are designed to facilitate an optimized tool environment while adhering to the tenets of the *Agile Manifesto*: individuals and interactions over processes and tools.

## Agility on the Organizational Level

In the following chapters concerning the management and organizational level issues on agile work, the authors deal with the decisions made by the management and the consequences agile work has for the structure and conditions of the organizations. In this sense, the contributions assemble perspectives on different managerial aspects such as strategies for implementing agility as a holistic framework, organizational culture and the strategy-making process itself. But as the employees and the design of the labour process are crucial on an organizational level, the section also includes perspectives from a more critical point of view, thereby contextualizing the discussion in a labour process debate.

In this context Stephanie Porschen-Hueck and Stefan Sauer focus on the organizational journey "*From Agile Teams and Organizations to Agile Business Ecosystems*". They address agile scaling as a bottom-up approach and business ecosystems as an outside-in approach for organizational change. These two different ways of challenging bureaucratic organization seem to be necessary to address challenges and chances within an innovative and complex platform economy, but bureaucratic structures seem to be a resilient opponent. The contribution thus sought to analyze implementation processes of agile management, agile work and business ecosystems in various companies, especially in Germany in small and medium-sized enterprises as well as in global corporations. The main question is how members of agile teams and (non-agile) managers, as well as customers and various stakeholders, can cooperate without organizational, structural frictions. Hence they analyze striking features for (more) agile management and a road to business ecosystems without denying existing structures, processes and organizational cultures. The central goal is to achieve good working conditions for (partly) self-organized and cooperative work. The thesis is that this could not be achieved with the implementation of single managerial concepts but requires ongoing management of contradictions which could be addressed by a developed concept containing several aspects like dealing with hierarchy and control vs. autonomy and self-organization as well as economization and participation vs. professionalization and pace.

In their chapter on "*Design Thinking as a Panacea? Towards a Symbiotic Understanding of Design Thinking and Organizational Culture*", Gordon Müller-Seitz and Werner Weiss develop a contextualized perspective on agile approaches and explore the role of organizational culture for employing design thinking as an agile management tool and reflect upon the benefits and challenges of doing so. By looking at a German small and medium-sized corporation in the field of omni-channel input management, the authors highlight the issue that the most difficult underlying task if design thinking is to succeed is to organize for self-organization. The chapter shows that design thinking cannot be employed successfully if the organizational culture does not allow such an agile management approach. This assertion is at least partially generalizable, allowing the presumption that other agile management approaches might also be dependent upon a fit with the respective organizational culture. Accordingly, the authors point to Scrum with its emphasis on self-organization and rapid iterative improvements. Such a managerial approach is also most likely to be contingent upon an organizational culture that is fitting. Ultimately, the contribution posits that the "one size fits all" premise in terms of design thinking is unlikely to hold true in managerial practice.

The chapter "*Strategility —A Challenging Alliance*" by Kerstin Pichel and Andrea Müller deals with agile strategy processes, which were investigated by means of interviews in eight companies and field research in another company. The developed concept of strategility focuses on three research parameters comprising practitioners, practices and the praxis itself. Within the empirical findings, a heterogeneous understanding of strategility was found, including the strategy-making process and the strategy content. Hypotheses for the differences were derived with regard to the empirical findings, the main hypothesis being that the paradigm of strategic management and that of agility are oppositional in some aspects and that this may create conflicts which have yet to be resolved. To cope with this, a maturity cluster for agile strategies was developed, comprising four types: agile activists and agile, easy-going emergent and traditional strategists. For a well-informed analysis and for further research, five core hypotheses about the new practice of agile strategy-making were detected, e.g. that strategility challenges long-term strategic management and is thus especially useful for medium-term decisions with strong and unknown influencing factors. Also, strategility demands tolerance for strategic decisions which not come about for some time.

In the last part of this section, Marion Flecher takes up thoughts from labour process theory and sheds light on "*Agile Organizations in Start-up Companies, the New Way of Controlling Work?*" The contribution looks at "new economy" companies, which are often seen as a driving force behind new work and management practices. The author's sociological perspective sees these companies as valuable laboratories for observing the changes affecting the world of work and organizations and concentrates on the modernist vision of management based on horizontality, autonomy and worker empowerment. By examining a start-up in the field of selling electronic devices in an online marketplace in France, the contribution draws on these debates about this vision. The chapter focuses on the implementation of agile methods, identifying the objectives of the adoption of such a form of project-based management within the software engineering department and seeking to understand how the organization reshapes the way employees are controlled. The examination shows that agile practices are still undermined by persistent hierarchical divisions, both in the decision-making process and in day-to-day interactions, while agile frameworks are seen as a new way of manufacturing consent.

## Agility on the Societal Level

In the final section, concerning agility on a societal level, the chapters deal with a more macro perspective on agile work. Besides institutional issues, this section also examines questions of political economy and capitalist development. While the previous section deals with the phenomenon of agile work in a narrower sense, this section shifts to an abstract level to examine the structure and reflection processes of agile work. The contributions contextualize agile work in broader discussions of management practices and their transformation.

In the first chapter to this section, Takahiro Endo, Masatoshi Fujiwara and Yuki Tsuboyama consider the issue of "*Travelling Management Ideas: Agility in Japan*". They show that management ideas do not exist in a vacuum and highlight that they need to be captured without losing the insights into dynamics. They are created, translated and implemented in different contexts. Such dynamics of ideas may need to be theorized by embracing vertical and horizontal factors. Here, vertical refers to long-term factors, while horizontal refers to trans-national ones. Such attention to vertical and horizontal factors is crucial, since emphasizing either one over the other may fail to embrace the entire picture concerning dynamics centred on management ideas. This article focuses on such vertical and horizontal dynamics concerning agile methodologies in Japan, which tends to be associated with car manufacturing in business and management studies. This background provides an interesting research site for embracing both vertical and horizontal factors. The authors retrieved and examined relevant newspaper articles in a leading economic newspaper over the past four decades. The examination revealed that "TPS" has provided a "common base" across the period. The newly introduced idea of "agility" did not replace it, but was "added on".

In their chapter "*What Do Workers get out of Agility? Examining Workers' Capability for Democratic Self-government of Work*", Olivier Jégou and Fyriel Souayah take up democratic elements of the agile imperative and emphasize that agility is a doctrine of management promoting decentralized autonomous teamwork with short and iterative work sequences, involving some level of end-user feedback all along the development process. Arguing for critical pessimism regarding the belief that agility makes an organization more democratic, the authors highlight that agility does not disrupt the institution of subordination peculiar to the employment relations and the domination it institutes. Building on Amartya Sen's capability approach, the text shows that agility still represents some interest in the promotion of a democratic society in that it contributes to the development of workers' capability for democratic self-government of work. This chapter relies on an ethnographic case study of Selecta Bank in Belgium. Understanding how the doctrine of agility is implemented at Selecta Bank and how it affects work practices, Jégou and Souayah describe and explain how workers make sense of agility in their daily working lives. They show that agility contributes to the development of professional self-awareness and to the institution of collective autonomy.

Taking up a critical perspective on neoliberal developments, in her chapter "*Agility of Affect in the Quantified Workplace*" Phoebe Moore highlights how sensory and tracking technologies are being introduced into workplaces in ways Taylor and the Gilbreths could only have imagined. New work design experiments merge wellness with productivity to measure and modulate the affective and emotional labour of resilience that is necessary to survive the turbulence of the widespread incorporation of agile management systems in which workers are expected to take symbolic direction from machines. By looking at the Quantified Workplace project in a multinational real estate company, a project carried out by a Dutch firm that fitted sensory algorithmic devices to workers' computers and bodies, this chapter argues that these devices identify agility via data collection. The collection reveals management practices that track affective and emotional labour, categorized in the project as stress, subjective productivity and wellbeing, which identify workers' so-called agility. Moore, however, concludes that agile as a system does not fully crystallize what is at stake for workers. The agile work design method attempts to convert areas of work capacities to facilitate the conversion of labour power into a source of value, but through quantification of unseen labour it can also result in alienation and abstraction. Participants' resistance to participation in the Quantified Workplace reveals tensions in the labour process when affect is measured in processes of corporate change.

## Three Levels of Perspectives on Agility—From Teams and Work to Organization and Management to Institutions and Society

Of course, we acknowledge that there is an interplay between the different levels mentioned above, and none of the articles focus strictly on only one level. The division of this book on a team, an organizational and a societal level is not intended to deny this interplay, but aims to provide special insights into the consequences of the agile movement within labour processes and cooperations, management and our societal way of thinking. According to this notion and the guiding question, namely whether the consequences of the agile imperative could be seen as fact or fiction, the contributions in the three sections reveal that agility is a fact: it happens, changes work and company cultures, has effects on teams and institutions. But agility is also a fiction: promises of self-management and emancipation of employees are kept, but also undermined, eroded, disappointed. If we look across the three levels of investigation, the three sections of the book, the different sectors, companies and countries in which the studies were conducted, three main findings emerge:

- Agility as fact and agility as fiction are contradictory, but not a contradiction: where self-management has inherent limits (because numbers and profits ultimately set the pace), but is indispensable (because this is the only way to innovate complex products in volatile markets), the fiction of agility is just as necessary as agility as a fact (be it with more or less self-management).
- In agile work, not only are fiction and fact as indissoluble as they are contradictory, but also the paradoxes of agile work cannot be resolved—it is the employees in the agile processes who have to deal with them most. The positive promises of agility come with systematic barbs. Dealing with these paradoxes on a daily basis becomes a day-to-day and concrete additional work demand.
- Agility is still new for many organizations, but the principles, ideas and methods of agility have a long history. If one wants to understand whether we are dealing with fact or fiction or whether true self-management can really be lived in the long term even in market-oriented and profit-driven companies, then—and this is also shown by the variety of contributions and perspectives gathered here—it is not enough to look at implementation processes and methods. Agility is sufficient fact and creates so much fiction that the analysis leaves the company and needs the triad of micro, meso and macro levels.

In this sense, this volume cannot and does not intend to close the analysis of agile work, but rather seeks to broaden the perspective. Many answers have been presented, from which, however, new and more far-reaching questions arise. Agility is here to stay. At the latest until it falters like its predecessor—classical project management—and a new fiction (new promises) and new facts (a changed lived working world) emerge and agility is seen as the old concept that is to be overcome. It is to be assumed that this will not come about without new paradoxes. Until then, however, much remains to be understood about what constitutes the qualitatively new aspect of agility. This volume, with its three-level perspective on agility, will certainly not be the last critical-analytical look at agility as fact and/or fiction.

Agility *is* an imperative. Actors on different levels are called upon and encourage others to become agile. Those who are in a decision-making position *cannot* refuse to become agile. Organizations can be less and *less non-agile*. Or at least call themselves that. The contributions gathered here also show this. Agility is, first and foremost, an imperative to employees: organize yourself! Act entrepreneurially! Be customer-oriented! Innovate in a two-week cycle! Put quality before everything else! And in doing so permanently increase the added value! The question remains whether an accumulation of imperatives does not create more control than hierarchy, more restrictions than bureaucracy, more management than "self" and more lonesome labour than collaboration. More lived agility will show this. And further research will help us understand the connections, dynamics and paradoxes even better. We hope that this volume will lay the foundations for further (in the agile sense) iterations of research on agility.

## References

Beck, K., Beedle, M., Bennekum A. v., Cockburn A., Cunningham W., Fowler, M., et al. (2001). *Agile manifesto*. http://agilemanifesto.org/. Accessed 11 July 2020.

Brunsson, N. (1989). *The organization of hypocrisy: Talk, decisions and actions in organizations* (2nd. ed.). Business School Press [u.a.].

Cicmil, S., & Hodgson, D. (2006). Making projects critical: An introduction. In S. Cicmil & D. Hodgson (Eds.), *Making Projects Critical* (pp. 1–25). Palgrave Macmillan.

Clegg, S. R., Cunha, J. V., & Cunha, M. P. (2002). Management paradoxes: A relational view. *Human Relations, 55*(5), 483–503.

Cockburn, A., & Highsmith, J. (2001). Agile software development, the people factor. *Computer, 34*(11), 131–133.

Cram, W. A., & Newell, S. (2016). Mindful revolution or mindless trend? Examining Agile development as a management fashion. *European Journal of Information Systems, 25*(2), 154–169. https://doi.org/10.1057/ejis.2015.13.

Grantham, C. (2000). *Future of work: The promise of the new digital work society*. McGraw-Hill.

Guillén, M. F. (1994). *Models of management: Work, authority, and organization in a comparative perspective*. University of Chicago Press.

Hall, P., & Soskice, D. (2001). *Varietes of capitalism: The institutional foundations of comparative advantage*. Oxford University Press.

Hobbs, B., & Petit, Y. (2017). Agile methods large organizations projects. *Project Management Journal, 48*(3), 3–19.

Hodgson, D., & Briand, L. (2013). Controlling the uncontrollable: 'Agile' teams and illusions of autonomy in creative work. *Work, Employment and Society, 27*(2), 308–325. https://doi.org/10.1177/0950017012460315.

Lee, G., & Xia, W. (2010). Toward Agile: An integrated analysis of quantitative and qualitative field data on software development Agility. *MIS Quarterly, 34*(1), 87–114. https://doi.org/10.2307/20721416.

Lundin, R. A., Arvidsson, N., Brady, T., Ekstedt, E., Midler, C., & Sydow, J. (2015). *Managing and working in project society: Institutional challenges of temporary organizations*. Cambridge University Press. https://doi.org/10.1017/CBO9781139939454.

Mann, C., & Maurer, F. (2005). A case study on the impact of scrum on overtime and customer satisfaction. *Agile Development Conference (ADC'05)*, 70–79. https://doi.org/10.1109/ADC.2005.1.

Moore, P. V. (2018). Tracking affective labour for Agility in the quantified workplace. *Body & Society, 24*(3), 39–67. https://doi.org/10.1177/1357034X18775203.

Overby, E., Bharadwaj, A., & Sambamurthy, V. (2006). Enterprise agility and the enabling role of information technology. *European Journal of Information Systems*, 15(2), 120–131. https://doi.org/10.1057/palgrave.ejis.3000600.

Prange, C., & Heracleous, L. (2018). *Agility.X: How organizations thrive in unpredictable times*. Cambridge University Press.

Russo, N., Fitzgerald, G., & Shams, S. (2013). Exploring adoption and use of Agile methods: A comparative case study. *AMCIS 2013 Proceedings*.

Sauer, S. (2017). *Wertschätzend selbst organisieren*. Springer Fachmedien Wiesbaden. https://doi.org/10.1007/978-3-658-15509-4.

Vijayasarathy, L., & Turk, D. (2008). Agile software development: A survey of early adopters. *Journal of Information Technology Management, 19*(2), 1–8.

West, D. (2011). *Water-scrum-fall is the reality of Agile for most organizations today*. http://www.storycology.com/uploads/1/1/4/9/11495720/water-scrum-fall.pdf. Accessed 12 Nov 2020.

Whitworth, E., & Biddle, R. (2007). The social nature of Agile teams. *AGILE, 2007*, 26–36. https://doi.org/10.1109/AGILE.2007.60.

PART I

# Agility on the Team Level

CHAPTER 2

# Antecedents and Consequences of Agility—On the Ongoing Invocation of Self-Organization

*Manuel Nicklich, Stefan Sauer, and Sabine Pfeiffer*

## Introduction

Due to increasingly volatile global markets, growing geopolitical risks, more dynamic value chains and ever shorter innovation cycles, both science and business practice have been observing a constant increase in complexity, contingency and uncertainty for decades. Strictly hierarchical structures are often seen as incapable of dealing with these challenges. As a solution, management concepts increasingly focus on the necessity

M. Nicklich (✉) · S. Sauer · S. Pfeiffer
Nuremberg Campus of Technology (NCT), Friedrich-Alexander-Universität Erlangen-Nürnberg, Nuremberg, Germany
e-mail: manuel.nicklich@fau.de

S. Sauer
e-mail: stefan.sauer@fau.de

S. Pfeiffer
e-mail: sabine.pfeiffer@fau.de



S. Pfeiffer et al. (eds.), *The Agile Imperative*, Dynamics of Virtual Work,
https://doi.org/10.1007/978-3-030-73994-2_2

of empowering employees, thereby giving them the opportunity to self-manage and self-organize their daily work. Comparatively quickly, it has become clear that this is not only a question of personal skills but also an issue of resources, organizational structures and structural support within the organizations.

Various concepts of project-based work combined with less authoritarian management approaches have long been considered the organizational response to this challenge. Combined with more result-oriented forms of organizational governance, these concepts are seen as the precondition for the self-management of employees. The most recent of these approaches is agile project management, in which self-management is to be made possible not only for individual employees but for entire teams. Given these considerations, in this chapter, we examine the antecedents and consequences of agile ideas and show that new concepts such as agile methodology are necessary for revitalizing the earlier discussion concerning the participation of employees and the self-organization of teams. According to claims of agile project management, empowerment (Bartunek & Spreitzer, 2006; Rappaport, 1981) of teams and—to some extent—individuals within organizations is both the anchor point and promise of organizing work and by this, successfully coping with complexity. In line with this, the literature states that "agile methodologies represent a 'people' centered approach" (Whitworth & Biddle, 2007) in which "the most important implication to managers working in the agile manner is that it places more emphasis on people factors in the project: amicability, talent, skill, and communication" (Cockburn & Hingsmith, 2001: 131). Among other things, the *Agile Manifesto* (Beck et al., 2001) underlines that projects need motivated individuals. Preconditions for this are the provision of an environment and the support these individuals need as well as a certain degree of trust that they will get the job done.

Interestingly, this is by no means a novel approach, but sounds like the realization of McGregor's ideas from his 1960s classic *The Human Side of the Enterprise* (McGregor, 1960), which were inspired by even earlier concepts in Human Relations Theory (Roethlisberger & Dickson, 1949). It seems that scholars have discussed aspects such as employee participation and self-organization in a more or less similar way for decades. Early management concepts in organizational research such as Likert's "System 4" realized in a "human organization" (1967) appear to be as important as (semi-)autonomous work teams in the eighties (Carnall, 1982; Pearson,

1992) or the discussion of post-bureaucratic organizations (Heckscher & Donnellon, 1994) in these debates. This array can be continued with approaches in the context of the new work debate (Cappelli & Rogovsky, 1994; Hackl et al., 2017).

Based on these considerations, we explore the links between agile management and its predecessors. By analyzing management literature in its historical development, we will trace the precursors of agile management and the development of these approaches over time. In doing so, we follow two theses: firstly, we assume that the recurrent emphasis on self-management and participation is not only explained by changing actors or management modes, but has systematic reasons, and secondly that these reasons lie in fundamental—i.e. unsolvable—paradoxes. In other words, our analysis sets out to show that the cause of the permanent—but obviously repeatedly disappointed—promise of self-empowerment is an expression of economic structures beyond the single organization or an individual management style.

Our analysis of the management literature of recent decades is therefore divided into two steps. First, we look at the rationale, dimensions and methods of the approaches which even before the advent of agile methods promised to increase the organization's self-management and ability to deal with complexity. Building on this foundation, in a second step we question agile approaches—precisely because their self-description is staged as a kind of countermovement to the previous approaches.

Finally, we combine both analysis steps in a thesis-like interpretation. Accordingly, the explanation for the eternally renewed cycle of never sufficiently redeemed self-organization is not to be found on the level of organization or management, but in the immanent logic of the capitalist economy.

More than ever, global and digital capitalism needs forms of organization and employees that are both capable of self-organization. Employees, as the only truly flexible component in organizations, are the last resort, so to speak. Only they enable even large and sluggish organizations to deal with the unexpected quickly and thus (economically) successfully.

However, by doing just that, it makes them more competent, confident and independent than individual employees. It also makes them more supportive and enables them to act collectively as a team. Employees become the real masters of complexity, they are the true conquerors of contingency—not the organization. But those who successfully pull the coals out of the fire and experience themselves as relevant and powerful in their everyday work also become more incalculable for the organization: the controllable recipient of orders disappears, but not control as a necessity for the organization. The actual source of value creation, the producer of numbers, is no longer a number itself. And in the long run, the most agile, open and modern organization cannot stand this, because it contradicts the basic principles of the capitalist organization.

Self-organization is an insuperable problem for this form of economy because hierarchy, control and inhuman demands are part of the inherent logic of capitalism. Management that enables and requires self-management suddenly becomes frightened by its own courage, and management concepts swing back to old motivations of control (perhaps disguised in new forms). That is why the debate continues, but under ever-new headings. The permanent invocation of self-organization and humane work is just a symptom of an underlying paradox: consequently, we come to the conclusion that there is more to organizational change towards agility and its paradoxes than organization theory observes.

## Theoretical Thoughts on the Development of Agile Ideas

### *Organizational Concepts as Antecedents of Agile Project Management*

If we speak about autonomy and self-organized work, a common and classical notion in the context of the sociology of work is that "capitalist firms try to reduce both complexity and autonomy so as to ensure lower costs and greater control" (Adler, 2007: 1314). With "changing contours of work" (Sweet & Meiksins, 2016) within a "project society" (Lundin et al., 2015), empirical observations seem to confirm this matter of course: "It seems that the changes in the organization of work of the last two decades have led to a decline in the workers' influence on when and how to do their work and, for most workers, also on the content of work" (Lopes et al., 2014a: 23). Besides the occurring institutional effects, which lend a different shape to this situation in European countries, there are also differences regarding skill levels (Lopes et al., 2014a). While this is not surprising, "contrary to all expectations, there has been an overall decline in work autonomy for all skill levels over the period [1999–2014]" (Lopes et al., 2014b: 348).

The issue of organization in this context is expressed by the following observation by Clegg et al.: "All organization is founded on paradox: on the one hand it contains free, creative, independent human subjects; on the other hand, the relation between these subjects aspires to be one of organization, order and control" (2002: 483). Indeed, research on organizations noted the negative consequences of top-down control decades ago (Argyris, 1964); especially in the course of "projectification" (Jensen et al., 2016; Midler, 1995), firms establish new organizational principles and techniques for organizing and managing work. In this context, projects "are regarded as the appropriate way to stimulate a learning environment and enhance creativity" (Cicmil & Hodgson, 2006: 6).

Besides the perceived benefits for firms, according to some scholars, moving beyond hierarchical organizations also offer emancipatory potentials for employees (Peters, 1992). Often these new principles are seen as positive with regard to self-organized work and the workers' self-esteem, their work motivation and their personal satisfaction with working life (Gagné & Deci, 2005; Grantham, 2000; Knudsen et al., 2011; Lopes et al., 2014b; Ryan & Deci, 2000, 2006). Consequently, the "promotion of self-managing teams" was one of the "'project-related' contemporary tendencies" that could be observed (Cicmil & Hodgson, 2006: 6). Not least the introduction of teamwork, it is argued, was a sign of the development in this direction. One central aim of the introduction of these kinds of principles was to reduce the "micromanaging" of employees by attempting to reorganize competence areas in which management became responsible only for setting the framework and making the decisions concerning the actual teamwork (Sweet & Meiksins, 2016: 41–44).

Interestingly, the tensions of subjects' creative potential and organizations' demand for control has been addressed by different theoretical approaches. Early examples of prominent management concepts in organizational research such as Douglas McGregor's (1960) "The human side of the enterprise", Rensis Likert's (1967) "System 4" realized in a "human organization" and "The Post-Bureaucratic Organization" by Charles Heckscher and Anne Donnellon (1994) appear to anticipate agile visions. In his seminal work, McGregor unfolds the idea that the traditional design of organizations usually follows the perspective on humans as opportunistic and unmotivated, unwilling to take responsibility and needing to be controlled during their work. This usually becomes a self-fulfilling prophecy and employees act like the organizations expects. In contrast to this perspective on humans, McGregor proposes a design of organizations in which employees are seen as motivated, creative and do not need control to accomplish tasks if these make sense for the employees. In the traditional organizational design—i.e. bureaucracy—however, this potential of subjects is neglected and organizations need to be designed in such a way—i.e. with decentralized decision-making, the delegation of responsibilities or decisions made by groups instead of individuals—that they foster opportunities for personal development. And Chris Argyris (1964) also argues along the same lines when he examines the negative consequences of top-down control by managers and the potential for organizational learning of alternative forms or organizing thereby eventually realizing the "integration of individuals and organizations".

And Likert's (1967) ideas too are a radical critique of bureaucratic models of organizations (which he describes as System 1). He also emphasizes the importance of team-based work and decision-making in which leaders rather play a supportive role. Especially the notion that decisions should be discussed on a team level and the opinion of every team member should be taken into account is a central characteristic of organizations based on the System 4 model. By developing an organizational model with cross-linking groups and cross-function work groups, he seems to be envisioning a Spotify model of the sixties. Consequently, System 4 organizations are organizations in which leaders have a high level of trust in their employees—not least manifested in a high degree of self-control—and continuously take into account their suggestions, the work and decision-making are based on teams and information flows in all directions within the firm.

In the early nineties, in *The Post-Bureaucratic Organization* Charles Heckscher and Anne Donnellon (1994) collected different contributions about the necessary transformation of organizations which need to overcome bureaucratic structures to guarantee dialogical decision-making. Like the approaches illustrated above, the starting point are the limitations of bureaucratic forms of organizations. The authors see the major problem of bureaucracy in the fact that people are only responsible for their own jobs, which leads to a waste of intelligence, underestimation and misspent potential of informal networks and crudeness in organizational change. Contrary to this, the concept of post-bureaucratic organization promotes "an organization in which everyone takes responsibility for the success of the whole" (Heckscher, 1994: 24). More precisely, the post-bureaucratic organization is seen as a form based on back-and-forth dialogue and informed consensus instead of authority and one-way communication. And instead of fixed rules, the organizations should only give principles that serve as a frame for decisions on the work level and the base for a continuously changing decision-making process. To prevent potential dangers, the organization needs to establish trust and awareness of interdependencies within the organization as well as frequent reviews of the existing principles (Heckscher, 1994: 24–28). Besides the empowerment of employees and decentralization of decision-making processes, the perception of time is another idea included in the concept which expresses an interesting parallel to the agile approach: "structural change in bureaucracy comes as something of a surprise, as a dramatic 'break' in the flow of events. A post-bureaucratic system, by contrast, builds in an expectation of constant change, and it therefore attaches timeframes to its actions. One element in structuring a process is to determine checkpoints for reviewing progress and for making corrections, and establishing a time period for re-evaluating the basic direction and principles of the effort" (Heckscher, 1994: 28). This is rather reminiscent of the idea of sprints, planning and reviews, which are central to the Scrum methodology.

This discussion—started after the Second World War—on autonomy and self-organization continued with approaches in the context of (semi-) autonomous work teams in the eighties (Carnall, 1982; Pearson, 1992) or the new work debate (Cappelli & Rogovsky, 1994; Hackl et al., 2017). A common ideal of all these approaches was to reduce the "micromanaging" of employees by attempting to reorganize competence areas in which the management only became responsible for setting the framework and making the decisions concerning the actual teamwork and moving beyond hierarchical organization.

Historically, these discussions on self-organization have forerunners in debates dealing with teamwork in the European automotive industry or the Japanese organization of work (Womack et al., 1991; on the parallels of agile approaches and Japanese management styles see Endo et al. in this volume). A key motivation regarding the introduction of teamwork in Japanese firms was not least to increase flexibility and to establish efficient and effective organization (Watanabe, 2000). Similar to ideas of agile methods, the system of Tanoko in Japan seeks to encourage shop floor workers' participation in problem-solving, since these workers are the most competent actors when it comes to dealing with practical problems (Aoki et al., 2014). Moreover—and also related to ideas of agility—with the introduction of semi-autonomous teamwork in the automotive industry, responsibility for planning and the flow of materials was shifted to the group level. In terms of consequences for employees, some of these previous studies interpreted the introduction of teamwork as an upgrading of work (Kern & Schumann, 1985; Piore & Sabel, 1984), while others considered the foundation of new patterns of solidarity to be difficult to control for the management (Vallas, 2003). Although the application of semi-autonomous teamwork started with production, it continuously spread to the administrative and research and development spheres. Others, however, see in these new and sophisticated principles of organizing work only new methods with which to (indirectly) control the work of (highly skilled) employees (Kunda, 2006). In this context, Barker (1993) for example speaks about how a system of "concertive control" of value-based normative rules is established that is even more powerful than hierarchical bureaucratic control. As these contrary perspectives are still virulent in the current debate, it remains controversially discussed whether these new forms of organizing work actually increase autonomy and the capacity for self-organized work.

Despite the critique that scholars place too much emphasis on autonomy (Anzola et al., 2017), the concept is worth examining more closely, since it is central to the context of self-organized work (Langfred, 2000). As a general definition, autonomy can be seen as the "the ability to exercise a degree of control over the content, timing, location, and performance of activities" (Mazmanian et al., 2013: 1337). But there is also critique of the use of the very term "autonomy". Adler, for instance, sums it up in a simple formula and highlights the fact that "autonomy is merely the converse of interdependence" (Adler, 2007: 1319). However, he argues, especially the current capitalist development—for example internationalization—is a movement away from local isolation and craft-based autonomy towards "universal interdependence". Hence under the present circumstances one should rather speak of and distinguish between collaborative and coercive interdependence than using the term "autonomy" (Adler, 2007). Nevertheless, some scholars observe new dynamics in which craft-like communities re-emerge. As an example, they mention skilled programmers, who sometimes operate like craft communities (Pietrykowski, 1999; Sweet & Meiksins, 2016: 42).

### *Development of Project Management and Agility as a Counter Movement?*

Originating in the sixties, project work became a widespread phenomenon during the eighties. First steps towards project management were even made with the Manhattan Project during the Second World War and the Apollo program that followed it (Cicmil & Hodgson, 2006). Initially, project management was first and foremost engineering sciences-oriented with a special interest in precise planning and controlling working processes by using different models (Kalkowski, 2013: 400). Back then, international project management associations were already beginning to develop special methods and trying to apply standards and norms for project management (Muzio et al., 2011). First located especially in research and development departments and implemented in organizations to increase the efficiency of product development processes, this form of work was also established in other parts of the companies, leading to circumstances which might be called "projectification" (Midler, 1995; Packendorff & Lindgren, 2014). That is, one could observe a "development towards the use of projects for handling complex tasks and creative renewal in contemporary organisations" (Packendorff & Lindgren, 2014: 8). Over the years, the focus changed: project management approaches increasingly turned away from the original intention of planning and controlling by models towards greater consideration of social aspects, which play a central role in the context of complexity and uncertainty (Lundin et al., 2015). This development was no coincidence: compared to traditional, hierarchal organization structures, project work promised greater chances for employees' self-management and sought to realize the flexibility assumed necessary under circumstances of high complexity (Heidling, 2018). Not least project work was seen as an opportunity to integrate dispersed knowledge under these circumstances (e.g. Mills & Treagust, 2003). The development of projects unfolds on different levels. There is a rather "narrow" perspective scholars call "organizational projectification", which focuses "mainly on the contents and consequences of organizational re-structuring initiatives taken in order to increase the primacy of projects within a firm and its immediate supply network" (Packendorff & Lindgren, 2014: 8).

Taking up this narrow perspective, one has to say that traditional forms of project management call for self-management and lateral authority (Dahlander & O'Mahony, 2010). According to Cicmil and Hodgson (2006: 5) projects "are promoted as universally applicable templates for integrating, by design, diverse functions of an organization that enable concentration of flexible, autonomous, and knowledgeable individuals in temporary project teams, for the focused accomplishment of goals efficiently, timely, and effectively, for customer satisfaction and company benefits". But it remains embedded in hierarchical structures in which concrete planning still plays a central role. Although there is a demand for self-organized work, the management still plans the objectives meticulously top down, which eventually leads to a "legacy of bureaucratic control in the post-bureaucratic organization" (Hodgson, 2004: 81). This means that the relationship of projects and the hierarchical structures in which they are embedded is essential for the degree of autonomy the project employees have (Heidling, 2018). Not uncommonly, unclear responsibilities and roles create tensions and are a source of stress for employees working in these projects (Cicmil et al., 2016; Hodgson, 2004; Pfeiffer et al., 2014). Especially the spreading of project work in often Tayloristically organized production in the seventies revealed tensions between bureaucratic organizations and project work. In these companies, the projects usually had the purpose to support the classical organizations and were seen as an extension of possible options. Additionally, top-down control still played an important role. Moreover, especially in recent decades, controlling and reporting have become increasingly important and one may ask who is controlling the controlling departments (Sauer, 2017).

But "projectification" also develops on a societal level and can be examined in a broader sense. In this perspective, projects are seen "as a central discursive theme in contemporary society" and "processes of projectification are becoming increasingly relevant for the understanding of almost any aspect of the contemporary economy" (Packendorff & Lindgren, 2014: 8). Some authors even speak about projects as a "human condition" (Jensen et al., 2016) and use the term "project society" to point "out specific changes in the organization of work and business activity as an important part of the overall transition from the Industrial Society without denying the continued importance of producing goods and services, the rapid and widespread diffusion of a revolutionary technology" (Lundin et al., 2015: ix). More precisely, project (management), which took on more importance, was seen as a newer solution for reconciling bureaucratic organizations with the flexibility to face challenges due to complexity. Boltanski and Chiapello (2006) in particular, in their groundbreaking work on the "New Spirit of Capitalism", talk about the formation of the "projective city", which is seen as a reaction to the unsatisfied needs of the previous epoch, such as the need for autonomy, creativity, spontaneity and mobility. Subjectification of work was thus both a need on the part of companies and a demand on the part of employees (Baethge, 1991). Within these settings, the tensions of common project management, the differences between claims and reality were becoming increasingly obvious. For this reason, these approaches were developed further in forms of agile management, as agile methodologies represent a "people"-centred approach including flat hierarchies and little documentation. Moreover, as "agile" is generally linked to speed and responsiveness, the terminology seems to be quite appealing for organizations too (Cram & Newell, 2018: 74). How this is realized in agile approaches today will be the subject of this chapter's following sub-section.

Besides methods such as eXtreme Programming (XP), Crystal Methods and Dynamic Software Development Method (DSDM), Scrum is the most popular manifestation of the agile idea. All of these approaches sought "to counter established waterfall-style project management processes" (Lynch, 2019). According to the "Status Quo Agile" (Komus, 2020), Scrum is the agile framework most in use, as a whole as well as in combination with other management approaches like Kanban. The Status Quo Agile indicates that 84% of agile working employees use Scrum—in its pure form or in combination with other agile frameworks (Komus, 2020). The development of Scrum and the typical claims in Scrum textbooks originate in Takeuchi and Nonaka's (1986) seminal text on "The New New Product Development Game". In their text, the authors examined companies in the USA and Japan and their flexibility, innovativeness and rapidness in delivering new products. They especially emphasize the role of self-organized teams in these processes. On the basis of these insights from manufacturing firms, Jeff Sutherland and Ken Schwaber adapted the core results for software development and developed the idea of Scrum in the mid-nineties (Schwaber, 1997). The central idea was to adopt "common good practices that had existed for many years into a framework for teams that self-organized and communicated and cooperated closely to develop software in an iterative and incremental way" (Keith, 2007: 26). Over the last fifteen years, Scrum has witnessed growing popularity. The starting point for a broader reception was the *Agile Manifesto* (Beck et al., 2001), which was published in 2001 and has since been translated into over sixty languages. Based on the manifesto, in 2002 the Scrum Alliance was founded and certification was established

(Lynch, 2019). The manifesto can be seen "as a widely-cited rhetorical discourse that justifies and promotes the use of the agile approach" (Cram & Newell, 2018: 74). It contains four core values and twelve principles. The authors seek to strengthen the development processes as well as cooperation with customers and avoid documentation overload and the "Taylorizationof software development". The principles of the *Agile Manifesto* places a strong focus on team-based work and self-organization: "The best architectures, requirements, and designs emerge from self-organizing teams". But the focus is not only on teams, but also on organizations and organizing: "Build projects around motivated individuals. Give them the environment and support they need, and trust them to get the job done". The agile team is thus the core element of the development process; management roles like the Scrum Master have the duty to support the agile team and to deal with impediments identified by the development team. All these aspects may seem to be in favour of self-organized and decent work. But three crucial issues were identified: first, Scrum points out that both acceleration and sustainable pace are very important and could be achieved by following the principles of Scrum. But it says only very little about how these seemingly contradictory elements could be brought together. Second, Scrum text books say nothing about solving issues within the team or with customers which could not be solved by the Scrum Master, who quite often is also a software developer. Due to empirical findings, Scrum teams need to be embedded in a supporting and coaching leadership approach without addressing it. And there is another very important issue when it comes to leadership and hierarchical structures. The Scrum approach focuses on agile teams, but it is rather unclear how these teams should fit into non-agile, hierarchical environments. This seems to be fine for start-ups, but the question arises as to how to deal with the agile approach within organizations—and especially within big companies.

Hence the crucial question is how these principles are realized in daily work under agile project management and how agile teams are embedded in bureaucratic organizations. A substantial problem is the legacy of waterfall and plan-driven, i.e. often hierarchical, elements that outlive the agile transformations (see also Cram & Newell, 2018), which often leads to parallel organizational structures. A Scrum Master told us, "I have to explain what I can do as a Scrum Master over and over again. I'm not a team leader, and the managers are not team leaders either. [...] I feel like a lightning-rod for the team". Therefore, many team members feel somewhat oppressed by the leadership positions that still exist. One developer told us, "I always ask myself: why do we have a team leader in an agile team? And why does he take part in agile meetings? These meetings are team meetings, nothing to do with him". In these contexts, one of the core responsibilities of Scrum Masters is to protect the development teams from overreaching managers and leaders. One core issue is managers (or also customers) who want to overreach sprint planning. Within a sprint planning meeting, the teams' plan—together with the Product Owner, who is responsible for the product and its progress—the tasks and the workload for the next sprint, which usually lasts two to four weeks. In some teams, sprint planning doesn't even take place within the team as a whole but only between some members known as "experts"– who are named by the management. To put it somewhat exaggeratedly, the core problem in these numerous cases is that agile frameworks like Scrum are not seen as a new way to organize work, but as a new way to organize teams.

Quite often, not only structures, but also duties and responsibilities are doubled. Agile documentation does not replace controlling duties, but is quite often added on top of (old-fashioned) bureaucratic practices. An interviewee told us: "There is no fit between agile tools and controlling tools. [...] I have my sprints and my sprint reviews, but I have to do reporting activities monthly". In this context, Cram and Newell (2018: 73) state that "in situations where agile is employed alongside a traditional development approach, challenges related to conflicting values, unclear employee expectations and confused management styles can surface". Different studies have therefore pointed out the existence of different types of agile deployment and rather hybrid forms of common approaches on a company level. While Cram and Newell (2018: 76) focus on the organizational level and distinguish the categories "crusader", "tailor" and "dabbler" based on the degree to which agile and traditional project management elements are used, Sauer and Pfeiffer (2018) look at the team level, differentiate ideal types and describe a range from the attempt to establish more and better communication processes within project teams to the attempt to ensure a protective and highly self-organized space for agile teams. Both contributions, however, emphasize the potential legacy of more traditional forms, which undermines the central idea of self-organization.

As a consequence, agility creates stress under circumstances of conflicting demands and standards rather than empowering teams and strengthening self-organization. According to our empirical findings, especially when it comes to workloads, agile teams are patronized: only 53.2% male and as few as 35.2% of the female employees think that their influence on their workload is very high or high. As a consequence, 56% of members of agile teams are often under time pressure and almost half of the agile workers regularly reach the limits of their capacity. A high proportion of agile workers show symptoms of stress: 44% of respondents are "often" or "frequently" unable to switch off during their time off work.

This means that we are at a tipping point regarding self-organization in which the question arises whether the introduction of agile methods is another failed attempt to escape hierarchical control. The core issue is that agile frameworks are quite often used on a team level, but the overall organizational structures still exist and overreach agile approaches whenever they are in conflict. Back to the Status Quo Agile, only 34% of the agile employees state that scaling approaches are also used in their working environment (Komus, 2020). These employees also claim that in the 93% in which a scaling approach is used, things get much better. This is crucial, especially because, as we have shown above, there were several management approaches which should help organizations deal with complexity and uncertainty; one may call these different types of management fashions. Today, several of them are seen as bureaucratic themselves and should be replaced by agile frameworks like Scrum. Hence the suspicion arises that all these approaches apply at the wrong level: could it be that we do not need more and more approaches to managing teams but need to stray from management and consultant supremacy? If this is the case, then the most important aims of agile frameworks like Scrum are those which are rarely implemented: empowering teams, opting for team-based self-organization and conceiving of management positions as internal service providers.

## Discussion

Agility is seen as a management concept for solving increasing complexity and uncertainty. In this context, the focus increasingly shifts towards the necessity to empower employees, thereby giving them the opportunity to self-manage and self-organize their daily work. Looking at the development of agile ideas and the antecedents of these ideas, one can see how history is repeating itself and contradictions are not dissolved but keep on culminating.

Our analysis of management literature reveals: the theoretical antecedents of agile work embrace literature regarding the relationship between organizations and individuals, the pending project work and project management. From early management concepts in organizational research to discussions on teamwork in the eighties to the development of diverse agile instruments at the beginning of this century, self-organization of employees has always played a central role in these debates. Going back along the time axis, it becomes clear that the idea of self-management appears again and again, then vanishes, only to come back with changed wording and seemingly new concepts (see Fig. 2.1).

Regarding the invocation of self-organization, all these different streams of debate share similar objectives.[1] Objectives ranging from moving beyond the hierarchical and highly bureaucratic organizations in organization theory, to consideration of employees' needs (such as autonomy, creativity, spontaneity, flexibility) within the context of project management to the agile promise of self-organized and team-based work.

Regardless of which time period or which management concepts we examine, the same problem (coping with complexity) is always defined as new and challenging. Furthermore, self-management is always proclaimed as a seemingly completely new answer. And the methods and instruments with which self-management is to be implemented are always recognizably influenced by the *Zeitgeist*.

Accordingly, while conventional project management was seen as a radical new idea legitimated by narratives of individualization (see also Boltanski & Chiapello, 2006) and started to overcome the contradictions of the hierarchical organization, Scrum is "sold" as a remedy for the same problems—which are, however, seen as problems of the old project management (although conventional project management in itself began with the same claim, namely that it was a remedy for the maladies of hierarchical organization).

Consequently, we see that there are still unresolved contradictions: just as the problems of hierarchical organization were not solved by conventional project management, its (very similar) problems cannot be solved

[1] Of course, the studies mentioned do not only focus on the above-mentioned objectives. But at this point we first and foremost concentrate on aspects of self-organization and degrees of autonomy for employees within organizations.

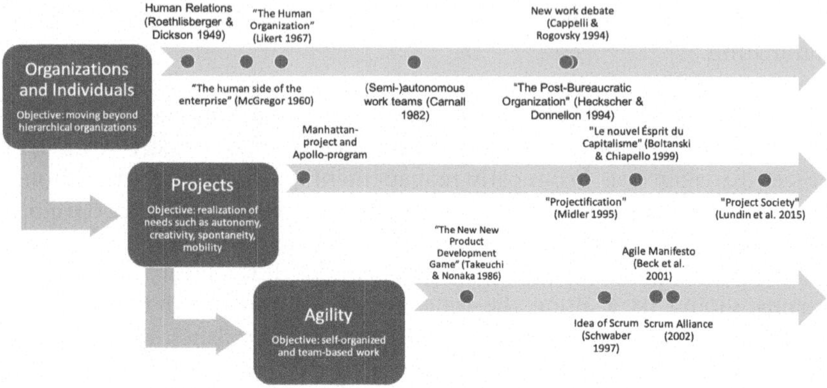


**Fig. 2.1** The ongoing invocation of self-organization (Own illustration)

by introducing agile project management. On the contrary: the contradictions that are always unsolved (or better: cannot be solved) culminate and come to a head. This can still only be observed empirically in rudimentary form, namely where agility is not only well implemented but has been consistently lived for a long time. Even there, the contradiction between self-organization as a claim and self-organization as a mere symptom minimizer is not resolved.

What applies logically and generally is therefore also true for agility: underlying contradictions are not solvable on the level of appearances. We can draw this conclusion on the basis of the data evaluated here. However, on this foundation alone it is not yet possible to conclusively clarify whether the ongoing history of the ever-new proclamation of self-management is not simply and quite banally the result of poorly designed introduction processes. Nor can it be clarified at this level whether Scrum is simply an inadequate method for solving the problems it claimed to overcome. Or whether Scrum became a hostage to the system whose organizational excesses it had ceased to eradicate.

Our thesis in this context is that the permanent invocation of self-organization and human work is a symptom of an underlying paradox: there are needs of the organizations and there are employees that are capable of self-organization but cannot abide it, because control and inhuman demands are part of its inherent logic. This shows that it is not only a question of firm-level adaptation (Cram & Newell, 2018), but is also related to a broader societal context.

However, there is more to organizational change towards agility and its paradoxes than organization theory observes. The contradictions of agile approaches in global capitalism are a phenomenon of the organizational paradox not only between self-organization needs and the control logic of economic valuation, but also between the use value the Agile Manifesto addresses and the exchange value the organization is obsessed with.

## References

Adler, P. S. (2007). The future of critical management studies: A paleo-marxist critique of labour process theory. *Organization Studies, 28*(9), 13–45.

Anzola, D., Barbrook-Johnson, P., & Cano, J. I. (2017). Self-organization and social science. *Computational and Mathematical Organization Theory, 23*(2), 221–257.

Aoki, K., Delbridge, R., & Endo, T. (2014). 'Japanese human resource management' in post-bubble japan. *The International Journal of Human Resource Management, 25*(18), 2551–2572.

Argyris, C. (1964). *Integrating the individual and the organization*. Wiley.

Baethge, M. (1991). Arbeit, Vergesellschaftung, Identität: Zur zunehmenden normativen Subjektivierung der Arbeit. *Soziale Welt, 42*(1), 6–19.

Barker, J. R. (1993). Tightening the iron cage: Concertive control in self-managing teams. *Administrative Science Quarterly, 38*(3), 408.

Bartunek, J. M., & Spreitzer, G. M. (2006). The Interdisciplinary career of a popular construct used in management: Empowerment in the late 20th century. *Journal of Management Inquiry, 15*(3), 255–273.

Beck, K., Beedle, M., Bennekum A. v., Cockburn A., Cunningham W., Fowler, M., et al. (2001). Agile manifesto. http://agilemanifesto.org/. Accessed 11 July 2020.

Boltanski, L., & Chiapello, E. (2006). *Der neue Geist des Kapitalismus*. Herbert von Halem Verlag.

Carnall, C. A. (1982). Semi-autonomous work groups and the social structure of the organization. *Journal of Management Studies, 19*(3), 277–294.

Cappelli, P., & Rogovsky, N. (1994). New work systems and skill requirements. *International Labour Review, 133*(2), 205–220.

Cicmil, S., & Hodgson, D. (2006). Making projects critical: An introduction. In S. Cicmil & D. Hodgson (Eds.), *Making Projects Critical* (pp. 1–25). Palgrave Macmillan.

Cicmil, S., Lindgren, M., & Packendorff, J. (2016). The project (management) discourse and its consequences: On vulnerability and unsustainability in project-based work. *New Technology, Work and Employment, 31*(1), 58–76.
Clegg, S. R., Cunha, J. V., & Cunha, M. P. (2002). Management paradoxes: A relational view. *Human Relations, 55*(5), 483–503.
Cockburn, A., & Highsmith, J. (2001). Agile software development, the people factor. *Computer, 34*(11), 131–133.
Cram, W. A., & Newell, S. (2018). Examining agile development as a management fashion*. In C. Prange & L. Heracleous (Eds.), *Agility.X* (pp. 71–84). Cambridge University Press.
Dahlander, L., & O'Mahony, S. (2010). Progressing to the center: Coordinating project work. *Organization Science, 22*(4), 961–979.
Gagné, M., & Deci, E. L. (2005). Self-determination theory and work motivation. *Journal of Organizational Behavior, 26*(4), 331–362.
Grantham, C. (2000). *Future of work: The promise of the new digital work society*. McGraw-Hill.
Hackl, B., Wagner, M., Attmer, L., & Baumann, D. (2017). *New work: Auf dem Weg zur neuen Arbeitswelt*. Springer Fachmedien Wiesbaden.
Heckscher, C. (1994). Defining the post-bureaucratic type. In C. Heckscher & A. Donnellon (Eds.), *The post-bureaucratic organization: New perspectives on organizational change* (pp. 14–62). Sage.
Heckscher, C., & Donnellon, A. (1994). *The post-bureaucratic organization: New perspectives on organizational change*. Sage.
Heidling, E. (2018). Projektarbeit. In F. Böhle, G. Voß, & G. Wachtler (Eds.), *Handbuch Arbeitssoziologie* (pp. 207–236). Springer Fachmedien Wiesbaden.
Hodgson, D. E. (2004). Project work: The legacy of bureaucratic control in the post-bureaucratic organization. *Organization, 11*(1), 81–100.
Jensen, A., Thuesen, C., & Geraldi, J. (2016). The projectification of everything: Projects as a human condition. *Project Management Journal, 47*(3), 21–34.
Kalkowski, P. (2013). Projekte (Projektarbeit, Projektmanagement). *Lexikon der Arbeits- und Industriesoziologie* (pp. 400–404). Nomos Verlagsgesellschaft.
Keith, C. (2007). Scrum rising. *Game Developer Magazine, 2007*(2), 21–26.
Kern, H., & Schumann, M. (1985). *Industriearbeit und Arbeiterbewußtsein: Eine empirische Untersuchung über den Einfluß der aktuellen technischen Entwicklung auf die industrielle Arbeit und das Arbeiterbewußtsein*. Suhrkamp.
Knudsen, H., Busck, O., & Lind, J. (2011). Work environment quality: The role of workplace participation and democracy. *Work, Employment and Society, 25*(3), 379–396.
Komus, A. (2020). *Status Quo (scaled) Agile*. https://www.hs-koblenz.de/bpm-labor/status-quo-scaled-agile-2020. Accessed 8 Nov 2020.
Kunda, G. (2006). *Engineering culture: Control and commitment in a high-tech corporation*. Temple University Press.

Langfred, C. W. (2000). The paradox of self-management: Individual and group autonomy in work groups. *Journal of Organizational Behavior, 21*(5), 563–585.

Likert, R. (1967). *The human organization: Its management and value.* MacGraw-Hill.

Lopes, H., Lagoa, S., & Calapez, T. (2014). Declining autonomy at work in the EU and its effect on civic behavior. *Economic and Industrial Democracy, 35*(2), 341–366.

Lopes, H., Lagoa, S., & Calapez, T. (2014). Work autonomy, work pressure, and job satisfaction: An analysis of european union countries. *The Economic and Labour Relations Review, 25*(2), 306–326.

Lundin, R. A., Arvidsson, N., Brady, T., Ekstedt, E., Midler, C., & Sydow, J. (2015). *Managing and working in project society: Institutional challenges of temporary organizations.* Cambridge University Press.

Lynch, W. (2019). The brief of history of scrum. https://medium.com/@warren2lynch/the-brief-of-history-of-scrum-15efb73b4701. Accessed 8 Nov 2020.

Mazmanian, M., Orlikowski, W. J., & Yates, J. (2013). The Autonomy paradox: The implications of mobile email devices for knowledge professionals. *Organization Science, 24*(5), 1337–1357.

McGregor, D. (1960). *The human side of the enterprise.* McGraw-Hill.

Midler, C. (1995). 'Projectification' of the firm: The Renault case. *Scandinavian Journal of Management, 11*(4), 363–375.

Mills, J., & Treagust, D (2003). Engineering education: Is problem-based or project-based learning the answer? *The Australasian Association for Engineering Education,* 2003–2004.

Muzio, D., Hodgson, D., Faulconbridge, J., Beaverstock, J., & Hall, S. (2011). Towards corporate professionalization: The case of project management, management consultancy and executive search. *Current Sociology, 59*(4), 443–464.

Packendorff, J., & Lindgren, M. (2014). Projectification and its consequences: Narrow and broad conceptualisations. *South African Journal of Economic and Management Sciences, 17*(1), 7–21.

Pearson, C. A. L. (1992). Autonomous workgroups: An evaluation at an industrial site. *Human Relations, 45*(9), 905–936.

Peters, T. (1992). *Liberation management.* Pan.

Pfeiffer, S., Sauer, S., & Ritter, T. (2014). Agile Methoden als Werkzeug des Belastungsmanagements?: Eine arbeitsvermögensbasierte Perspektive. *Arbeit : Zeitschrift Für Arbeitsforschung, Arbeitsgestaltung Und Arbeitspolitik, 23*(2), 119–132.

Pietrykowski, B. (1999). Beyond the fordist/post-fordist dichotomy: Working through 'the second industrial divide'. *Review of Social Economy, 57*(2), 177–198.

Piore, M. J., & Sabel, C. F. (1984). *The second industrial divide: Possibilities for prosperity*. Basic Books.

Rappaport, J. (1981). In praise of paradox: A social policy of empowerment over prevention. *American Journal of Community Psychology, 9*(1), 1–25.

Roethlisberger, F. J., & Dickson, W. J. (1949). *Management and the worker: An account of a research program conducted by the western electric company, hawthorne works*. Harvard University Press.

Ryan, R. M., & Deci, E. L. (2000). Intrinsic and extrinsic motivations: Classic definitions and new directions. *Contemporary Educational Psychology, 25*(1), 54–67.

Ryan, R. M., & Deci, E. L. (2006). Self-regulation and the problem of human autonomy: Does psychology need choice, self-determination, and will? *Journal of Personality, 74*(6), 1557–1586.

Sauer, S. (2017). *Wertschätzend selbst organisieren*. Springer Fachmedien Wiesbaden.

Sauer, S., & Pfeiffer, S. (2018). Innovation meets agility: Four ideal types of a combination of agility and innovation. *International Journal of Strategic Management, 18*(1), 33–40.

Schwaber, K. (1997). SCRUM development process. In J. Sutherland, C. Casanave, J. Miller, P. Patel, & G. Hollowell (Eds.), *Business Object Design and Implementation* (pp. 117–34). Springer.

Sweet, S., & Meiksins, P. (2016). *Changing contours of work: Jobs and opportunities in the new economy*. Sage.

Takeuchi, H., & Nonaka, I. (1986). The new new product development game. *Harvard Business Review, 64*(1), 137–146.

Vallas, S. P. (2003). The adventures of managerial hegemony: Teamwork, ideology, and worker resistance. *Social Problems, 50*(2), 204–225.

Watanabe, S. (2000). The Japan Model and the future of employment and wage systems. *International Labour Review, 39*(3), 307–333.

Whitworth, E., & Biddle, R. (2007). The social nature of agile teams. In J. Eckstein, F. Maurer, R. Davies, G. Melnik, & G. Pollice (Eds.), *AGILE 2007*, 26–36. Los Alamitos: IEEE. https://doi.org/10.1109/AGILE.2007.60.

Womack, J. P., Jones, D. T., & Roos, D. (1991). *The machine that changed the world: How Japan's secret weapon in the global auto wars will revolutionize western industry*. Harper Perennial.

CHAPTER 3

# Agile Software Development: Practices, Self-Organization, and Satisfaction

*Robert Biddle, Martin Kropp, Andreas Meier, and Craig Anslow*

## Introduction

In the Manifesto for Agile Software Development (Agile Manifesto Signatories, 2001), one of the principles specifies self-organizing teams. At many early conferences on the Agile software development, emphasis was on adoption, and resistance to self-organization was a common concern. In the years afterwards, research involved study of the many human

R. Biddle (✉)
Carleton University, Ottawa, ON, Canada
e-mail: robert.biddle@carleton.ca

M. Kropp
University of Applied Sciences and Arts Northwestern Switzerland, Brugg, Switzerland

A. Meier
Zurich University of Applied Sciences, Winterthur, Switzerland

C. Anslow
Victoria University of Wellington, Wellington, New Zealand



S. Pfeiffer et al. (eds.), *The Agile Imperative*, Dynamics of Virtual Work,
https://doi.org/10.1007/978-3-030-73994-2_3

aspects of agile processes, including the social nature of agile teams (Whitworth & Biddle, 2007b). Team bonds were found to be impressively strong, involving cohesion and a sense of identity that led to self-efficacy. This kind of environment may not be easy to create and support, and more recent qualitative studies by Hoda, Noble, and Marshall show the challenges and strategies that can be involved (Hoda et al., 2012a, 2012b).

Agile software development is no longer new, and the *Agile Manifesto* is now 20 years old. In recent work, we have examined the state of applied practice using data from a study of software professionals in Switzerland (Kropp & Meier, 2017). In particular, we examined the issue of overall satisfaction with their development methodology (Kropp et al., 2020). We looked at a range of practices and how they influenced projects, but the most striking single correlation to satisfaction was the level of adoption of self-organization.

While self-organizing teams are a principle of Agile software development, the day-to-day activities involve practices of various kinds. In this paper we explore the relationships between these practices, self-organization, and satisfaction. To do this, we examine the data from the Swiss Agile Study surveys conducted over the three years 2012, 2014, and 2016, and consider the consistency of the results and relationships over those surveys. Was satisfaction based only on collaborative processes and self-organization?

We begin by outlining the background to our work, with the findings of Whitworth about the social nature of Agile teams, identifying some of the key practices commonly employed in Agile software development, and then providing an overview of the Swiss Agile Study surveys. We then present the results of the surveys for satisfaction, self-organization, and the key practices. With that understood, we explore the relationships between these results and reflect on our findings.

## Background

### *The Social Nature of Agile Teams*

Elizabeth Whitworth's studies were motivated by the widespread feeling that Agile processes represented an exciting and significant change to the software development workplace. Her research question was simply "What is the experience of being in an Agile software development team?"

She conducted in-depth interviews with developers at conferences and in the community in several countries in Europe and North America, and she conducted rigorous analysis using the grounded theory method (Whitworth, 2006; Whitworth & Biddle, 2007a, 2007b). What she found was that Agile teams had a strong culture of communication and collaboration within teams, with relatively little structure imposed from without, but with a focus on ensuring quality and concern for what customers really wanted and needed. This environment led to feelings of trust, mutual respect, and empowerment.

> You feel like you get things done. And you feel like, you know, you've ticked things off and you feel like not only have you done it but the business says you have done it, you know. You have met the acceptance criteria that was suggested in the beginning and you talk to your business. Rather than just delivering something and they go "Mmm that's not what I want now" and that sort of thing. So you feel a bit of a buzz, and there is also a buzz about you know when it goes live, but that's of every project, but it's quite nice to sort of see it go quickly you know.
> —Whitworth (Whitworth, 2006) quoting a study participant

At the same time, Whitworth also found the demands of the Agile workplace could be draining, stemming from the constant openness and mutual accountability. She recalls the study by Barker (1993), suggesting that, without care, self-organizing teams can become stressful to team members. Barker recalls the work of Weber and the concept known in English translation as "the iron cage" (original in German: stahlhartes Gehäuse), meaning a structure in which individuals can feel trapped by social expectations.

> This isn't a place you go to hide.
> —Study participant (Whitworth, 2006)

> Even more than in non-agile software development teams, the need for individuals to be "on" and "in" the entire day was seen to have additional effects such as the lack of privacy and down time to make personal calls and run errands.
> —Whitworth (Whitworth, 2006)

### *Agile Software Development Practices*

The term "Agile" was adopted in the *Agile Manifesto* in 2001 (Agile Manifesto Signatories, 2001) to identify an approach to software development that was gaining much attention. The lead statement of the manifesto articulated the essence of the approach:

> Individuals and interactions over processes and tools.
> Working software over comprehensive documentation
> Customer collaboration over contract negotiation.
> Responding to change over following a plan.
> —*Agile Manifesto* (Agile Manifesto Signatories, 2001)

Several established processes emphasized many of these ideas, and "Agile" became an umbrella term for these processes and their elements. The processes themselves varied in several ways, in particular with the emphasis on more technical aspects or more human aspects of software development. Since 2006, the company "Version One" and its successors have conducted and published surveys that identify the most popular processes. In 2006, the survey (VersionOne Inc., 2006) showed the two most popular single processes reported were Scrum (Schwaber & Beedle, 2002), which emphasized a simple iterative and collaborative structure, and XP (Extreme Programming) (Beck, 2000; Beck & Andres, 2004), which also included several technical practices, such as unit testing, refactoring, and continuous integration. XP also emphasized work-life balance by insisting on a "sustainable" pace. The same survey, however, showed a hybrid of both those processes was really most common. In the most recent survey in the same series (Digital.ai Inc., 2020), Scrum is by far the most dominant process identified, but in truth most teams employ a variety of practices, including some stemming from XP, some from other processes, and some emerging from the vibrant professional community.

### *Swiss Agile Studies*

In 2012, the Swiss Agile Study (SAS) started to survey the state of Agile Software Development in Switzerland, and similar surveys were conducted in 2014, 2016, and most recently in 2018. The surveys covered various aspects of the software development process, asking about the use of technical practices, management or collaborative practices, as well as outcomes experienced and reflections. The reports on each survey provide full details of how the surveys were conducted and the descriptive results (Kropp & Meier, 2012, 2015, 2017).

These results offer a mirror available to the community, but later in-depth analysis has suggested a variety of interesting insights. For example, it was found that newcomers to Agile processes reported more emphasis on technical practices, and an emphasis on collaborative practices developed more slowly over time (Kropp et al., 2016). Stress was also seen to be higher for newcomers, and was still not entirely resolved even by those with more experience (Meier et al., 2018). Overall, in analysis of the 2016 survey, satisfaction in Agile software development seemed to relate most closely to collaborative practices and self-organization (Kropp et al., 2018, 2020). Not only was this practice the strongest single indicator of satisfaction, but related matters suggested the same finding, for example, showing that the strongest hindrances to satisfaction were a lack of ability to change organizational culture, and lack of management support. It is clear that the issue of self-organization is still contentious.

## Satisfaction, Self-Organization, and Practices

In this section we explore the subject of satisfaction and self-organization, and especially their relationship with various Agile practices. We use the results of the SAS surveys over time, looking at the 2012, 2014, and 2016 surveys. In each of these years there were in fact two surveys. One was for senior people in organizations, responding on behalf of their organization. The other was for individual professionals, responding on their own behalf: in this paper we are interested in the perspective of individual professionals, so we consider only the results of those surveys. The data therefore comes from responses from the 348, 280, and 294 individual professionals in the years 2012, 2014, and 2016, respectively.

### *Satisfaction, Self-Organization, and Balance*

We begin with responses to a simple question near the beginning of each survey, asking how satisfied participants were with their development methodology, offering a 4-point Likert scale for responses, from 1 (unsatisfied), 2 (somewhat satisfied), 3 (satisfied), and 4 (very satisfied). The responses for each year are shown in Fig. 3.1. As can be seen, the results show a range of responses, but are fairly consistent over the three

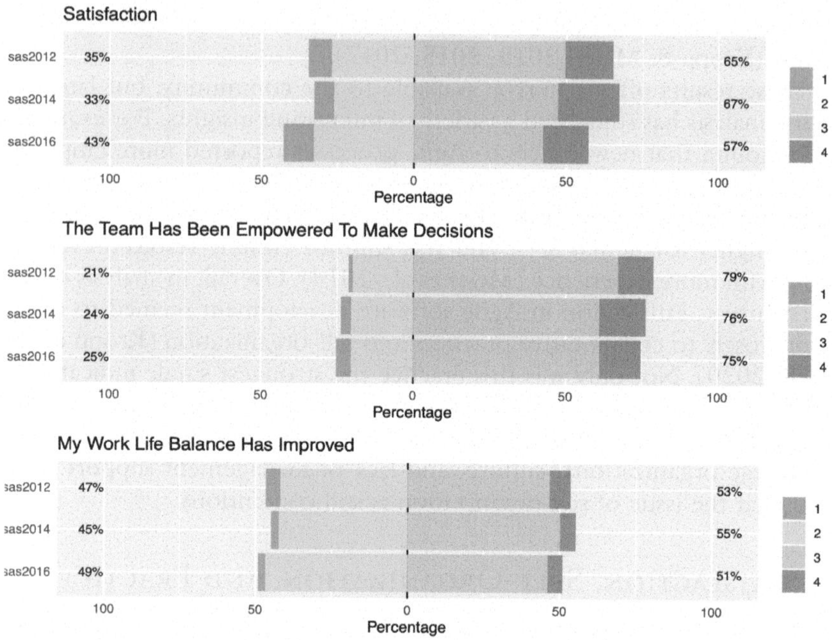


**Fig. 3.1** Responses to questions about satisfaction, self-organization, and work-life balance (1 is low, 4 is high)

surveys. For self-organization we asked about agreement with the statement "The team has been empowered to make decisions about how to do their work and execute on those decisions without outside interference". They reported on a scale of agreement from 1 (very low) to 4 (very high), and there was consistency over the surveys—but the pattern was somewhat different to that of satisfaction. Clearly, satisfaction is not only about self-organization. We also asked about any improvements to work–life balance with Agile adoption, and responses were very balanced: as many people disagreed as agreed.

### *Practices*

Next we consider practices, beginning with some technical practices. We asked participants how important various technical practices were in their adoption, offering a 5-point Likert scale, with 1 being of least, and 5 of most importance in their environment. Here we particularly look at several of the most common technical Agile practices: unit testing, refactoring, automated builds, and continuous integration.

All these relate to a core concept of agility: being able to change or add system functionality throughout development. Unit testing emphasizes rigorous testing of new or changed units in isolation, ensuring that they process a range of input correctly producing the intended behaviour. Refactoring means that any changes or additions are accommodated harmoniously with existing software to ensure the resulting software is well structured. Continuous integration means that any changes or additions to software are integrated on an ongoing basis, to ensure that overall functionality is always correct. Automated builds involve testing and integration of new or changed software being done automatically, rather than requiring special effort, so as to support ease of following the practices just mentioned.

As can be seen in Fig. 3.2, these are all rated fairly consistently in all three surveys.

We also considered various collaborative practices in Agile software development. For example, we asked about the importance to participants of daily "stand-up" meetings, open work areas, shared taskboards, and team retrospectives.

These too are strongly emphasized in Agile processes. Daily stand-up meetings ensure that all team members are aware of what others are working on, and any problems that are being experienced. In this way the practice provides situation awareness, though the meeting is brief (hence "stand-up") and so any follow-up discussion will thus happen later as appropriate. Open work areas are intended to maintain situation awareness, so that team members learn about other ongoing work, success, and frustration, without a need for timetabled meetings. Shared taskboards typically show the state of overall development, including tasks ready for work, those in progress, and those completed. As well as providing visibility to the whole team, such taskboards also facilitate discussions by team members, either casual or scheduled, as they share experience and expectations (Gossage et al., 2015). Team retrospectives are held at the

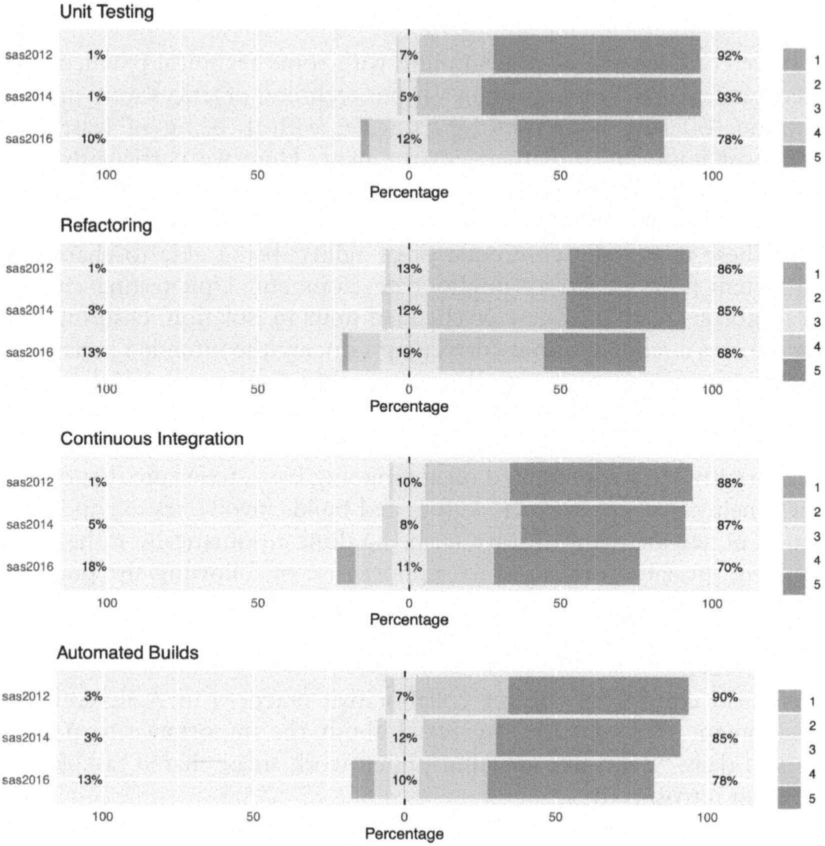


**Fig. 3.2** Technical practice importance as rated by participants: 1 is low, and 5 is high

conclusion of development cycles to reflect on the work just completed, and to share what has been learned and to discuss ideas for improvement (Derby et al., 2006). Again, all seem rated by participants consistently across the years: see Fig. 3.3.

Another collaborative practice that goes beyond the development team requires that the person responsible for business value, the "customer" or "product-owner" be "on-site", co-located with the development team. The idea is that questions can be asked and issues addressed very quickly,

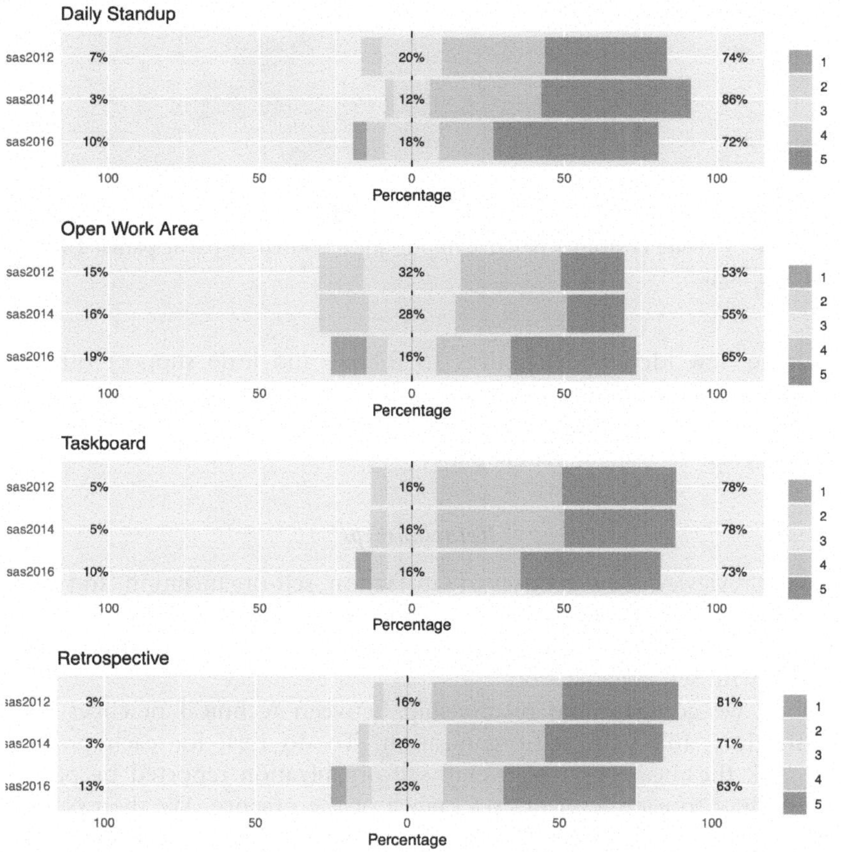


**Fig. 3.3** Collaborative practices importance as rated by participants: 1 is low, and 5 is high

with progress demonstrated for immediate comment and feedback, and collaborative learning and trust enhanced. The importance and usage of this practice drew more equivocal responses, still similar across the years: see Fig. 3.4. The practice was emphasized in the Agile method XP (Extreme Programming), but not in other methods such as Scrum, whereas the "product owner" role is less explicitly involved during a development cycle. Even where adopted, the on-site customer practice has proven challenging. In particular, there is little advice on understanding

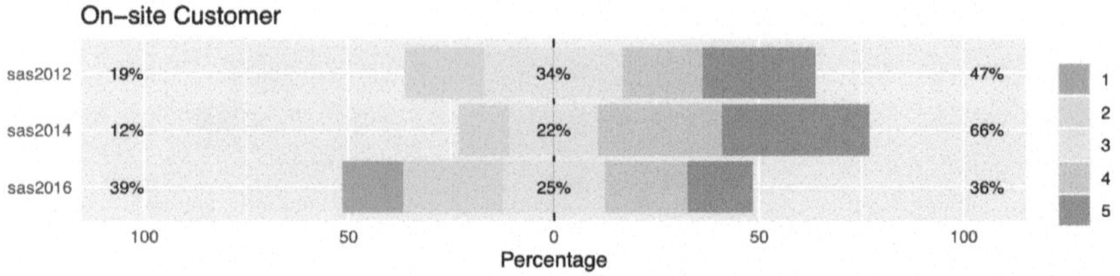


**Fig. 3.4** On-site customer practice importance as rated by participants: 1 is low, and 5 is high

the role, few identified practices to follow, and little support offered. Studies have identified and explored all these issues and suggested ways to improve customer collaboration (Martin et al., 2009a, 2009b), but the issue appears to remain problematic.

### *Relationships*

Having reviewed the responses to satisfaction, self-organization, and practices, we now consider how they might be related. Based on the earlier work, we thought that the collaborative practices might correspond most closely with self-organization.

First we compare the relationship between technical practices with satisfaction, and with self-organization. To do this, for each practice we took the mean level of overall self-organization reported by people responding to each level of importance of the practice. We then plotted the result, showing whether there was any change in satisfaction and in self-organization associated with differing levels of importance of a practice. The top row of Fig. 3.5 shows the results for continuous integration, which are representative. We can see the same pattern over all three surveys, showing that higher levels of usage of the practice were associated with higher levels of satisfaction, but with only a small difference.

Next we look at the relationship between collaborative practices with satisfaction and self-organization, using the same approach: see the bottom row of Fig. 3.5. We show the results for shared taskboards, which was the strongest pattern. For other collaborative practices the relationship was milder, but for shared taskboards it was clearer, showing higher usage is associated with higher overall satisfaction. Again the patterns over the years are similar.

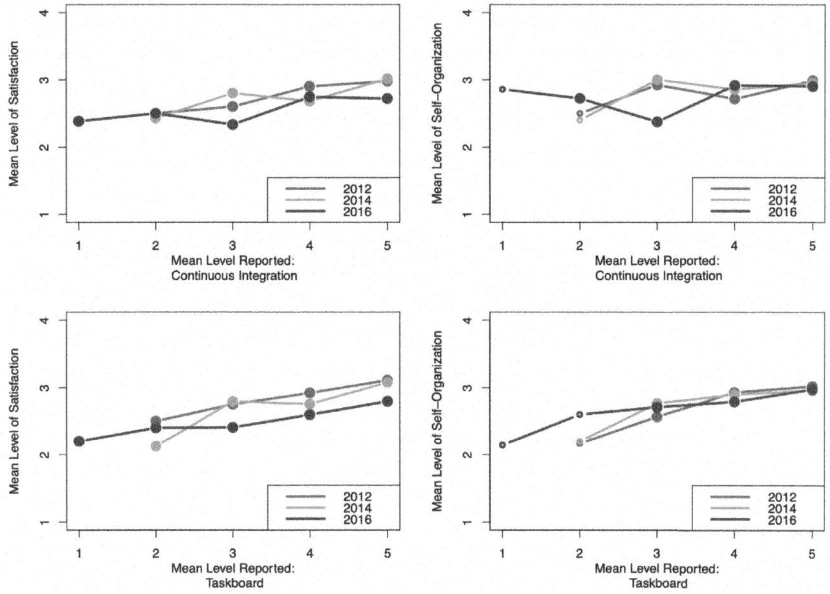


**Fig. 3.5** Practices and relationships with satisfaction (on the left) and self-organization (on the right). Each line shows the mean result for each level of practice reported. Small hollow points indicate means based on less than 5% of the sample

Overall, what we see is that there is a small positive relationship between all practices and both satisfaction and self-organization. The taskboard practice is the clearest, suggesting again that a shared taskboard has a stronger impact than might be expected. However, it seems that neither collaborative nor technical practices, nor any single practice by itself, is related to much higher satisfaction or self-organization. If we look at the data more closely, when both collaborative *and* technical practices are rated highly, both satisfaction and self-organization are higher still. This perhaps shows that identifying practices as "technical" or "collaborative" is naïve. On reflection, all the technical practices we discussed are not merely technical. Unit testing requires checking that a unit meets the requirements to function correctly as expected by units created or being worked on by other team members. Continuous integration ensures that the overall system, the work of the whole team, is as expected. Refactoring involves restructuring changed code so as to ease understanding and potential later modification. Automated builds facilitate all these practices for anyone in the team. In truth, all the Agile "technical" practices we considered here also involve collaboration and indeed self-organization.

### *Outcomes*

Satisfaction might be regarded as a general way of assessing the outcome of practices and even self-organization. But there are also other, and more specific, outcomes we can consider. In the three surveys, we asked several questions about these, and now review the most salient relationships.

The relationships between some of these outcomes and both satisfaction and self-organization are shown in Fig. 3.6. We can see that team member initiative is related to satisfaction, and strongly related to self-organization. The latter is not very surprising, as it can be seen as essential to self-organization, but the former suggests that satisfaction involves other factors as well. We asked about several outcomes involving aspects of business value, and the most interesting relationships were with "time to market". As the graphs show, there is a strong relationship between time to market and satisfaction, though less with self-organization. We also asked about "Work–life balance", and it can be seen as related to both satisfaction, and again less so with self-organization. We must remember the overall response to our question on work–life balance seen earlier in Fig. 3.1. Improved work–life balance is related to satisfaction, but, in general, overall work–life balance has not been improved.

## Discussion and Conclusion

In the 20 years since the *Agile Manifesto*, Agile processes and practices have had a tremendous impact on how software development is conducted. Indeed, Agile is now commonplace, and it is now difficult now to find workplaces that do not claim to be following at least some Agile practices. In the early period after the *Manifesto*, as reported by Whitworth (Whitworth, 2006; Whitworth & Biddle, 2007a, 2007b), individual developers showed real excitement, involving both pride in the quality of their work and a spirit of cohesion and empowerment. The Swiss Agile Study surveys allow us to look at a later period, and explore the relationships between the practices and outcomes, self-organization, and satisfaction. In our analysis of the 2016 survey, we

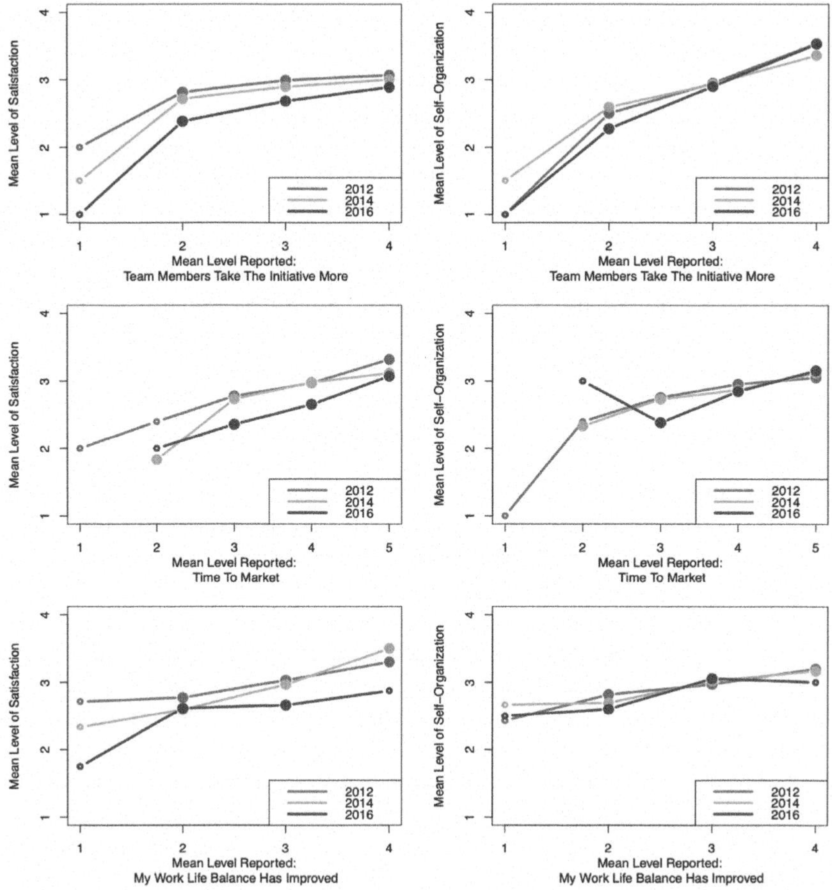


**Fig. 3.6** Outcomes and relationships with satisfaction (on the left) and self-organization (on the right). Each line shows the mean result for each level of outcome reported. Small hollow points indicate means based on less than 5% of the sample

found that satisfaction was most related to collaborative practices and self-organization.

In this chapter, we looked at the results from Swiss Agile Study surveys of individual professionals in 2012, 2014, as well as 2016, and explored the subject in more depth. We found consistency between the three surveys, and results that showed a variety of relationships between practices and outcomes. We started by seeing that self-organization in software development was common, satisfaction somewhat less so, and responses about work-life balance change were equivocal. Both technical and collaborative practices were related to self-organization and satisfaction, but each alone was not enough to explain satisfaction. A combination of both technical and collaborative practices was better. On reflection, it occurred to us that many "technical" practices necessarily involve collaboration, in ways that show the deep connections between "Agile", meaning iterative and incremental, and self-organization. Shared taskboards were more strongly related to satisfaction than other collaborative practices, showing they have more impact than might be expected. As observed in other studies (e.g. Gossage et al., 2015), as well as allowing visibility of work and progress across team members, they engender discussion, reflection, and shared understanding, speculation, and expectation. Even with strong technical and collaborative practices, however, satisfaction is not always ensured. Software development has goals of creating timely and successful products and services; and those results matter. As we saw, time to market is also strongly linked to satisfaction.

Our intent in this paper was exploratory, making use of the data already collected in the Swiss Agile Study surveys of software professionals from 2012, 2014, and 2016. Our enquiry was not a priori, but rather retrospective, based on observations in earlier analysis. Moreover, although these surveys welcomed participation from any software professional, the focus of the survey on Agile processes may have resulted in bias in the self-selection of participants. Finally, we should not assume that any relationship shown indicates causality: but our findings suggest the study of causality might be worthwhile.

In the last twenty years, Agile processes have made a huge impact on software development. At the same time, software development has become an ever-important kind of work, directly involving millions of people, and indirectly affecting everyone in the world. We still need to learn much more about this kind of work, and how Agile practices affect both the workplace and the products and services that result. Agile methods are now also being applied in non-IT domains, so these issues are of even wider importance. A key aspect relates to self-organization, the practices that support it, and the outcomes that result.

**Acknowledgments** We especially thank the Swiss Agile Study participants for their most valuable responses, and the Swiss IT organizations swissICT and SWEN for supporting and funding the studies.

## References

Agile Manifesto Signatories. (2001). *Agile Manifesto*. http://agilemanifesto.org. Accessed 11 Nov 2020.

Barker, J. R. (1993). Tightening the iron cage: Concertive control in self-managing teams. *Administrative Science Quarterly, 38*(3), 408–437. https://doi.org/10.2307/2393374.

Beck, K. (2000). *Extreme programming explained: Embrace change*. Addison-Wesley Longman Publishing.

Beck, K., & Andres, C. (2004). *Extreme programming explained: Embrace change*. Addison-Wesley Professional.

Derby, E., Larsen, D., & Schwaber, K. (2006). *Agile retrospectives: Making good teams great*. Pragmatic Bookshelf.

Digital.ai Inc. (2020). *14th Annual state of Agile report*. https://stateofagile.com. Accessed 11 Nov 2020.

Gossage, S., Brown, J. M., & Biddle, R. (2015). Understanding digital card-wall usage. In *2015 Agile Conference* (pp. 21–30). https://doi.org/10.1109/Agile.2015.16.

Hoda, R., Noble, J., & Marshall, S. (2012a). Developing a grounded theory to explain the practices of self-organizing Agile teams. *Empirical Software Engineering, 17*(6), 609–639. https://doi.org/10.1007/s10664-011-9161-0.

Hoda, R., Noble, J., & Marshall, S. (2012b). Self-organizing roles on Agile software development teams. *IEEE Transactions on Software Engineering, 39*(3), 422–444.

Kropp, M., & Meier, A. (2012). *Swiss Agile study 2012*. ISSN: 2296–2476.

Kropp, M., & Meier, A. (2015). *Swiss Agile study 2014*. ISSN: 2296–2476.

Kropp, M., & Meier, A. (2017). *Swiss Agile study 2016*. ISSN: 2296–2476.

Kropp, M., Meier, A., & Biddle, R. (2016). Agile practices, collaboration and experience: An empirical study about the effect of experience in Agile software development. In P. Abrahamsson, A. Jedlitschka, A. Nguyen Duc, M. Felderer, S. Amasaki, & T. Mikkonen (Eds.), *Product-focused software process improvement: 17th international conference, Profes 2016, Trondheim, Norway, November 22–24, 2016, Proceedings 17*, 416–431. https://doi.org/10.1007/978-3-319-49094-6_28.

Kropp, M., Meier, A., Anslow, C., & Biddle, R. (2018). Satisfaction, practices, and influences in Agile software development. In *Proceedings of the 22nd International Conference on Evaluation and Assessment in Software Engineering* (pp. 112–121).

Kropp, M., Meier, A., Anslow, C., & Biddle, R. (2020). Satisfaction and its correlates in Agile software development. *Journal of Systems and Software,* 164. https://doi.org/10.1016/j.jss.2020.110544.

Martin, A., Noble, J., & Biddle, R. (2009a). XP customer practices: A grounded theory. In *AGILE Conference* (pp. 33–40). https://doi.org/10.1109/AGILE.2009.68.

Martin, A., Noble, J., & Biddle, R. (2009b). The XP customer team: A grounded theory. *AGILE Conference*, 57–64. https://doi.org/10.1109/AGILE.2009.70.

Meier, A., Kropp, M., Anslow, C., & Biddle, R. (2018). Stress in Agile software development: Practices and outcomes. In J. Garbajosa, X. Wang, & A. Aguiar (Eds.), *Agile processes in software engineering and extreme programming* (pp. 259–266). Springer International Publishing.

Schwaber, K., & Beedle, M. (2002). *Agile software development with Scrum.* Prentice Hall.

VersionOne Inc. (2006). *The state of Agile development*. https://www.infoq.com/news/versionone-agile-survey/.

Whitworth, E. (2006). *Agile experience: Communication and collaboration in Agile software development teams. Master's thesis*. Carleton University.

Whitworth, E., & Biddle, R. (2007a). Motivation and Cohesion in Agile teams. In G. Concas, E. Damiani, M. Scotto, & G. Succi (Eds.), *Agile processes in software engineering and extreme programming* (pp. 62–69). Berlin, Heidelberg: Springer Berlin Heidelberg.

Whitworth, E., & Biddle, R. (2007b). The social nature of Agile teams. In J. Eckstein, F. Maurer, R. Davies, G. Melnik, & G.Pollice (Eds.), AGILE 2007, 26–36. Los Alamitos: IEEE. https://doi.org/10.1109/AGILE.2007.60.

CHAPTER 4

# Agile Software Tools in the Field: The Need for a Tool Reflection Process

*Azuka Mordi*

## Introduction

Organizations regard agility to be a central element for successful projects and acknowledge the strong relevance for their future business (Tseng & Lin, 2011). The agile concepts originated in the 1990s, inspired by the advancements of agile manufacturing and lean development and the realization that traditional project management approaches are insufficiently inadequate for software development (Dybå & Dingsøyr, 2008). The new approaches, initially called "lightweight" approaches (Fowler, 2001), were officially introduced by the inception of the *Agile Manifesto* in 2001, in which software developers created a set of values and principles as guidelines for practitioners to create better software (Beck et al., 2001). The basic idea of agile concepts is to frequently incorporate changes through iterative development steps and improved customer communication, and achieve continuous improvement by routine reflection and optimizations incorporated in the process (Nerur et al., 2005).

A. Mordi (✉)
University of Hohenheim, Stuttgart, Germany
e-mail: azuka.mordi@uni-hohenheim.de



S. Pfeiffer et al. (eds.), *The Agile Imperative*, Dynamics of Virtual Work,
https://doi.org/10.1007/978-3-030-73994-2_4

Agile methods contain a new set of procedures and activities within projects and between stakeholders (Dybå et al., 2014). This makes it necessary for people involved to adopt relevant changes and adjust previous behaviour. The changes in procedures and behaviour necessitate new instruments dedicated to supporting the communication-driven and collaboration-based agile approaches. Consequently, software tools and their appropriate use are key factors for successful agile projects (Nerur et al., 2005). They are highly relevant, especially in distributed settings, which do not enable co-located teamwork and face-to-face interaction (Calefato & Ebert, 2019). There are a large amount of software tools in the market and with this comes a large variety of ways in which teams may operate and conduct their daily activities. Yet, in the area of software tools, there are gaps in the research related to the use of software applications and non-digital tools in agile projects. Early studies provide first initial insights into tools, features and user needs associated with the use of software tools in agile contexts (Azizyan et al., 2011). Commercial websites and tool vendors cater to the needs of practitioners by listing available software on the market, offering feature selection and delivering tool recommendations (Capterra, 2020). However, in science and practice there still remains a lack of understanding regarding how tools are actually used in agile projects. Therefore, further investigation is needed in order to identify aspects of software tool usage embedded in the different scenarios and contexts of agile projects. The findings then allow researchers and practitioners alike to better understand the circumstances in which agile teams operate, how software tools are utilized and how they can be optimized to provide the assistance these tools should actually be intended to: to support help agile practitioners perform in the spirit of the *Agile Manifesto*. Thus, the following research questions are posed: (1) how are software tools used in agile projects? and (2) how is the software tool selection conducted?

The objective of this paper is to provide insights into software usage in agile projects the way they present themselves in the studied scenarios. Further, the findings that emerge can be used by practitioners and researchers to reflect on and discuss what is needed to improve and adjust shortcomings in the current situations. This includes deliberations on how to use affects and conflicts with the values of the *Agile Manifesto*. These reflections ensure that research plays an active part in continuous improvement towards better implementation of agility. The study is structured as follows: the second section provides a brief overview of relevant studies on software tools in agile projects. In the third section, the methodology of the research approach and its explorative nature is described. The fourth section presents the results of the study, followed by a detailed discussion of the results in section five. The study concludes with an outlook in the final section.

## Background

There is a large amount of software commercially available that is advertised for agile contexts (Capterra, 2020). Although the origins of agile methods lie in software engineering, they have successfully transcended into other domains. This applies to agile software tools as well, which were originally designed for software developers but now serve all types of practitioners in the agile community, also in areas outside of product development, like marketing and human resources (Rigby et al., 2016). In order to proceed with the study, certain clarifications and definitions need to be made. First, the term software tools is based on a software engineering definition but adapted to suit modern applications. According to that definition, "software tools are computer programs that support the development of software" (Hildebrand, 1990). Expanding the area of application to all domains, our updated definition reads as follows: software tools are tools that are made from software and used to create an outcome. Second, the term "tool" follows the common definition as a general device or implement used to carry out particular functions (Oxford Dictionary, 2020). Third, when the term "agile software tool" is used, it signifies software tools that are deployed in agile contexts, which is a more precise description. Finally, unless stated otherwise, when the single term "tool" is used, it refers to a software tool as described above. Pertaining to agile methods, "method" is used in the broad sense accepted in information systems development of being more than a set of rules, as idea and enactment (Conboy, 2009).

The advent of agility introduced the need for a new set of tools, as the new agile methodologies require a different way of working, including novel procedures and activities. Additionally, the improvements and innovations evolving from ever-advancing computer technology allow new features and functionalities to be developed and integrated into software. Since Scrum is currently the most widespread method used in organizations (Digital.ai, 2020), many software tools are designed around its methods and characteristics, for instance, by addressing the sprint process, the Scrum events or generating metrics. Further, the marketplace has transformed into a global economy, an environment in which people and teams are geographically distributed yet tied by shared projects and activities in organizations (Shrivastava & Rathod, 2014). This creates additional challenges and expectations towards software in global or distributed settings. According to the tenets of the *Agile Manifesto*, agile teams are supposed to be co-located (Beck et al., 2001). However, the reality of businesses today is that economic pressure impels many companies to adopt distributed project teams and individuals, especially in areas such as software development, where deliverables exist in digital form (Noll et al., 2010). Despite their disadvantages and the fact that they are considered an irregularity by the origins of agility, distributed settings qualify as agile (Ramesh et al., 2006). A report indicates that reduced face-to-face contact in distributed agile teams is not detrimental when other appropriate modes of communication are available in situations with small time-zone differences (Robinson, 2019). On the other hand, the *Agile Manifesto* clearly positions personal interactions over tools, prompting the question as to how tools can be used without conflicting with said reasoning. Ultimately, the reality of geographical distribution and the highly integrated globalized activities of organizations makes software tools that enable and support distributed teams all the more relevant.

What then do we know about agile software tools and how they are used in agile projects? Azizyan et al. (2011) contribute to a basic understanding of what kind of tools are used in agile projects, the issues associated with them and users' needs. They find that physical walls are still largely used by both co-located and distributed teams. Another finding is that there seems to be a void in the tool market between the extremes of sophisticated tools with many features and complicated interfaces and simple tools with limited functionalities. The importance of human factors is highlighted by the discovery that human interactions cannot be standardized via tools and that tools limit creativity (Azizyan et al., 2011). In a more recent study, the researchers set out to learn how project management tools are used in practice (Raith et al., 2017). An interesting approach here is the distinction of geographically divided teams into two categories: dispersed and distributed teams. Dispersed means one or more teams each with members in geographically different places, whereas distributed means two or more teams are in separate locations but the members within each team are co-located. Dispersed teams are more dependent on software tools than the distributed counterparts, who can use both physical and software tools. Regarding communication and collaboration, distributed teams experience more transparency and informal exchange among each other than is possible in dispersed settings (Raith et al., 2017). In their findings, a benefit of software tools is that they allow documents and key data to be connected with tasks, help visualize key information and allow information to be shared more comfortably. Physical boards on the other hand act as a meeting space and facilitate transparency and discussions. The researchers highlight that there are few guidelines on how to combine physical with digital tools and that there is no one-for-all solution that suites all contexts (Raith et al., 2017).

Other research studies focus on the actual software tools used in global software development and map them into categories (Chadli et al., 2016). One insight is that the most common features of the tools studied are related to human factors such as support for informal communication and social awareness (Portillo-Rodríguez et al., 2012). The concept of awareness has been highlighted as a crucial factor in projects, because the inherently cooperative nature of projects relies on a shared understanding of tasks, artefacts and the activities of all members (Omoronyia et al., 2010). In distributed teams, acquiring and sharing awareness information is more challenging than in co-located settings. This circumstance inspired researchers to study how best to support teams to gain awareness through software solutions. Ideas generated by the researchers include a platform that would support users in selecting the most appropriate form of communication depending on the actual situation and includes features displaying peoples' moods (Dullemond et al., 2012). In agile software development, user stories (Cohn, 2004) as a means of requirements management are very popular and have become widely accepted. Therefore, user story management plays an important role in agile projects, making corresponding software vital for teams. Dimitrijević et al. (2015) show that users prefer simple visual tangible tools that are easy to learn and easy to set up and use, highlighting usability as a key requisite.

An aspect related to agility and software tool usage is that of workspace design and IT infrastructure. Workspace design has an impact on work relationships (Khazanchi et al., 2018), which is relevant if people are to communicate and collaborate in an agile way. IT infrastructure plays an important role in collaborative digital environments (Dery et al., 2017). Transitioning from waterfall to agile should therefore be accompanied by redesign considerations and changes to the physical workspace (Cockburn, 2007). This is a challenging task, as there is a conflict inherent to trying to accommodate distraction-free space for the individual and space for a group to interact and work together, critical aspects that need to be balanced (Heerwagen et al., 2004). To address this matter, a conceptual model of office space arrangement for agile Scrum projects has been proposed which sketches a honeycomb layout with public and private work areas and allows full scalability to meet the needs of the diversity of project teams (Rola et al., 2016). Although workspace design is not a particular focus of the current study, it is important to consider this area of human interaction and create awareness of it. Hence in this study, IT infrastructure and collaboration workspace will receive minor attention in order to complement the investigation of software use in agile projects.

As outlined in this section, although software tools have been studied, this has been isolated to specific areas like tool distribution, type of tools, tool features or user needs. What has been missing is an overall view of agile software tools in the field, covering many aspects of tool use and how practitioners actually interact with the software tools in their agile projects within their organizations.

## Methodology

The research approach of this investigation follows the interpretivist research paradigm and is designed as an explorative study (Walsham, 1995). The approach incorporates three steps, each of which can be associated with a different level of project environments: management, team and individual (Fig. 4.1). The first step consists of 15 semi-structured interviews with participants from five different companies and involves multiple roles, including management roles. The team level is addressed via video observation of two teams with 13 participants from

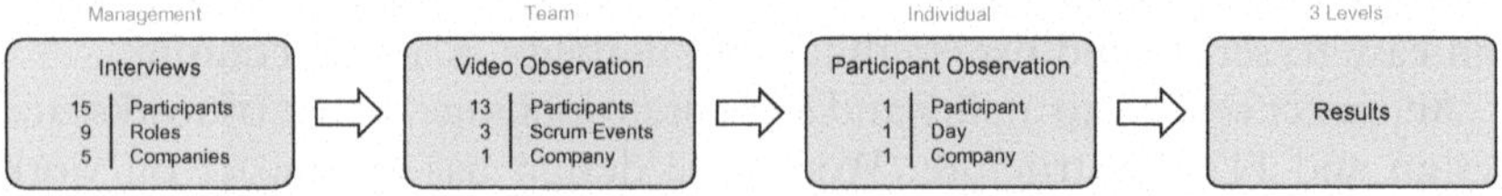


**Fig. 4.1** Research process including three data collection steps

one company. The individual level was studied in a participant observation with one project member at a different company to that in the video observation.

The approach taken follows a case study design and its strategy (Benbasat et al., 1987). Further guiding the research design is the understanding of case studies as holistic concepts (Verschuren, 2003), and hence three data collection steps were included, all of which were carried out in situ. The research proceeded by collecting and evaluating the data in the corresponding three steps described above. The following sections elucidate the methodology applied for each step.

### *Interviews*

The semi-structured interviews were conducted with agile practitioners who were acquired via a research project on developing standards for good agile projects. The interview process and respective preparations followed recommended guidelines (Gläser & Laudel, 2010). In total, fifteen individuals representing five companies were involved. All companies are active in the IT industry, ranging from small and medium-sized enterprises (SMEs) to large ones. Agile adoption had been initiated in all companies between two and seven years prior to the interviews, resulting in different levels of maturity and experience with agile methods. Interviewee selection was based on achieving a broad representation of different roles involved in agile projects. The roles included are Developer, Scrum Master, Product Owner, Technical Consultant, Agile Coach, Program Manager and Manager (first-line and upper management). Additionally, a founder and CEO of a software tool company was interviewed. All participants volunteered to the interviews (Table 4.1).

Of the 15 interviews, 14 were conducted face to face on site at the respective company locations and one via telephone. All interviews were recorded via voice recorder, 12 being held in German and three in English. The recordings were all transcribed by external professionals and kept in the recorded language. The transcriptions were coded using qualitative content analysis, utilizing a mix of deductive and inductive categories (Mayring, 2014; Schreier, 2014).

**Table 4.1** Interview participants and their project roles

| # | *Role* | *Agile experience* | *Company size* | *Industry/Field* |
|---|---|---|---|---|
| 1 | Developer | 3 years | SME | Information Technology |
| 2 | Program Manager | 10 years | Large Enterprise | Information Technology |
| 3 | Scrum Master | 5 years | Large Enterprise | Information Technology |
| 4 | Developer | 6 years | SME | Information Technology |
| 5 | Technical Consultant | 6 years | SME | Information Technology |
| 6 | Product Owner | 3 years | Large Enterprise | Information Technology |
| 7 | Scrum Master | 2 years | SME | Information Technology |
| 8 | Manager | 6 years | SME | Information Technology |
| 9 | Scrum Master | 2 years | Large Enterprise | Information Technology |
| 10 | Manager | 6 years | SME | Information Technology |
| 11 | Scrum Master | 3 years | Large Enterprise | Information Technology |
| 12 | Manager | 6 years | SME | Information Technology |
| 13 | Scrum Master | 2 years | Large Enterprise | Information Technology |
| 14 | CEO & Founder | 4 years | SME | Information Technology |
| 15 | Manager | 13 years | Large Enterprise | Information Technology |

### *Video Observation*

The video observation was conducted via video recording in one location of a distributed Scrum project. Three events were recorded in a meeting room: a daily stand-up meeting, a refinement meeting and a follow-up meeting. The recordings had a total runtime of 110 minutes. The daily stand-up had a length of 8:22 minutes and included 13 participants in two locations within the European Union (EU), five in the recorded location and eight in another location. The refinement meeting had a length of 64:38 minutes and included five participants at the recorded location and seven at the other site. The follow-up meeting had a length of 28:14 minutes and included one participant at the recorded location and two at the other one. The events were recorded in the course of the joint research project. Data analysis was conducted following recommended guidelines for video analysis (Mayring et al., 2005), using incident segmentation (Greve et al., 1997). The scope of analysis was centred on software use and the respective activities, emotions and other behavioural aspects of the participants were not part of the analysis. The following information was captured during the sessions: start and end time of each incident segment; software tools and visible hardware used; participant activities and how technology devices and software were utilized. The coding scheme applied deductive category assignment, as the categories had been developed from previous data collection steps.

### *Participant Observation*

The observation took place at a single location, where one participant was observed during a short working day from 8:45 am until 3 pm. It was conducted in a meeting room that had been reserved for the duration of the observation. In a normal setting, the participant would have switched between the meeting room for virtual meetings and a desk space in the open office for individual work. The participant had volunteered to participate in the observation after taking part in one of the interviews. The role of a technical consultant was described as an interface between Product Owners, Customers, Scrum Masters and the development team—in short: a person who understands both the customer and the business side as well as the deep technological aspects of the software product. The observation was implemented in an open participatory manner with contemporaneous analysis of entity and phenomena as well as corresponding documentation (Seidel & Prenzl, 2010). The entire session was logged via incident logging, following the same pattern described above. Directly after the session concluded, details and further information were added to the log from immediate memory. The data was coded primarily following an inductive approach, blended by deductive coding (Skjott Linneberg & Korsgaard, 2019).

### *Validity Procedures*

Qualitative exploration mandates scientific rigour and attendance to validity procedures (Goldkuhl, 2012). One way of achieving this is by research design; hence this research applied triangulation by employing different datasets and techniques (Golafshani, 2003). It included interviews, video observation and participant observation, involving multiple participants and five different companies. The participants themselves represent diverse cultural and professional backgrounds from companies of various sizes, locations and markets. The interviews were conducted on-site, permitting the participants the comfort of familiar surroundings. Transcriptions were executed by external professionals who were unrelated to the interviews. All transcriptions were compared with the original audio recordings and cross-checked for accuracy. First coding was carried out by a researcher unfamiliar with the interviews; afterwards, the data were coded by the interviewing researcher. The observations focussed strictly on software use and activities: no emotions or behavioural cues were considered or evaluated. The video observation was first coded individually by multiple researchers in a group session facilitating intercoder reliability. For the participant observation, building rapport with the participant was initiated early (Kawulich, 2004).

## Results

The results are assembled in the same structure as the methodology, following the three data collection steps. Discussions and evaluations of the results follow afterwards.

### *Interviews*

Many aspects and scenarios of software tool used in agile projects were described in the interviews. These results were grouped into six categories (Fig. 4.2) and will be presented accordingly.

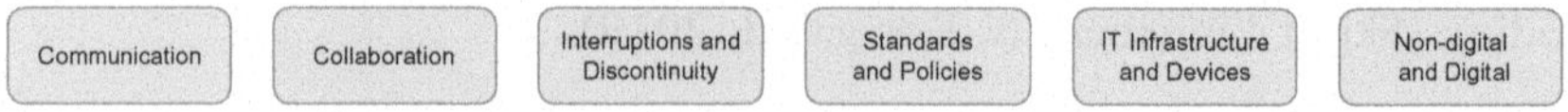


**Fig. 4.2** Six categories of scenarios related to tool use

*Communication*

Communication played an important role in the projects described by the interviewees. Communication was largely done via computer-based audio and video tools. In case of singular interaction telephones or mobile phones for audio calls were also used, complemented by occasional use of text messaging (P11, Scrum Master). Email was also named as part of regular communication; interestingly, this was often mentioned only after an explicit inquiry about the use of email: "I didn't think of that, it is so natural" (P11, Scrum Master). Smartphone-based messaging services like Whatsapp seemed to be problematic, depending on the nature of communication and company policies. Many interviewees stated compliance and data security issues related to the exchange of project information, so only in a few cases was communication unrelated to the project shared on these platforms (P6, Product Owner). Communication via chat tools was stated as very important by all interviewees; in all projects they were an essential part of the communication routine (P1, Developer). In rare cases, chat was conducted via comments linked to tasks in the taskboard application (P11, Scrum Master). The use of tools seemed to follow other patterns in projects involving higher management, as indicated in the interviews. In agile projects on the management level, a strong focus on the telephone as means of exchange was mentioned, with almost no use of chat, as the managers were on the move very often and employed a quick transfer of information that did not require desk location. In the study, interviewees mentioned a new type of communication tool used in some of their projects and within the organization, called Mentimeter (Mentimeter, 2020). It was used to generate quick feedback loops via immediate surveys. In this study, it will be referred to as an Instant Feedback Tool (IFT), but can appear under different names in the literature, such as, inter alia, Audience Response Systems (ARS) or Classroom Response Systems (CRS) (Fies & Marshall, 2006). The tool was rated very useful by all respondents acquainted with it; they cited the potential for anonymous feedback as one of the beneficial factors. It was used for applications such as polling the agenda for upcoming meetings and retrospectives, requesting feedback during or after events or workshops (P15, Manager), or more intricate tasks such as identifying problems in the team. Through skilful anonymous questioning, the Scrum Master can disclose delicate issues that probably would not have been uncovered in a setting without the tool (P3, Scrum Master).

*Collaboration*

Agile project management is based on collaboration by people within projects and also with external stakeholders. One tendency that became apparent in the study was the use of the popular market leaders Jira and Confluence as standard tools for task management and documentation. In most cases there was a clear distinction between the use of the two tools; tasks were managed in Jira and documented in Confluence, although some situations were described differently; for instance, one team used Jira for documentation too. The team added information to the tasks via comments and attachments and only used Confluence to store information seen as non-essential, such as screenshots of implemented features no longer used (P11, Scrum Master). The general approach in that project was described as a culture of a low level of documentation with respect to the actual documentation as the results visible in the delivered increments. Documentation habits in another project expanded into recording various pieces of information surrounding the project activities in Confluence, for example, recommended meeting rooms at different company locations, who to contact in case of catering needs or where to find templates and documents (P15, Manager). Another aspect that emerged in the study was the prominent use of the tool OneNote. It was used as a digital notepad for jotting down notes and as a shared documentation space besides Confluence. Because of its ease of use and free availability, it is also suitable for non-project members who do not have the fee-based software Confluence (P9, Scrum Master). The interviewee further noted that OneNote is also used for personally managing topics related to the role as a Scrum Master, like collecting ideas and new methods for retrospectives, tracking team and human relations topics and information related to other stakeholders. A strong advocate of OneNote even went so far as to declare: "Life without OneNote is unimaginable" (P3, Scrum Master), praising it as a simple yet powerful tool that could even replace most other tools, since some users even run their Kanban with it (P3, Scrum Master). Collaboration with project-external partners often requires other solutions, as the integration of outside stakeholders with the existing toolset might conflict with confidentiality concerns. In some scenarios, data exchange platforms like Sharepoint were introduced while still maintaining frequent use of emails to share data (P11, Scrum Master), to the extent that in some cases, over 90% of data exchange occurred via email and only in exceptional cases were drives established to exchange large files (P4, Technical Consultant). A different approach was chosen in another project, where the team created an environment of trust and transparency with the customer, who used the same Jira boards as the project team (P9, Scrum Master). This reduced the amount of tools needed for both parties, thereby increasing efficiency.

*Interruptions and Discontinuity*

An issue raised in connection with software use was that of workflow interruptions and tool discontinuity. In many reported cases, the information needed to be extracted from the Jira taskboard and transferred to other tools, for instance in order to calculate KPIs in a spreadsheet (P2, Programme Manager) or to create presentations (P3, Scrum Master). Working with outside stakeholders also produced tool discontinuity. Data exchange needed to be conducted through different means, either by copy-and-pasting information from internal task boards or wikis to OneNote (P3, Scrum Master), or by using emails by following a similar copy-and-paste process (P13, Scrum Master). Customers often expected arrangements to be made in a format convenient to them, resulting in project teams having to adopt and manage additional customer tools and having to keep both project and customer information synchronized (P4, Technical Consultant). Specific challenges were pointed out in the interviews when it came to requests by other company departments. Invoicing, for example, involved transfer of information to other applications using multiple steps and tools (P6, Product Owner). External access to human resources programs was restricted, so that additional tools like SAP needed to be updated (P3, Scrum Master). The overall consensus in the study was that the ideal setting would be to have as few tools as possible, because complexity and work demands increase with the addition of tools (P9, Scrum Master). One solution for reducing tool interruptions and the number of tools was implemented in a project providing regular top management reports. Acquisition of a Jira plugin for a large sum of money allowed the report-creating process to be automated (P3, Scrum Master). The decision to invest in the plugin was motivated by the Scrum Master's persistence in enforcing agile values and principles by questioning the value of management reports, ultimately freeing the project team to focus on real value-added activities.

*Standards and Policies*

The use of software tools is often subject to company policies and standards. Some are designed to adhere to legal requirements like the GDPR (EU, 2016) or to protect company interests such as data security and intellectual property. In the interviews, these topics were addressed particularly in connection with communication and collaboration tools. An example is the use of a chat tool called RocketChat instead of other more popular tools because they do not allow company-hosting and store data in countries outside the European Union that do not underlie the GDPR (P10, Manager). An interesting case exists in one company that has different regulations within the organization, depending on the location. One team in Germany has restrictions and cannot use the chat tool Slack, while the other team in a location outside the EU uses it. This creates a big challenge for collaboration in a distributed setting, as it is not easy to bring together different customs and tool traditions manifested in each location (P6, Product Owner). Documentation is equally affected by company standards and policies. In one project, new solutions needed to be implemented, as documentation is only allowed up to a specific level of confidentiality, excluding vital high-level classified information from the existing tool Confluence and mandating that data be transferred to secure drives (P3, Scrum Master). A reaction to these circumstances can be changing tools, a measure that was implemented by moving from a Kanban tool with a public cloud solution to a self-hosted one (P3, Scrum Master) and moving from the chat tool Skype to another more compliant solution by customer request (P1, Developer). Another area generating restrictions in projects is standards and workflows that emerged from previous projects which are the default setting for new projects. For a project requiring variability and changes in workflow, the predefined stages for taskboard elements made necessary adjustments impossible without altering global permissions, thereby affecting all other projects (P2, Programme Manager). A workaround was then created to map a different amount of stages into the taskboard's fixed set of stages. Another interviewee referred to problems with standards related to centrally pre-set task priorities (critical, high and low) that could not be changed within a project and limited all projects equally to the three choices (P1, Developer).

*IT Infrastructure and Devices*

An aspect of software use that needs to be considered is IT infrastructure, the technology devices on which the software is run and the impact it has on tool use. In the interviews, devices were mentioned in various examples, one being managers' extensive use of mobile phones to shift tasks on the taskboard of their mobile app. As they are on the move and travel frequently, desk time is limited, making mobile phone use essential. A reported downside is that documentation falls short and is often forgotten, making it necessary for the Scrum Master to move the tasks back to the previous state and force the managers to complete documentation before a task status can be changed (P3, Scrum Master). This scenario is an example of heavy mobile phone use, as opposed to most projects described in the study, in which nearly all project activities were computer or laptop-based and mobile phones were only used for phone calls (P2, Programme Manager, P10, Manager). Two other situations were portrayed related to mobile phone use, one being the advantage of using them for "Planning Poker" sessions, including co-located sessions, whereby the smartphone app allows more comfort than handling physical cards (P13, Scrum Master). The other was related to testing; mobile phones and tablets were used to check and verify the responsive design, testing whether apps and features were performing accordingly (P6, Product Owner). One interviewee emphasized the comfort of using the smartphone to take screenshots of detected bugs of an app and directly link those snapshots to tasks and tickets in Jira on the phone, without having to switch to a laptop and create a ticket and transfer the screenshot to the computer (P4, Technical Consultant). The same interviewee also praised the convenience of a mobile phone for monitoring the activities in the project, as the phone rings when changes are made to tickets, allowing a causal tracking of progress during the sprints (P4, Technical Consultant). Other than that, tablets were almost of no relevance whatsoever in the projects investigated. Besides devices, computer hardware was also mentioned as relevant. A need was vocalized for well-equipped video conferencing rooms that contain large screens or video walls that enable simultaneous full-size teleconferencing and full-size screen sharing on different screens (P2, Programme Manager). A challenge noted by a manager was finding the right number of screens. Although the advantages of multiple screens in certain scenarios were explicitly acknowledged, at some point a screen limit needs to be set in order to prevent developers from adding screens for each application and creating screen overabundance (P10, Manager). Clearly, the general trend apparent in the interviews was the evident need for enhanced communication infrastructure, to be made available via sufficient well-equipped video conferencing rooms, expressed tellingly by the comment: "you know, like in Star Trek" (P8, Manager).

*Non-digital and Digital*

A large amount of work is done via digital tools, yet non-digital tools still play an important role. Physical taskboards, for example, can be seen as superior to digital taskboards, due to improved communication and subsequently team performance (P12, Manager). However, this can be disputed. Advantages of digital taskboards in distributed or dispersed settings can be seen in the enhanced flexibility of attaching relevant information to tasks, such as comments, screenshots and links to other applications. This applies to any geographic team setting (P8, Manager). Independent of the controversy, one Scrum Master characterized a positive personal view on physical taskboards by stating: "It suddenly became clear as day to me what great presence such a physical board has. You cannot click it away. It is always there, you see it. It is something completely different" (P2, Programme Manager). Use of non-digital tools also extends to individual note-taking. One interviewee developed his own portable taskboard, using a folder and sticky notes to record tasks and personal notes. Citing regular interruptions over the course of a working day, it represents the best way for the interviewee to manage the influx of information and tasks, something that cannot be reproduced digitally (P5, Technical Consultant). Opposing views also exist. For some, digital tools are key to their management of information, even in private contexts: "I haven't used pen and paper for years now… and if I had to, it would be a real challenge because I would need to get used to it again" (P1, Developer). An argument brought up was the issue of having to be able to read one's own handwriting when things are jotted down hastily. Scenarios where non-digital tools came to bear were in the context of project kick-offs (P13, Scrum Master), workshops (P15, Manager) or meetings with clients (P6, Product Owner). In these situations, the advantages of physical tools and face-to-face interaction were fully utilized. The results of these events were later transformed into corresponding digital representations in taskboards or wikis. Interestingly, the need to print rarely arose. Although it was recognized as useful, the printing feature was not valued as important and was rarely used (P9, Scrum Master).

### *Video Observation*

In the three observed sessions, four different tools were used in the exchange between the locations. The central tool used was the browser, in which the taskboard, documentation and the majority of applications were executed. Skype was used for video as well as audio communication. It was activated in the beginning of each meeting to open the communication channel and deactivated at the end. During the sessions, the applications were controlled by one team member, mostly the Scrum Master. In general, the meetings were largely communication driven; there were not many switches between software tools once the basic setup had been established upon starting. The daily stand-up revolved around the Jira taskboard, the refinement meeting around the Confluence workspace. During the refinement meeting and while discussing functional extensions of a certain feature, the team switched between the Confluence workspace and a search engine. They discussed how the feature could look by comparing different graphs and images that were displayed as results of their keyword search. This activity lasted roughly four of the total 64 min; afterwards the meeting proceeded after screenshots of sample images were added to the documentation and tasks updated on the board.

From a workspace and IT infrastructure perspective, the meetings in the observed location all took place in a small meeting room that is shown in Fig. 4.3. The room had a table and seating for 6 people and contained one 40-inch TV screen with a webcam placed on top and an audio conferencing telephone system. The screen and webcam were connected to a laptop, which the Scrum Master brought to the meeting. As only one TV

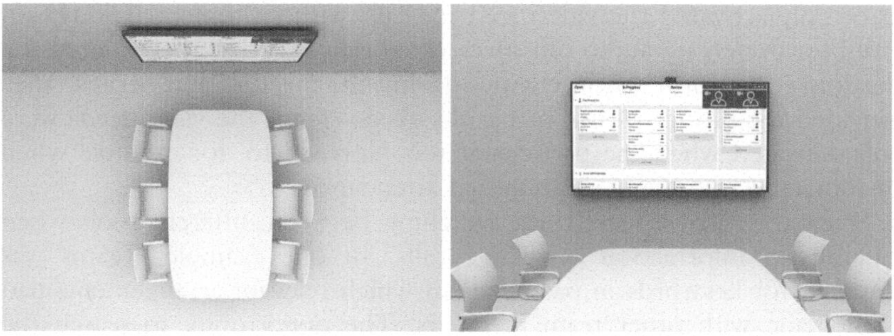

**Fig. 4.3** Layout of meeting room, from above and from a front screen view

screen was available, screen sharing and video feeds had to be split within the single screen, leading to a roughly 90:10 split, 90% for the shared laptop screen displaying the respective software application and 10% for the dual video feed, each location pictured in the upper right-hand corner of the TV screen.

### *Participant Observation*

14 different tools were employed over the course of the observation. The central application used was the browser, from which most applications were launched. There were usually around 35 tabs open, the participant stating that personal use was often made of a feature within the browser that provides quick access to recently accessed pages. During the entire working day, the participant used a portable folder in which sticky notes containing tasks and memos were placed, basically a personal taskboard containing all tasks that accrued over the day. Tasks were noted during meetings and while working on individual topics. The participant claimed it was the most efficient and pleasant way of keeping track, first because of speed and ease of writing and second because of the pleasure and ability to crunch and throw away the piece of paper upon completion. Another observation was the participant's flexible use of multiple tools, switching applications in case problems occurred with a specific tool. After a team member expressed problems logging on to Teams, Skype was used instead, making an easy changeover to another screen-sharing tool in the process. In total, six conference calls were made during the observation, one with customers and five with team members. What became apparent was that although video was the default setting in the meetings, the participant only activated the video feed for calls with customers. The reason given for preferring audio calls over video calls was that they offered the freedom to perform other activities during the meeting and because they provided the privacy of not being observed. Hence the video feeds were only activated when the participant was "forced" to, for example when customers were present and required attendance.

What was also observed was switching between different tools when looking up information on active calls. In one example, Teams was searched for keywords in past chats in which relevant arrangements had been made with other team members. The opportunity to search the text in chat tools was cited as a very valuable feature. In the multi-project environment in which the participant operated it was important to be able to quickly access data via keywords. Additionally, as mentioned above, in conference calls open tabs in the browser proved an important means to discuss appearances of features and images for the projects at hand. In one internal call with developers there was a frequent change of screens between tasks in VSTS, Wireframe Sketcher and Bitbucket, as an implemented feature was discussed and put to the test. The participant repeatedly emphasized the importance of keeping many channels open in the browser so as to be able to act and react quickly. Towards the end of the sessions, the participant clocked the time spent in each project in the tool Timecamp, stating that this is needed internally for invoicing and also to keep track of resources and related KPIs (key performance indicators) in the projects. Another finding was that despite the participant having a smartphone and a tablet readily available, no use was made of them for any project-related activities.

### *Tool Selection*

A formal or structured tool selection process was not reported by any interviewee, for any project. Most software tools are present for all projects and only certain types of tools can be chosen or changed by the teams. Despite the default tool portfolio, there were steps described on an individual, team and organization level that bear resemblance to a structured tool selection approach. One possibility was described by a Scrum Master who conducted a search for a retrospective tool that would meet his demands for virtual settings (P13, Scrum Master). First, all potentially relevant tools for retrospectives were identified on the internet. Second, all tools were personally tested by simulating a retrospective session and trying out all relevant functions and features. In a final step, a list of the pros and cons of each tool was created and the tool with the most benefits selected. The list was subsequently made available to an internal group of Scrum Masters and Agile Coaches, who in turn were encouraged to expand the list with new tools and their own ratings. On a team level, a search was made by two project teams to find an appropriate "Planning Poker" tool. One team had the challenge of finding an application that provides sufficient data security (P15, Manager) and the other team was searching for an application that provides a better and more appealing user interface than the standard tool (P3, Scrum Master). Both cases followed a detailed but rather casual search process compared to a structured and systematic approach. On an organizational level, the only reference to a similar concept of systematic tool search was given in one case within a bi-annual company-wide employee survey. In the questionnaire they are given the opportunity to provide personal feedback on a variety of topics, including tools (P12, Manager). How the employee feedback is processed and integrated in company strategy and decisions were not mentioned and remains unclear. From a company perspective, the common platform for recommending or initiating tool discussions would be the regular team meetings, where these ideas have been shared previously.

Although not the result of a systematic tool search, it is worth taking a brief look at tool choices that were made in the projects and how they originated. One example of an individual effort was made by a Product Owner. After having gained many positive experiences with Jira, the tool was recommended to a group of fellow Product Owners who had expressed dissatisfaction with the current solutions they were using (P6, Product Owner). Another example is provided by a Scrum Master previously introducing OneNote as a collaboration tool to former teams that have now completely embraced it: “yes, our tool, only OneNote” (P3, Scrum Master). On a team level, an Agile Coach reported how teams were encouraged to make suggestions for tools or any tool improvements they see, as long as they do not collide with company policies, explicitly granting teams the freedom to conduct tool searches (P11, Scrum Master). An example of organization-related tool decisions is also reported in the interviews. In search of a tool capable of visualizing both tickets and user stories, top management rolled out Jira as a standard tool after screening the market (P10, Manager). The details of the procedure and the decision-making process are unreported. Concluding this section, two findings are noteworthy. The first is an argument made by a Scrum Master who advocates a careful balance of new and old tools, pointing to the positive aspects of learning curves and maturity that come with the use of standard tools: “we do not need to reinvent everything” (P2, Programme Manager). The second is the remark that even if a superior and useful tool were discovered, it would be unclear how to proceed or whom to contact in order to make a suggestion to the central IT department (P9, Scrum Master). In essence, a systematic tool selection process in the agile projects did not exist in the companies reviewed for this study.

## Discussion

The goal of this research is to present the use and selection of agile software tools as they occur in real project settings. The study's results provide ample examples for discussion, which will be elucidated below.

### *Software Tool Usage*

Communication played an important role in these projects. This holds for both text-based communication and audio and video communication. Emails are ubiquitous and can be regarded as the common standard. Potentially, they could become obsolete, as one respondent daringly proclaimed them to be a relic from the past, "like a postcard", and recommended switching to other means like telephone and chats (P3, Scrum Master). A more prominent role was assumed by chat tools, which were prevalent in all projects. Studies have confirmed the importance of chat tools and provide guidelines on how best to utilize these tools under the challenges of human factors within project teams (Stray et al., 2019). Challenges of chat communication relate to conflicts with standards and policies, which will be highlighted later in this section.

Using video conferencing to facilitate communication was standard practice in all projects, yet its implementation appeared limited compared to the technological capabilities and modern examples. At the company Google, project teams using always-on video connections have shown how video portals are used effectively and that they exhibit strong benefits for spontaneous communication, integrating remote team members and facilitating easy access and consulting services with peers, all of this at low cost and easy to set up (Karis et al., 2016). In contrast, as obvious in Fig. 4.3, the full potential of video technology is underutilized in many projects. With only one screen, the limitations of the meeting room force the teams to use small windows for the video feed, rendering the idea of video facilitating communication ineffective. Sensing body language and other emotional cues is arduous without sufficient screen presence, the goal of creating good team chemistry becoming a real challenge. This leads to a general observation of this study. It appeared that workspace design, office layout and hardware infrastructure in the studied projects did not resonate with the agility principles of empowering communication and collaboration. Research findings advocate open environments, good visibility and communal space (Mishra et al., 2012) or more elaborate conceptual models with a honeycomb design containing public spaces, social and chill-out areas, team cells driving knowledge exchange, close product owner cells and well-equipped conference rooms (Rola et al., 2016). When those recommendations are compared with the conditions found, there is an evident gap. Although a respondent reported that special workspaces with large-screen video conferencing systems exist, they were limited to few rooms at headquarters that are practically unavailable (P2, Programme Manager). The findings of this study translate into a scenario in which agile teams are expected to work according to agile principles within the confinements of non-agile workspaces, an obvious contradiction.

Collaboration via software tools took place in various manners. Interestingly, all projects used the software tools Jira and Confluence by default, despite their relatively high costs (see P3, Scrum Master) and perceived limitations and drawbacks (P13, Scrum Master, P2, Programme Manager). The question of physical boards versus digital boards clearly revealed a preference for digital solutions, as all teams reported using software tools like Jira for task management. In line with previous studies, the present investigation delivered similar arguments for and against digital taskboards, such as availability and connectivity of project data versus reduced communication and accessibility (Katsma et al., 2013). Although digital taskboards do not sufficiently enable a collaborative agile work environment (Kropp et al., 2017), they are necessary if team members are to effectively work together over distances in distributed or dispersed settings. Research provides some ideas on what collaboration could look like with modern tools that merge the best of both worlds, the digital and the physical. One example is a Wall, a large digital multi-touch screen that emulates the comfort of a physical board (Kropp et al., 2017). Another idea is a digital scrum board that allows control via hand motion, using a device that recognizes finger and hand gestures (Rittitum et al., 2016). An alternative to upstanding boards is a digital tabletop that is designed for planning sessions (Wang et al., 2010). Some tools attempt to include more human-related aspects in their solutions. Scrumpy, or instance, was developed as an all-in-one tool that integrates social aspects of the team through profile pages, avatars and chats (Eckhart & Feiner, 2016). One further step is a capability-centric tool that aims to support agile teams by pairing professionals according to capabilities and roles, providing better allocation of resources (Vishnubhotla et al., 2018).

As creativity can suffer in digital environments with current whiteboard tools, retrospectives are at risk of becoming tedious (P11, Scrum Master). In order to facilitate retrospectives, researchers present an AI-based tool as an easy-to-use solution for voice-activated retrospectives, building on components capable of voice control like Amazon Alexa or Google Assistant (Gaikwad et al., 2019). These solutions are not currently viable options for immediate use but are an indication of future products and technologies. The participants in the present study did not make use of novel collaboration tools available today, including a type of tool that can be described as a collaborative whiteboard, a platform that provides an endless canvas and is designed to accommodate and integrate various types of data, formats and applications. Examples are Miro (Miro, 2020) and Deon (Deon, 2020), which according to their own testimony are used in a wide array of businesses worldwide. Another type of tool not mentioned by the participants is workflow and automation tools like Zapier (Zapier, 2020), which are intended to support the existing tool portfolio by connecting different applications to reduce tool discontinuity issues.

In some cases, tool interruptions are self-inflicted and can be solved in a witty manner. In one example, the Product Owner billed the company for all the monthly costs for a team member assigned to create spreadsheets for senior management, after which management abandoned the practice, freeing the team and other projects from requiring spreadsheet reports (P6, Product Owner). Another area of concern that does not provide simple solutions is company standards and policies conflicting with tools, affecting all types of software tools, as exemplified in the study. One factor that explains the lack of certain tools in the study is the policies and standards that prohibit their use. In one company, the general attitude towards new tools could be described as reluctant and can be ascribed to the experience that many new tools conflict with company policies and are therefore rejected. This feeds into an atmosphere of restraint that could persist in projects out of fear of negative reactions towards innovative tools, which, one could argue, works against the spirit of agility. Software companies, especially those outside the EU, should consider these issues when developing solutions in order to allow for various scenarios, for example by providing secure self-hosting solutions to the companies. This situation is aggravated by the recent invalidation of the EU–US Data Protection Shield, commonly referred to as the privacy shield (EU, 2020). This results in more software tools being made exempt from agile teams, creating more challenges for tool selection.

### *Tool Selection*

The studied entities showed that software tools and their use are not subject to systematic reflection and consideration. Very often they are accepted as a given or historically adopted (P9, Scrum Master). In all, there was no reported systematic and comprehensive tool selection process in the agile teams, neither on a project level nor on an organizational level. Anecdotal reports and personal experience with technology companies indicate similar situations in other projects around the world, a condition for which there are presumably several reasons, including unawareness of the impact of inadequate tool configuration. Research has demonstrated the importance of employing appropriate media for certain types of tasks in teams (Hollingshead et al., 1993), and hence using the right tools should be an important matter for project teams. Academics further explicate the need for practitioners to consider the advantages and disadvantages of different technologies in virtual settings (Kirkman & Mathieu, 2005), which raises the question whether the teams studied operate at an adequate level, given the fact that no such considerations have been reported. Adding to this is the circumstance that tool use is highly individual. This makes it all the more important to take context and individuals into account, since due to different needs of coordination and interaction, performance will be improved when individuals use a variety of media to perform a task (Dennis et al., 2008). In summary, tool selection emerges as a neglected aspect in agile teams, which needs to be addressed in a straightforward manner.

### *Recommendations*

This research study concludes with the following two recommendations for agile projects: (1) integration of a recurring tool reflection process, and (2) the integration of a role responsible for tools. The overall idea of the two recommendations is to create awareness of the importance of tool fit and to facilitate an optimized tool portfolio in agile projects. Both recommendations represent an initial proposal which should encourage researchers and practitioners to reflect, discuss and expand the concept (Fig. 4.4).

**Fig. 4.4** Tool Reflection Concept to be integrated in organizations

### Tool Reflection Process

The Tool Reflection Process is a concept that can be integrated in regular agile practices, starting at project kick-off and continuing in the retrospectives. The aim is to scrutinize the intended or current toolset, assess team and individual satisfaction with it and discuss possible improvements. Project teams underlie fluctuations and project environments change. This precipitates change to contexts and in individuals, which can affect tool fit. The goal of the tool reflection is to provide the team and relevant stakeholders with a fitting tool portfolio, according to the current and anticipated project contexts. In a first step, independent of tools, the team needs to agree on methods and activities the members intend to put into practice. In a second step, the team should discuss potential software tools that accommodate the aforementioned methods and practices. Discussion and evaluation of software tools can take place employing the categories of software usage identified in the results: Communication, Collaboration, Interruptions and Discontinuity, Standards and Policies, IT Infrastructure and Devices and Non-digital and Digital. After thorough and collective discussions considering the six categories, taking into account context factors such as team size, locations, geographical distribution, agile maturity level and external ties to name a few, a first agreement on software tools can be made. The third step is to implement the defined software tools with all necessary organizational levels and stakeholders. This process may be reiterated regularly or according to demand in order to adapt to change over the lifecycle of projects, ultimately cultivating a mindset of tool reflection. A memorable statement was made by the creator of a software tool: "Most project management tools are data-driven and designed around forms, they are not visually appealing. For novice users they can be overwhelming and too complicated. That is why we created our own software, we wanted a project management solution that everyone immediately wants to work with" (P14, CEO & Founder). This is an aspect that should be considered in the reflection process, providing software that is appealing and that does not discourage use.

Theoretically, any team member can already initiate and manage the Tool Reflection Process. The Scrum Master or another dedicated role can accommodate tool reflections in the existing process. Yet without explicitly distinguishing tool reflection as its own relevant domain there is a danger that the process will be ignored. To mitigate this risk, the second recommendation is to create a role responsible for all tool-related topics, called the Tool Guide.

### *Tool Guide*

This role can be assumed by any team member or be defined as a standalone role, depending on the team setting and the willingness of the organization. As the name Tool Guide suggests, the role should guide tool-related topics in agile teams, not necessarily be an expert on tools. Being a tool expert is an added benefit, but is dependent on training, personal ambition and other factors determined by the organization. The tasks of the Tool Guide include preventing situations in which individuals and teams are unaware that certain tools even exist in their organization. Furthermore, the role can facilitate transition to tools by enforcing a change in habits described in an interview for managers to cling to emails to distribute meeting minutes despite the arrangements to use agreed-upon documentation tools (P11, Scrum Master). Tool Guides could also drive tool change processes in the organization as ambassadors for tools and tool innovations. In addition, they could organize themselves in Communities of Practice (CoPs), a concept that shows benefits for individuals, teams and organizations and could gain strong relevance for scaling agile (Smite et al., 2020). Table 4.2 displays suggested tasks and responsibilities. It is important that the Tool Guide be equipped with sufficient authority in order to be able to execute the tasks and accept the responsibilities the role entails. These provisions for the Tool Guide must be made by the team and the organization.

An interesting aspect brought up by one study is that if methods and tools are introduced at the same time, the process might be learned from the tool, including its flaws (Eckhart & Feiner, 2016). In this context, this means that agile values, principles and practices should be established prior to tools and adherence observed from an early stage. This leads to a very important aspect: Tool Reflection Process and Tool Guide must adhere to the tenets of the *Agile Manifesto*: individuals and interactions over processes and tools. Since tool use can be reduced in teams that have

**Table 4.2** Suggested tasks and responsibilities of the new role Tool Guide

| *Tasks* | *Responsibilities* |
|---|---|
| • Facilitate Tool Reflection Process<br>• Support research of current and future tools<br>• Facilitate reflection of habits, behaviours and tools (on individual, team and organizational levels)<br>• Support implementation of agreed tools within the team and the organization<br>• Support and create awareness for tool reflection, tool fit and required changes within the organization as well as with customers and suppliers<br>• Enforce and preserve adherence to agile values, in line with the philosophy behind "individuals and interactions over processes and tools" | • Ensure implementation of a Tool Reflection Process<br>• Ensure that the tool portfolio has been reflected and agreed upon by the team |

gained agile maturity (P3, Scrum Master), the ultimate goal is to have as few tools as possible while keeping the correct tools. The Tool Guide and project team need to find a balance between tools and individuals in order to prevent technostress (Sellberg & Susi, 2014), especially if smartphones and future devices extend their omnipresence into organizational settings (Lee et al., 2014). The idea is to become an enforcer of the agile values by ensuring that tool use occurs within the principles. Without this enforcement and awareness, there is a potential danger that business dynamics thwart the original intentions and unobtrusively lead to agile projects operating outside the actual agile concept, and that this condition eventually becomes accepted over time. Ultimately, the existence of the Tool Reflection Concept is a contribution to enabling and preserving agility as conceived by the founders and embedded in the values and principles.

### *Limitations*

This research was designed as an explorative study, and hence the limitations of the case study design apply. The organizations studied are companies with headquarters based in Germany and the majority of respondents reside in Germany. Therefore, there is a potential bias due to the German cultural background. One of the five companies had a labour union, which impacts company policies and standards. EU regulations like the GDPR and data security concerns that were voiced in all organizations affect company culture and ultimately team culture. As stated previously, public cloud solutions offered by many non-EU vendors are almost entirely excluded from official company use, meaning that a large amount of software tools are unavailable to agile teams in German companies, at least in their EU locations. This fact can be one reason why the type of tools and their use exhibited in this study is potentially limited. A recommendation would be to conduct this research in non-EU locations and in companies more inclined to adopt new tools and technologies. Besides the potential biases and behaviours of the participants being skewed towards German cultural and legal norms, there are additional limitations to point out. The participant observation was conducted by a single researcher at one company location involving one participant, meaning that researcher bias might be at play (Kawulich, 2004). As evident in the study, tool use is highly individual, and hence the insights gained are potentially limited to the specific individuals and contexts. Although the Hawthorne effect is scientifically ambiguous, it should be mentioned that psychological and social variables might have affected the outcome of both the participant and the video observations (Wickström & Bendix, 2000). Another aspect is that given the explorative nature of the investigation, this research represents a broad study. The research questions allow a range of information to be considered and thus when not all aspects of software tool usage are included. In order to gain a detailed view, longitudinal studies would be necessary, as would a very narrowly defined view of a specified software tool.

## Conclusion and Outlook

The contributions of this study are manifold. First, the results have opened up ample opportunities for further investigation into more detailed use of software tools and varying contexts. Second, many aspects of concern and the problems associated with tool use have been pointed out, which in today's highly connected environment is important for academics and practitioners alike. Future tools and workspaces need to address the restrictions that could exist across the globe, depending on legal regulations or company policies. Third, the inception of a Tool Reflection Process and the corresponding role of Tool Guide provides practitioners with an idea with which to experiment and researchers with a platform for further investigation. In order to leverage agility appropriately, some interviewees advocated going back to co-located teams and rethinking the cost-centric team allocation strategies in favour of focussing on creating teams from people in one location (P13, Scrum Master). Ultimately, adhering to agile values and principles is key. Tool reflection and a Tool Guide are by no means a contradiction to the agile philosophy; instead they replicate the idea of the founders by aiming to support individuals and teams in the best way possible within the constraints of performing with digital tools.

Today, technology devices and software tools are ubiquitous and play a very different role in organizational and private settings than twenty years ago, when the agile principles were formalized. At the inception of the *Agile Manifesto*, technology was in a very different state: 3G Networks were just about to be introduced commercially (Ratliff, 2002) and smartphones and the corresponding ecosystem were in their infancy and unknown to most end consumers (Goggin, 2009). Many devices, software tools and standards we know today had yet to be invented. Technological advances are phenomena to be reckoned with, allowing new tools with novel features to emerge with high frequency. Therefore, in line with an agile mindset (Mordi & Schoop, 2020), it is wise to anticipate change and react accordingly (Denning, 2018). This, among other things, motivates the creation of the Tool Reflection Process and the Tool Guide. As costs and payoffs play an important role when organizations consider new technology (Fitzgerald et al., 2013), the outcomes of the study are potentially limited by the reluctance of companies to invest in novel tools, especially if others are already available. Yet companies should be more experimental, even if some ideas do not work out. An interesting attempt to virtually merge two locations was made in one organization in which a dedicated team room was installed in each location to improve team communication by simulating cross-location water cooler and coffee break environments. This was done by providing live audio and video feeds of each location's team room on a large TV screen (P10, Manager). The experiment was stopped after a while, as certain habits like speaking the local language as opposed to English prevailed and prevented lasting success. From an agile point of view, it can still be seen as an achievement, since the attempt was made to overcome the distance and value the team.

To date, colocation cannot be replaced (Karis et al., 2016). New technologies are on the horizon, making workplace technology perhaps the new area of disruption, similar to how the iPhone changed the electronic consumer market. The coronavirus pandemic could accelerate this situation even further, as many companies are considering a general increase in virtual and remote work (Johnson & McKinsey, 2020; Suskewicz, 2020). Already, it is imaginable that chat could become the primary tool of communication (Cardon & Marshall, 2015). This leads to an interesting future research question that extends Conway's Law (Conway, 1968; Herbsleb & Grinter, 1999) to software tools: "Are the tools used in the development process mirrored in the results of agile projects?" Whatever happens in the future, the agile precept is irrevocable: individuals and interactions over processes and tools.

**Acknowledgments** This work was supported by the German Federal Ministry of Education and Research (BMBF) and the European Social Fund (ESF) under grant 02L15A300. I would like to thank all people involved in the project, including all supporting roles; together they all made this possible.

## References

Azizyan, G., Magarian, M. K., & Kajko-Matsson, M. (2011). Survey of agile tool usage and needs. *2011 AGILE Conference*, 29–38. IEEE.

Beck, K., Beedle, M., Bennekum A. v., Cockburn A., Cunningham W., Fowler, M., et al. (2001). *Agile manifesto*. http://agilemanifesto.org/. Accessed 15 Sept 2019.

Benbasat, I., Goldstein, D. K., & Mead, M. (1987). The case research strategy in studies of information systems. *MIS Quarterly, 11*(3), 369–386.

Calefato, F., & Ebert, C. (2019). Agile collaboration for distributed teams. *IEEE Software, 36*(1), 72–78.

Capterra. (2020). *Software & software reviews for business & nonprofit*. https://www.capterra.com/. Accessed 20 April 2020.

Cardon, P. W., & Marshall, B. (2015). The hype and reality of social media use for work collaboration and team communication. *International Journal of Business Communication, 52*(3), 273–293.

Chadli, S. Y., Idri, A., Ros, J. N., Fernández-Alemán, J. L., de Gea, J. M. C., & Toval, A. (2016). Software project management tools in global software development: A systematic mapping study. *Springerplus, 5*(1), 2006.

Cockburn, A. (2007). *Agile software development: The cooperative game* (2nd ed.). Addison-Wesley.

Cohn, M. (2004). *User stories applied: For agile software development*. Addison-Wesley.

Conboy, K. (2009). Agility from first principles: reconstructing the concept of agility in information systems development. *Information Systems Research, 20*(3), 329–354.

Conway, M. (1968). How do committees invent? *Datamation, 14*(5), 28–31.

Denning, S. (2018). Ten agile axioms that make conventional managers anxious. *Strategy & Leadership, 46*(5), 10–16.

Dennis, A. R., Fuller, R. M., & Valacich, J. S. (2008). Media, tasks, and communication processes: A theory of media synchronicity. *MIS Quarterly, 32*(3), 575.

Deon. (2020). *The visual collaboration platform*. https://deon.de/. Accessed 20 July 2020.

Dery, K., Sebastian, I. M., & van der Meulen, N. (2017). The digital workplace is key to digital innovation. *MIS Quarterly Executive, 16*(2), 135–152.

Digital.ai (2020). *14th Annual State of Agile Report*. https://stateofagile.com. Accessed 20 April 2020.

Dimitrijević, S., Jovanović, J., & Devedžić, V. (2015). A comparative study of software tools for user story management. *Information and Software Technology, 57*, 352–368.

Dullemond, K., van Gameren, B., & van Solingen, R. (2012). Supporting distributed software engineering in a fully distributed organization. *5th International Workshop on Co-operative and Human Aspects of Software Engineering (CHASE)*, 30–36. IEEE.

Dybå, T., & Dingsøyr, T. (2008). Empirical studies of agile software development: A systematic review. *Information and Software Technology, 50*(9–10), 833–859.

Dybå, T., Dingsøyr, T., & Moe, N. B. (2014). Agile project management. In G. Ruhe & C. Wohlin (Eds.), *Software project management in a changing world* (pp. 277–300). Springer.

Eckhart, M., & Feiner, J. (2016). How scrum tools may change your agile software development approach. In D. Winkler, S. Biffl, & J. Bergsmann (Eds.), *Software quality: The future of systems- and software development: 8th International Conference, SWQD 2016* (pp. 17–36). Springer.

EU. (2016). General Data Protection Regulation: Regulation (EU) 2016/679.

EU. (2020). The Court of Justice invalidates Decision 2016/1250 on the adequacy of the protection provided by the EU-US Data Protection Shield: Judgment in Case C-311/18. PRESS RELEASE No 91/20. Luxembourg.

Fies, C., & Marshall, J. (2006). Classroom response systems: A review of the literature. *Journal of Science Education and Technology, 15*(1), 101–109.

Fitzgerald, M., Kruschwitz, N., Bonnet, D., & Welch, M. (2013). Embracing digital technology: A new strategic imperative. *MIT Sloan Review Research Report*.

Fowler, M. (2001). The new methodology. *Wuhan University Journal of Natural Sciences, 6*(1–2), 12–24.

Gaikwad, P. K., Jayakumar, C. T., Tilve, E., Bohra, N., Yu, W., & Spichkova, M. (2019). Voice-activated solutions for agile retrospective sessions. *Procedia Computer Science, 159*, 2414–2423.

Gläser, J., & Laudel, G. (2010). *Experteninterviews und qualitative Inhaltsanalyse: Als Instrumente rekonstruierender Untersuchungen* (4th ed.). Springer VS.

Goggin, G. (2009). Adapting the mobile phone: The iPhone and its consumption. *Continuum, 23*(2), 231–244.

Golafshani, N. (2003). Understanding reliability and validity in qualitative research. *Qualitative Report, 8*(4), 597–607.

Goldkuhl, G. (2012). Pragmatism vs interpretivism in qualitative information systems research. *European Journal of Information Systems, 21*(2), 135–146.

Greve, W., Wentura, D., & Gräser, H. (1997). *Wissenschaftliche Beobachtung: Eine Einführung* (2nd ed.). Beltz, PVU.

Heerwagen, J. H., Kampschroer, K., Powell, K. M., & Loftness, V. (2004). Collaborative knowledge work environments. *Building Research & Information, 32*(6), 510–528.

Herbsleb, J. D., & Grinter, R. E. (1999). Splitting the organization and integrating the code. In B. Boehm, D. Garlan, & J. Kramer (Eds.), *Proceedings of the 1999 international conference on software engineering* (pp. 85–95). IEEE.

Hildebrand, K. (1990). *Software Tools: Automatisierung im Software Engineering*. Springer Berlin Heidelberg.

Hollingshead, A. B., Mcgrath, J. E., & O'Connor, K. M. (1993). Group task performance and communication technology. *Small Group Research, 24*(3), 307–333.

Johnson, M.W., & Suskewicz, J. (2020). *Does your company have a long-term plan for remote work?* https://hbr.org/2020/07/does-your-company-have-a-long-term-plan-for-remote-work. Accessed 28 July 2020.

Karis, D., Wildman, D., & Mané, A. (2016). Improving remote collaboration with video conferencing and video portals. *Human-Computer Interaction, 31*(1), 1–58.

Katsma, C., Amrit, C., Hillegersberg, J., & van Sikkel, K. (2013). Can agile software tools bring the benefits of a task board to globally distributed teams? In W. van der Aalst, J. Mylopoulos, M. Rosemann, M.J. Shaw, C. Szyperski, I. Oshri, et al. (Eds.) (1st ed.), *Advances in global sourcing: Models, governance, and relationships. 7th Global Sourcing Workshop 2013, Val d'Isere, France, March 11–14, 2013, Revised Selected Papers* (pp. 163–179). Springer.

Kawulich, B. B. (2004). *Participant observation as a data collection method*. https://www.qualitative-research.net/index.php/fqs/article/view/466/996. Accessed 20 June 2020.

Khazanchi, S., Sprinkle, T. A., Masterson, S. S., & Tong, N. (2018). A spatial model of work relationships: The relationship-building and relationship-straining effects of workspace design. *Academy of Management Review, 43*(4), 590–609.

Kirkman, B. L., & Mathieu, J. E. (2005). The Dimensions and antecedents of team virtuality. *Journal of Management, 31*(5), 700–718.

Kropp, M., Anslow, C., Mateescu, M., Burkhard, R., Vischi, D., & Zahn, C. (2017). Enhancing agile team collaboration through the use of large digital multi-touch Cardwalls. In H. Baumeister, H. Lichter, & M. Riebisch (Eds.), *Agile processes in software engineering and extreme programming: 18th International Conference, XP 2017, Cologne, Germany, May 22–26, 2017, Proceedings* (pp. 119–134). Springer.

Lee, Y. K., Chang, C. T., Lin, Y., & Cheng, Z. H. (2014). The dark side of smartphone usage: Psychological traits, compulsive behavior and technostress. *Computers in Human Behavior, 31*, 373–383.

Mayring, P. (2014). *Qualitative content analysis: Theoretical foundation, basic procedures and software solution.* Beltz Verlag.

Mayring, P., Gläser-Zikuda, M., & Ziegelbauer, S. (2005). Auswertung von Videoaufnahmen mit Hilfe der Qualitativen Inhaltsanalyse - ein Beispiel aus der Unterrichtsforschung. *MedienPädagogik: Zeitschrift für Theorie und Praxis der Medienbildung*, 9 (Visuelle Methoden), 1–17.

McKinsey. (2020). *Reimagining the office and work life after COVID-19.* https://www.mckinsey.com/business-functions/organization/our-insights/reimagining-the-office-and-work-life-after-covid-19. Accessed 28 July 2020.

Mentimeter. (2020). *Interactive presentation software.* https://www.mentimeter.com/. Accessed 20 July 2020.

Miro. (2020). Free online collaborative whiteboard platform. https://miro.com/. Accessed 20 July 2020.

Mishra, D., Mishra, A., & Ostrovska, S. (2012). Impact of physical ambiance on communication, collaboration and coordination in agile software development: An empirical evaluation. *Information and Software Technology, 54*(10), 1067–1078.

Mordi, A., & M. Schoop (2020). Making it tangible—creating a definiton of agile mindset. *Proceedings of the 28th European Conference on Information Systems*. 15–17.

Nerur, S., Mahapatra, R., & Mangalaraj, G. (2005). Challenges of migrating to agile methodologies. *Communications of the ACM, 48*(5), 72–78.

Noll, J., Beecham, S., & Richardson, I. (2010). Global software development and collaboration. *ACM Inroads, 1*(3), 66–78.

Omoronyia, I., Ferguson, J., Roper, M., & Wood, M. (2010). A review of awareness in distributed collaborative software engineering. *Software: Practice and Experience, 40*(12), 1107–1133.

Oxford Dictionary. (2020). *Definition of tool*. https://www.lexico.com/definition/tool. Accessed 13 April 2020.

Portillo-Rodríguez, J., Vizcaíno, A., Piattini, M., & Beecham, S. (2012). Tools used in global software engineering: A systematic mapping review. *Information and Software Technology, 54*(7), 663–685.

Raith, F., Richter, I., & Lindermeier, R. (2017). How project-management-tools are used in agile practice. In *IDEAS 2017: Proceedings of the 21st International Database Engineering & Applications Symposium* (pp. 30–39). New York: Association for Computing Machinery.

Ramesh, B., Cao, L., Mohan, K., & Xu, P. (2006). Can distributed software development be agile? *Communications of the ACM, 49*(10), 41–46.

Ratliff, J. M. (2002). NTT DoCoMo and its i-mode success: Origins and implications. *California Management Review, 44*(3), 55–71.

Rigby, D. K., Sutherland, J., & Takeuchi, H. (2016). Embracing agile: How to master the process that's transforming management. *Harvard Business Review, 94*(5), 40–50.

Rittitum, P., Vatanawood, W., & Thongtak, A. (2016). Digital scrum board using leap motion. In *2016 IEEE/ACIS 15th International Conference on Computer and Information Science (ICIS)6/26/2016—6/29/2016, Okayama, Japan* (pp. 1–4). IEEE.

Robinson, P. T. (2019). Communication network in an agile distributed software development team. In *2019 ACM/IEEE 14th International Conference on Global Software Engineering: ICGSE 2019: Montréal, Canada, 25–26 May 2019: proceedings.5/25/2019—5/26/2019, Montreal, QC, Canada* (pp. 100–104). IEEE.

Rola, P., Kuchta, D., & Kopczyk, D. (2016). Conceptual model of working space for Agile (Scrum) project team. *Journal of Systems and Software, 118*, 49–63.

Schreier, M. (2014). Varianten qualitativer Inhaltsanalyse: Ein Wegweiser im Dickicht der Begrifflichkeiten. *Forum: Qualitative Social Research, 15*(1).

Seidel, T., & Prenzl, M. (2010). Beobachtungsverfahren. In H. Holling & B. Schmitz (Eds.), *Handbuch Statistik, Methoden und Evaluation* (pp. 139–152). Hogrefe.

Sellberg, C., & Susi, T. (2014). Technostress in the office: A distributed cognition perspective on human–technology interaction. *Cognition, Technology & Work, 16*(2), 187–201.

Shrivastava, S. V., & Rathod, U. (2014). Categorization of risk factors for distributed agile projects. *Information and Software Technology, 58*, 373–387.

Skjott Linneberg, M., & Korsgaard, S. (2019). Coding qualitative data: A synthesis guiding the novice. *Qualitative Research Journal, 19*(3), 259–270.

Smite, D., Moe, N. B., Floryan, M., Levinta, G., & Chatzipetrou, P. (2020). Spotify guilds. *Communications of the ACM, 63*(3), 56–61.

Stray, V., Moe, N. B., & Noroozi, M. (2019). Slack me if you can! Using enterprise social networking tools in virtual agile teams. In *2019 ACM/IEEE 14th International Conference on Global Software Engineering: ICGSE 2019: Montréal, Canada, 25–26 May 2019: Proceedings. 5/25/2019—5/26/2019, Montreal, QC, Canada* (pp. 111–121). IEEE.

Tseng, Y. H., & Lin, C. T. (2011). Enhancing enterprise agility by deploying agile drivers, capabilities and providers. *Information Sciences, 181*(17), 3693–3708.

Verschuren, P. (2003). Case study as a research strategy: Some ambiguities and opportunities. *International Journal of Social Research Methodology, 6*(2), 121–139.

Vishnubhotla, S. D., Mendes, E., & Lundberg, L. (2018). Designing a capability-centric web tool to support agile team composition and task allocation. In *2018 ACM/IEEE 11th International Workshop on Cooperative and Human Aspects of Software Engineering: CHASE 2018: 27 May 2018, Gothenburg, Sweden: proceedings. Ed. by A./I.I.W.o.C.a.H.A.o.S. Engineering. 5/27/2018—5/27/2018, Gothenburg, Sweden* (pp. 41–44). IEEE.

Walsham, G. (1995). Interpretive case studies in IS research: Nature and method. *European Journal of Information Systems, 4*(2), 74–81.

Wang, X., Maurer, F., Morgan, R., & Oliveira, J. (2010). Tools for supporting distributed agile project planning. In D. Šmite, N. B. Moe, & P. J. Ågerfalk (Eds.), *Agility across time and space: Implementing agile methods in global software projects* (pp. 183–199). Springer.

Wickström, G., & Bendix, T. (2000). The "Hawthorne effect"–What did the original Hawthorne studies actually show? *Scandinavian Journal of Work, Environment & Health, 26*(4), 363–367.

Zapier. (2020). *The easiest way to automate your work*. https://zapier.com/. Accessed 20 July 2020.

PART II

# Agility on the Organizational Level

CHAPTER 5

# From Agile Teams and Organizations to Agile Business Ecosystems? Contradiction Management as a Requirement of Agile Scaling and Transformation Processes

*Stephanie Porschen-Hueck and Stefan Sauer*

## Introduction: Current Tendencies (Not Only) in Software Development

Currently, agile approaches to management and organization that are remarkable in at least two respects are gaining momentum. On the one hand, they promise to follow through with self-organization and flexibilization by creating radically new structures intended to supersede established models of hierarchy, leadership and organization. On the other

S. Porschen-Hueck (✉)
Institute for Social Science Research (ISF), Munich, Germany
e-mail: stephanie.porschen-hueck@isf-muenchen.de

S. Sauer
Nuremberg Campus of Technology (NCT), Friedrich-Alexander-Universität Erlangen-Nürnberg, Nuremberg, Germany
e-mail: stefan.sauer@fau.de



S. Pfeiffer et al. (eds.), *The Agile Imperative*, Dynamics of Virtual Work,
https://doi.org/10.1007/978-3-030-73994-2_5

hand, they share a number of problems with previous approaches to reorganization aiming at de-centralization and self-organization. In addition, by challenging top-down decision-making channels, bureaucratic procedures and even organizational boundaries, they radicalize tendencies for blurring and even dissolution of boundaries. Whereas organizations tend to respond to VUCA through agile approaches as far as their internal structures and processes are concerned, they increasingly make use of ecosystem approaches with respect to their external relationships. Within business ecosystems, complex individualized products are provided via networking, which means that a company is not compelled to keep all the resources and competencies to itself. Thus, similar to the de-centralized agile organization with its pitfalls, de-centralized orchestration on equal terms (as opposed to the accustomed centralized orchestration) is an essential challenge for the shaping of adaptational and collaborative ecosystems.

Therefore, on the one hand, one might ask whether these new approaches are again confronted with limits and obstacles fundamentally counteracting a re-invention of company organization—or whether they actually harbour the potential to overcome hierarchy or even the problems of contradictory work requirements, workplace stress, etc. On the other hand, besides the issue of business ecosystem potentials, the question arises whether new areas of tension are emerging concerning issues of definition, control and governance. Such issues should become increasingly relevant in the context of platform-based business models that seem to be becoming increasingly important. In this chapter, we shall try to find answers to these questions regarding Agile Scaling and platform-based Business Ecosystems.

We examine these questions from the perspective of the sociology of work and organization, using empirical and conceptual examples from ongoing research projects to develop insights into contradiction management of organizational opening and flexibilization strategies bottom-up (agile scaling) and outside-in (organizational environment). The crux is the question whether and how agility can be embedded in an organization that relies on hierarchical structures for the rest of its activities, and whether agility can serve as a starting point for a business ecosystem which must be initiated by someone in the first place. In the following section, we shall provide a concise overview of new concepts concerning agility in organizations and inter-organizational collaboration in ecosystems (Section "New Approaches to Management and Organization:

Agile Scaling and Business Ecosystems"). Next, we shall shed empirical light on the interaction of these agility concepts with and within organizations characterized by historically evolved bureaucratic structures (Section "Empirical Highlights: On the Way to an Agile and Environment-Related Organization"). On the basis of our findings, we shall then derive preliminary principles for an active contradiction management suitable to processing these approaches in the sense of "good work" (Section "Conceptual Interventions: Active Processing of Contradictions in Participatory Ecosystems and Good Agile Work"). The final Section ("Outlook") is devoted to a preliminary conclusion.[1]

## New Approaches to Management and Organization: Agile Scaling and Business Ecosystems

In agile approaches of recent years, a paradigmatic re-orientation can be observed: they assume that limits of plannability exist, taking the fundamental complexity and contingency of causes and effects within and beyond organizations as their starting point. This includes concepts of learning (e.g. Argyris & Schön, 2008; Senge, 2011) and agile (e.g. Grund, 2015; Meyer, 2014), integral evolutionary (Laloux, 2014), holocratic (Robertson, 2015) or swarm organizations (e.g. Neef & Burmeister, 2005). These approaches replace the traditional striving for (nearly) comprehensive planning by a striving for agency, an effort to make employees and managers capable of acting in complex situations. Forms of distributive, collaborative or integral leadership and decision processes in self-organized teams in which all members are on equal terms take centre stage. In this way, organizations try to cope with increasing uncertainties and growing complexity in more and more volatile markets, in an effort to deal with frequent ambiguities and to gain pro-active agency. Similar objectives are being pursued with the building of business ecosystems. In this context, organizations increasingly make use of

[1] We owe thanks to Sophia Rossmann for her most helpful research and working papers on the topic of agile organization and scaling and Kurt Rachlitz for his valuable research, empirical and conceptual work and also his discussion of the topics of platforms and business ecosystems. Many thanks also to Frank Seiß for valuable editing and the translation. This article draws on previous joint discussions on the topic of agile work and organizations and is based on the joint expert dialog about the "new" challenges of making platform-based business ecosystems more agile and participatory towards the stakeholders. It builds on the joint work with Judith Neumer on "agile scaling" (Neumer et al., 2018).

three kinds of resources: (a) persons and their subject potentials; (b) technology, particularly platform and cloud technologies; and (c) meta-organizations or business ecosystems. Below, we shall outline ideas and concepts of Agile Scaling (roll-out of agile principles from single units into the overall organization) and Business Ecosystems (network organizations for the creation of complementary products or services).

## *Agile Scaling*

The starting point for approaches of agile scaling is to be found in self-organized teamwork in agile software development. Since Scrum is considered the agile approach most in use (Komus, 2020), we shall focus on two scaling approaches originating from the use of Scrum. In our description we draw on Spearman and Dolman (2016) and their Agile Scaling Knowledgebase Decision Matrix created to compare nine frameworks for agile scaling, thus ensuring that the description is oriented towards the empirical relevance of the approaches. The most popular frameworks emerging from this matrix are Scrum-of-Scrums (SoS) and the Scaled Agile Framework (SAFe) (Leffingwell, 2007). Radigan (2016) explains the Scrum-of-Scrums framework: if several Scrum teams cooperate in a big project, Scrum-of-Scrums is the next step towards an extension of agile methods. The main element of Scrum-of-Scrums is a stand-up meeting with several teams, meaning a short meeting that serves to keep participants in the whole organization informed about important events in the complete portfolio. In a first step, each team determines a member, ideally a member with a technical function, to represent the team in the Scrum-of-Scrums. The Scrum-of-Scrums is a democratic meeting and its procedure is the same as in any team stand-up meeting. The idea is to inform technical stakeholders at an early date and provide a forum in which they can share their views. Some companies also make a point of adopting other Scrum ceremonies in the Scrum-of-Scrums, such as Sprint Planning and Retrospective. The team representatives meet immediately before the Sprint Planning meetings of their respective teams, discussing which tasks should be dealt with in the upcoming Sprints. Thus, it is possible to avoid worrying dependencies between the teams or address integration problems even before they become really virulent. If a Retrospective is part of the Scrum-of-Scrums, it takes place after the Sprint Retrospectives of the respective teams. In the Retrospective, the participants talk about tasks that might make coordination beyond teams necessary.

The "Scaled Agile Framework" (SAFe) is another well-known approach to scaling agile methods in big companies (Leffingwell, 2007). It offers more structure for the extension of agile methods than Scrum-of-Scrums. SAFe defines three levels within the company: Portfolio, Program and Team. This structure is usually attractive for larger enterprises, as SAFe has a multi-level approach to delivering work. Larger areas of connected tasks are called "Themes", which are again allocated to what are known as "Epics", related to business issues and architectural issues. Business Epics describe customer-oriented initiatives, such as the introduction of a new product. Architectural Epics are technological initiatives, for instance, a migration from windows-based to linux-based servers. From these Epics, the Portfolio Backlog[2] is compiled. As soon as a company starts to execute the Portfolio Backlog under the priorities established by the product management and the technical management, the Business Epics or Architectural Epics involved are transformed into an agile Program with an "Agile Release Train"[3] of its own. This means that several teams within the company collaborate to execute the respective Program. All Programs include several features and architectural task elements forming the Program Backlog. On the team level, each team has a Team Backlog of its own, derived from the Program Backlog. The teams work together in order to deliver usable software after each Sprint and to ensure coordination with other teams within the Program.

Both frameworks share the underlying approach of structured self-organization with institutionalized coordination procedures but also

[2] Within the context of agile methods, the concept of backlog means a composition of tasks and technical requirements relevant for the creation of the final product. The backlog is changeable according to the project progression; its maintenance is the task of the Product Owner. In the context of SAFe, the backlog is also applied on the level of the organization as a whole.

[3] The Agile Release Train can be defined according to the Blogger Anshuman Singh: "The Agile Release Train (ART) is the primary value delivery construct in SAFe®. The Agile Release Train is a long lived, self-organizing team of Agile Teams, a virtual organization (5–12 teams) that plans, commits, and executes together. ARTs are organized around the enterprise's significant Value Streams and live solely to realize the promise of that value by building solutions that deliver benefit to the end user. Hence, an ART is basically a team of Teams responsible for the regular release of Features and business benefits" (https://www.digite.com/blog/agile-release-train-art/).

leeway for development. The orchestration of different organizations in the business ecosystems is described below.

### *Business Ecosystems*

To an increasing extent, organizations are not only changing in terms of their internal structure but also in terms of their relationship to the external organizational environment. This can be interpreted as the next step in a historical process beginning with the marketization of enterprises and the establishment of "indirect control" mechanisms. In a nutshell: within a "traditional" enterprise, the management responded to market requirements by formulating top-down commandments and passing them on to their employees, who acted within a sealed-off space of value creation and manufacturing. When the organizations were increasingly opened to market influences, this direct control was increasingly replaced by indirect control and the internal procedures and relationships underwent a process of marketization. Presently, the opening process is reaching a higher level, with the objective to actively interact with the organizational environment and even to co-create and shape this environment.[4] An effort to accomplish this goal is cooperative service networks (Huchler et al., 2018) or business ecosystems. According to the definition of Peltoniemi and Vuori (2005), a business ecosystem is a "dynamic structure which consists of an interconnected population of organizations" (cit. Semolic, 2012: 6). The objective to co-create and shape the organizational environment by forming a business ecosystem means that striving for complementarity with assets of other organizations takes centre stage, as opposed to the strategic use of the assets owned by the organization itself: "strategy is becoming, to an increasing extent, the art of managing assets that one does not own" (Lansiti & Levien, 2004: 1). The same authors (2004: 221f.) emphasize that the effective use of distributed competences is crucial: "From a world of vertical integration, internal capabilities, internal R&D, internal projects, and internal infrastructure, we have come to a world of mutual dependencies, distributed innovation, technology integration, trading collaboration, and on-demand capabilities. Leveraging the distributed assets of an extended network of business

[4] The question whether this implies a distancing from indicator-based stipulations and controlling methods is an empirical one and has to be answered on the basis of empirical data.

partners has opened the way to unprecedented innovation and operational flexibility".

Platform business models provide the preconditions for business ecosystems on a new comprehensive basis. Business ecosystems focus on the value of the ecosystem as a whole, rather than the isolated customer value. According to Alstyne et al. (2016), business ecosystems concentrate on orchestration of resources, rather than control of resources and on external interaction rather than internal optimization: "The network of producers and consumers is the chief asset" (ibid.: 5). Ecosystems can be conceptualized around a product and they can be interpreted as primarily mediated by technology: a platform. On the other hand, a business ecosystem can also be conceived as a focal entity with a company at its core which is surrounded by other companies or organizations (Jacobides et al., 2018). In any case, enterprises are increasingly challenged to answer the question as to how and where they want (or have) to locate themselves in an ecosystem and how they can find a strategical place for themselves in their value creation processes.

It is obvious that the idea of business ecosystems is closely related to the concepts of virtual enterprises (Nazarenko & Camarinha-Matos, 2019) and network organizations. Whereas the discussions about business ecosystems tend to focus on value creation, the debates about network organizations highlight issues like inter-organizational collaboration (Sydow et al., 2016) or Inter-Organizational Relations (IOR) management practices (Wilkinson et al., 2013).[5] Other important themes are the "key predictors of effectiveness of network governance forms" (Provan & Kenis, 2008: 237) and, more generally, the problem of ecosystem governance (Adner, 2017; Gawer, 2014; Uludag et al., 2016; Wareham et al., 2014), as well as "potential sources of dialectical tensions in alliances" (Bouchikhi, 1998; De Rond & Bouchikhi, 2004: 66). We refer to them here because they prove to be crucial areas of conflict in our empirical cases. Hence, they are also essential references for our concept of contradiction management.

[5] For similarities and distinctions between networks and ecosystems, see Shipilov and Gawer (2020).

## Empirical Highlights: On the Way to an Agile and Environment-Related Organization

In this section, we present our empirical findings concerning the scaling of agile methods in enterprises on the basis of two case studies from business-to-business software development. In addition, we present some results from a case study from both the business-to-business and business-to-customer software industry that deals with the challenges of building a business ecosystem.

### *Agile Scaling*

We conducted 30 expert interviews with employees in agile projects, managers and agility coaches and condensed them to enterprise case studies in the sense of case study research in sociology of work and industry (Yin, 2013). The findings gathered were fed back to the employees at a feedback workshop in order to gather further empirical material, to verify the findings and to initiate organizational change as part of the integrated research-and-design process (Huchler & Sauer, 2015; Porschen-Hueck & Neumer, 2015; Sauer, 2017).

The case studies are highly contrastive: in the medium-sized company *mesize* with about 450 employees, the development teams work out systemic solutions for communication and management of customer companies. For a number of years, they have been using agile methods. They make a point of not only implementing the agile project management framework Scrum but also permanently modifying and adapting it to the work processes of the teams. The scope of action allotted to the teams is considerable, although the company as a whole is not completely agile, as will be shown below. The company *macorp*, on the other hand, is a major corporation with more than 20,000 employees developing IT infrastructure for business customers. The development unit also uses teams, but more along the lines of a traditional waterfall model. In recent years, the agile framework Scrum has been increasingly introduced. However, the employees experience the implementation process as highly customer-driven: the tenor of the interviews is that the company has become more agile because the customers demand agility.

A feature common to both companies, in spite of their considerable differences, is that agile teams are more or less embedded in an environment which is, at the very least, not decidedly agile. Certainly, *mesize* is characterized by flat hierarchies and an informal corporate culture, but also has hierarchical leadership roles, as is the case in *macorp*. *Macorp* moreover tends to have a bureaucratic leadership culture, orientated towards a zero-error policy. The companies differ with respect to the roles of the managers and the scope of action allotted to the teams, particularly their opportunities for shaping agile methods in a self-organized way. Agile Scaling in the sense of the approaches outlined above (Section "New Approaches to Management and Organization: Agile Scaling and Business Ecosystems"), which tend to focus on ideal procedures without considering historically grown structures and cultures, does not take place in either of the case companies. Hence, rather than looking at Agile Scaling as an ideal-typical implementation of a scaling framework, we shall present the actual proceedings in both case companies with special reference to the scaling process (a) by reference to the relationship of the Scrum roles to managers/superiors, and the situatedness of the teams within the organization as a whole, and (b) by reference to customer relations.

Above the level of the Scrum teams and the Scrum roles (Scrum Master, Product Owner, developers), *mesize* has executives who are not elected or delegated by the teams but are appointed top-down, in a traditional way. Above this first level of superiors, we have the top management, consisting of the three owners of the company. In spite of this structural hierarchy, the interactions within the company are described as very collegial, without much hierarchical influence. This feature is very clearly evident in a team consisting of many young developers. This team is assigned to an executive who has been in the company for many years and, for this reason, has very good knowledge of the company's basic product, which is the basis for the customer solutions it has developed. Owing to this excellent product knowledge, this executive participates in some of the agile meetings but is only permitted to inject himself into the debate if requested to do so by the team. This is a prime example of how *mesize* strives to combine agile methods not with a pull-out of leadership but rather with an orientation towards supporting and coaching leadership. Thus the teams and the Scrum roles maintain a high status in spite of their embeddedness within a company that is ultimately hierarchically structured. Here, the place of agile scaling is taken by a high acceptance of the agile roles and particularly the agile teams, who are appreciated as the heart of the organization. There are only two levels of management. The leaders do not come from the teams but they seriously strive for close contact with them in the sense of participatory and supportive leadership.

However, the lack of Agile Scaling engenders severe limitations for interaction between the teams and the customers. If the customer company is not able or willing to proceed in an agile way, which is quite often the case, the agile teams are obliged to find a flexible response. In this case, they try to organize cooperation “as agilely as possible” given the customer demands, for instance by means of a Kanban board. As employees said in the interviews, this may result in “flexibility overload”, for instance, if customers don’t accept the Sprint as a necessary protective space for the developer teams but permanently demand changes to planning or re-planning according to their specifications. The managers’ reaction is to pledge that in this case, potential grievances on the part of the customers will be disregarded in performance reviews and appraisals. This means that credit of trust is granted to the employees in the internal relationships. However, the pressure from the outside remains; the leadership level pulls out here and doesn’t intervene actively in the negotiation processes with the customer. This is a problematic experience for the employees, particularly concerning the resources the team has at its disposal.

To sum up, although *mesize* is ultimately hierarchically structured, the enterprise places high value on the freedom of action for the teams and the teams’ needs are placed at the heart of organizational action, in line with Agile Scaling. However, customer negotiations usually come first and therefore customer demands simply have to be because of the idea of “focus on customers”. This may lead to a form of “decreed over-flexibility” which causes much stress, both in the daily dealings and in decreed temporary stand-ins in other projects. And these features are obstacles for comprehensive and consistent Agile Scaling.

*Macorp*, on the other hand, has a strictly hierarchical and fairly pronounced bureaucratic structure, in combination with a zero-error orientation. The isolated agile teams are integrated into these structures and their members are socialized accordingly. The consequence is that all agile roles are implemented but above the team level a project leader(ship) exists, in bigger projects even complemented by leaders for development, testing and planning one level below. A striking feature in this company is that the Product Owner is usually not just one person but a team, often barely greater in number than the developers’ team itself. This is an indication of a very marked planning paradigm, both above and within the agile structures. The example shows that if agile scaling is not taken seriously, this can engender severe consequences: not only do rigid hierarchies prevail beyond the teams, but hierarchical structures also diffuse into the teams, on both the cultural and the structural level (e.g. PO teams).

The people we interviewed consider the customers the main drivers of the implementation of agile methods: "We are agile if the customer wants us to be agile". In this perspective, the customer appears as both an enabler and a guarantor of agile procedures. The customer's interpretation of agility in real daily cooperation is, however, often wayward and self-centred, as described above in the case of *mesize*. In this interpretation, agility often implies the idea of unlimited flexibility on the part of the team, including short-term requirements to change demanded by the customer during an ongoing Sprint. These demands have to be staved off by the team, the Scrum Master and the Product Owner—otherwise they have to be flexibly integrated into the Sprints. The latter is possible if the customer suggests few changes that make sense functionally and professionally—and if he is ready to make concessions himself. For instance, if a new requirement is accepted during an ongoing Sprint, another requirement, at least equally time-consuming, can be postponed to the next Sprint. This openness on the part of the customer is necessary and it depends essentially, according to the interviewees, on the personal and structural willingness of the customers' employees to cooperate closely with the *macorp* teams.

In summary, *macorp* is indeed conscious of the necessity and the value of Agile Scaling and steps in this direction are in planning. For instance, there is a plan to make the sales department more agile, not only in the sense that they should take into account the agile proceedings of developer teams but also in the sense that salespeople should themselves work in an agile framework, as agile sales teams. This would be a very important development for the agile developer teams, because customers are the main drivers of agility in this company, as mentioned above. An agile sales department might be able to support agile customer cooperation.

In both case studies, it could be observed that the customer is highly relevant for the handling of agility. The customer's potential relevance for agile proceedings is a strong indication of growing integration of customers. This integration often happens in the form of Business Ecosystems.

### *Business Ecosystems*

Within the framework of a qualitative research design to investigate the building and shaping of platform-based business ecosystems, approximately thirty interviews were conducted with diverse partners to discuss their ideas and conceptions of a participatory ecosystem. Some of the findings of this project will be presented here.[6]

Business ecosystems, as agile teams, are not necessarily built from scratch. Often they are initiated by enterprises that already have a historically grown organization which might be more or less agile.[7] The crucial point in the establishment of ecosystems is the systematic development of the orchestrator role, which is closely linked to the question as to how the design of a participatory governance structure is defined.

An empirical example demonstrates that the solution of these decisive questions can lag far behind technological platform development. In the case example, an experimental and iterative approach has been adopted in this respect, getting the ecosystem partners on board one by one. The "lead organization" of this platform-based ecosystem has its starting point in a historically evolved network. The idea is that this network should develop into an ecosystem operating in line with diverse criteria which are still in the process of negotiation. Thus a network relying on contract relationships is to be transformed into a participatory business ecosystem for value-adding network partners which can also integrate new partners. Participation rights are to be designated in the sense of an expert democracy, thus creating a counterbalance to hierarchy. For the identity of the network, a "Commons" culture is intended, which implies the distribution of shares, the re-investment of the lion's share of the profits into the ecosystem, and the development of an overarching space for learning.

[6] These findings could be established in the course of a broad-based study within the framework of the experimental space SmartGenoLab, funded by the Federal Ministry of Labour and Social Affairs as a part of the INQA initiative (duration 11/2018 to 11/2021).

[7] Oesterreich and Schröder point out in their collegial leadership model, frequently cited in German-language literature, that the design of the framework and the reconfiguration itself have to be initiated by the top management of the firm. Afterwards, a body of experts can take on this responsibility, as can other members, where appropriate (Oestereich & Schröder, 2016: 59ff.). The transformation from an ecosystem conceived by a central body into an ecosystem under more or less decentralized control is a demanding task, necessitating effective contradiction management.

For the transformation process, the case company is intensely engaged in the "six keys to unlock ecosystem advantage", enumerated by Williamson and De Meyer (2012):

1. Pinpointing where value is created
2. Defining an architecture of differential partner roles
3. Stimulating complementary partner investments
4. Reducing transaction costs
5. Facilitating joint learning across the network
6. Engineering effective ways to capture profit.

There are extensive activities to perform these "key tasks", for instance, technological adaptations, a change of revenue model, skill development, etc.

Moreover, the issue of ecosystem governance (Adner, 2017; Gawer, 2014; Uludag et al., 2016; Wareham et al., 2014) is essential for the potential participation by the ecosystem partners. After all, the very idea of the process of enterprises opening up towards a business ecosystem is mutual propagation along the lines of "I give that you may give" (do ut des). In the case example, expectations of the ecosystem partners prove to be rather diverse. Members (including potential future members) harbour, for instance, very different ideas as to the centralized or de-centralized design of the orchestrator role. The tensions between "demands for centralized network control" and "claims for autonomy and participation" are a prominent area of dispute. Further contradictions, corresponding to those of Agile Scaling, are added. They will be described in the following section under the heading of "intervention issues".

## Conceptual Interventions: Active Processing of Contradictions in Participatory Ecosystems and Good Agile Work

The empirically based and theory-guided considerations on reflexive agile scaling and business ecosystems in this section are not aimed at constructing another business model or providing a best-practice example of these organization and business model processes. Rather, we intend to outline principles of a culture of active contradiction management, devised to create the ability to shape agile scaling and business ecosystems in the sense of integration in order to enable good work. In order to establish the necessary integrating framework for agile scaling and business ecosystems, it is essential to understand and handle organizational contradictions or areas of tension in the context of self-organized work. The idea is to permit "good work" and to avoid the confrontation of self-organized work with too many contradictory influences from outside that cannot be solved by self-organized action. Examples of typical contradictions are the following[8]:

a. *Hierarchy and control vs. self-organization and autonomy*: The hierarchically structured bureaucratic organization with its correspondent division of work on the one hand and a self-organized de-centralized work mode on the other are characterized by contradictory logics. Self-organization implies a more informal mode of working than hierarchical-bureaucratic organization. In a formalized framework, self-organization is regularly stretched to its limits. Moreover, self-organization is often actually coupled with a (re-) introduction of formalization by means of *both* direct and indirect control or governance of work organization and meta-organization through organizational rules as well as technology/digital systems. This is one of the most virulent areas of tension: self-organization is demanded from above but only supported to a limited extent. Rather, a kind of "limited self-organization" is practised to rope self-organization in. All the same, in modern organizations the general trend is towards self-organization and there is a great interest in informal solutions beyond rigid rules and extensive meetings.

[8] The following systematization of tensions is an extended version of a systematization previously developed by the PräFo project in cooperation with Margit Weihrich and Marc Jungtäubl (University of Augsburg) on the basis of comprehensive empirical surveys in the fields of technological engineering work and service work. The PräFo project aimed to establish preventive measures for occupational health and safety in formalized self-responsible work. Reflexive scaling is an important concept in this project. PräFo stands for Prevention of Stress in Formalized Work in Services and Technological Engineering. Our subproject was Prevention of Stress in Formalized Work in Technological Engineering. The project was funded by the German Ministry of Education and Research and supervised by the PTKA Project Management Agency in Karlsruhe. It ran from November 2015 to May 2019.

Moreover, coming to terms with participatory self-organization is a special challenge in business ecosystems. Here, it is not only the integration of distinct cultures of work and organization that is a demanding task. It is also important to identify the relevant control or steering points (see Ziegler, 2020: 229) and to establish a governance structure that reflects the interests of the ecosystem members.

In our case example (see above, Section "Business Ecosystems") there are conflicting and even contradictory ideas regarding this issue. On the one hand, there are demands for the existence of a promoter or central orchestrator who initiates and sets a canon of value, revenue and pricing models, road maps, learning platforms and communities. This orchestrator role is associated with ideas of a powerful actor protecting interests, allocating projects, designating planning parameters, setting standards, defining distinguishing features for differentiation between the centre and the periphery, permanently developing the platform technology further, and so on. On the other hand, potential stakeholders expect that exclusivity is precluded (multihoming) and spaces for joint priorization and theme setting are opened and warranted. On one hand, there is a desire for all partners to be on equal terms, independent of their specific roles. On the other hand, interested parties tend to opt for open and voluntary participation and cooperation and claim to have a say in strategic decisions (as questions of product, technology, participation, roadmaps, etc.). This observation confirms findings from a large-scale research and development project devoted to the development of a cooperative service network in health economy.[9] The establishment and maintenance of such ecosystems engenders high demands to coordinate the network cooperation in a way that both the stakeholders ' respective interests and the objectives of the ecosystem as a whole, in the sense of a cooperative surplus value, are

[9] The FISnet project (Flexible, Individualized Service Networks. Models of Preventive Health Services in the Region of Augsburg/Schwaben), funded by the Federal Ministry of Education and Research and supervised by the PTKA Project Management Agency (duration 11/2014 to 10/2018) investigated aspects of interactive coordination and networking work design and analyzed the preconditions and difficulties of the establishment of an ecosystem on equal terms. Over 12 main partners from research and practice took part in this project. The implementation of these models involved many additional partners.

satisfied. This involves typical coordination problems concerning, for instance, communication and understanding, contribution and distribution, which all have to be efficiently solved in the interests of the ecosystem, but also questions of definitory power (Huchler et al., 2018: 131ff.).

b. *Cooperation & trust vs. competition & contract*: Self-organization is generally based on cooperation (unless the term is used for individual work by individual people). In the context of the approaches discussed here, cooperation refers to several entities and people: cooperation as the principle of work in individual working teams and in teams composed of members of several organizations, cooperation with customers, cooperation with upstream and downstream units within the organization and cooperation of organizations with their environment. Such cooperation requires responsibilities, skills and material and temporal resources. It also requires trust as a fundamental building block of interaction processes. Hence preconditions of a legal, factual and social nature have to be warranted to permit successful cooperation on all levels. Contradictions between cooperation requirements and competition principles have to be avoided or managed, and resources (such as time) have to be provided in sufficient measure. Competitive relationships jeopardizing cooperation may occur between or within teams, for instance, if teams or even individual team members are compared to one another via very close-meshed controlling processes or if trust is undermined by conflicts of interests and perspectives. But the danger of competitive relationships is particularly relevant in cross-company cooperation within business ecosystems, reflected in the much-used term "coopetition". As far as new business models are concerned, the question of an exploitation strategy is very relevant for the keystone player: how do I succeed in achieving valuable network effects with my partners on the platform? Conversely, the partners will also have to assess the risk that the promoter might ultimately try to reclaim independence, taking over interesting developments for his or her own business and thus narrowing the partners' scope for action regarding products or technology.

c. *Economization & participation vs. professionalization & speed*: Conflicts between controlling level and working level and between organizational structures are also relevant to this issue. The credo that measurability is a necessary precondition of economic efficiency is a powerful driver of formalization in all of its aspects. Another important credo is participation: all stakeholders have to be involved and are interested in comprehensive information and participation in decision-making processes. However, these ideas are not always consistent with the requirements of product development from a professional point of view. Work intensification and acceleration of product delivery e.g. in sprints are not necessarily compatible with the motivation to create well-engineered products, and from a professional point of view not all stakeholders are necessarily able to contribute on an equally informed level. The experts' professionalism and their assessment of the "right" speed tend to collide both with imperatives of economic control and with the idea of participation of all partners on equal terms. These contradictions show up in our empirical results in both approaches: in the case of Agile Scaling they manifest in unsuitable cycles for the discussion of releasable part products with the customer; in the case of Business Ecosystems they become apparent in the integration of stakeholders who are unable to contribute to a concrete development process—at least at certain points in time—or who don't possess the necessary competencies in certain strategic questions. On one hand, it is important to avoid a one-sided focus on speed and economy, especially in the implementation stages of the approaches and the initial finding stages of projects. On the other hand, unproductive time-consuming meetings with too many partners and processes yielding only poor results should also be avoided. It is necessary to mediate between excessive speed and dysfunctional delay.

d. *Formal processes vs. material needs*: This contradiction refers to a fundamental paradox inherent to all organizations (Clegg et al., 2002). On the one hand, organizations depend on formalization of processes and bureaucratic structures, but, on the other hand, they depend on their employees' subject potentials such as creativity and self-organization. This paradox cannot be dissolved, neither through agility (see Nicklich et al. in this volume) nor through business ecosystems. But these approaches do change the setting in which this paradox can be dealt with by conceptually expanding the space for the realization of subject potentials. However, this expansion often takes on a one-sided shape in companies, manifesting in demands placed on employees without the provision of sufficient resources and competencies. A well-known example is quality management that requires that so much effort be devoted to documentation that it ultimately thwarts the actual goal of optimizing the production process and/or the (material or immaterial) product. Another example: in software development for embedded systems, formal adherence to a two-week Sprint rhythm may be inappropriate if the hardware end requires longer development cycles due to its material properties. In business ecosystems, again, on the one hand there may be a contradiction between formalization of coordination and situated informal exchange. On the other hand, participatory structures may necessitate additional formalization processes. New participation approaches may collide with informal customs of partner integration (and privileges) and path dependencies in partner management. Both examples demonstrate the need for formal procedures that guarantee quality standards, make goals tangible and promote sustainability principles without becoming an end in themselves and losing sight of the material core.

e. *Tools/ "toolism" vs. processes*: Part of the formalization of organizations is the installation of processes to support productive work. Tools are used to make the work easier. However, the use of tools may also have the opposite effect: complicating work activities and causing extra effort. For instance, the use of the software tool JIRA,[10] often installed to support agile processes, may under certain circumstances prove more irritating than supportive, especially in the introduction stage of an agile process. JIRA establishes a comprehensive transparency and new control options over the work process which may contribute to a sceptical attitude on the part of the employees. Hence under such circumstances the "analogous" whiteboard might be a much more practical tool. However, for large and distributed cooperation, the chances for non-virtual hands-on solutions are not so good. In any case, in order to avoid "toolism", it is necessary to repeatedly compare the actual current state with

[10] JIRA is the most applied software package for issue tracking, as Stettina and Heijstek (2011) explored in 79 software engineers from eight teams located in 13 different countries (pp. 3 and 5). The authors also pointed out that documentation is seen rather as a burden than as a co-created (core) artefact and found support for the perceptions in the literature that without ensuring a proper documentation process agile, methods can cause major knowledge loss during or after system development (p. 7). This shows that documentation (and documentation requirements) are not always seen as a counter-productive formalization.

the actual needs of all participants. In the case of business ecosystems, this also means reviewing the overall orientation. A system should not be one-sidedly tailored to the needs of platform technology and the development environment but should also support the community by providing platforms for exchange and learning as well as opportunities for in-person meetings. Such opportunities are important for the development of mutual trust.

## Outlook

The concepts of Agile Scaling in organizations and business ecosystems in organizational environments seem to be both promising and necessary. Promising because of their focus on supporting self-organized work, necessary because they are needed to meet the challenges of VUCA and positioning a company within the value-added process of a digital economy. Both approaches share attractive features: extensive self-organization of work; participation opportunities far beyond the range of influence traditionally given; and cooperation-oriented proceedings in business ecosystems. But as we demonstrated above in our analysis, a lot of conditions have to be met to successfully implement them, especially in mutual integration of both approaches. Bureaucratic structures, centralized control of networks and organizational cultures tend to be persistent; they cannot be changed in the blink of an eye. For an "agile value system", it is advisable not to rely solely on tools and strategies oriented around economic and administrative needs but to also be mindful of the time necessary for the integration process and its accompaniment (Eckstein & Buck, 2018). In our empirical analysis, we could establish a number of contradictions that have to be negotiated time and again. This is especially true in implementation stages, but will also prove necessary far beyond this phase. The approaches of Agile Scaling and business ecosystems offer good opportunities for such negotiation processes due to the idea of participation that is fundamental to both of them. But they will certainly also need permanent monitoring, for instance within the framework of Retrospectives, an agile meeting format that is often mentioned in this context. In the case of building a business ecosystem, a specifically adapted institutional reflexity will be a sustainable building block, including e.g. instances of self-observation and critique, systematic resort to third-party observation, communicative reference to external perceptions, open evaluation of consequences of actions, and drafts of alternative scenarios (see Moldaschl, 2005: 368).

## References

Adner, R. (2017). Ecosystem as structure: An actionable construct for strategy. *Journal of Management, 43*(1), 39–58. https://doi.org/10.1177/0149206316678451.

Alstyne, M. W. Van, Parker, G. G., & Choudary, S. P. (2016). Pipelines, platforms, and the new rules of strategy. *Harvard Business Review, 94*(4).

Argyris, C., & Schön, D. (2008). *Die Lernende Organisation: Grundlagen, Methode, Praxis*. Klett-Cotta.

Bouchikhi, H. (1998). Living with and building on complexity: A constructivist perspective on organizations. *Organizations, 5*(2), 217–232. https://doi.org/10.1177/135050849852004.

Clegg, S. R., Cunha, J. V., & Cunha, M. P. (2002). Management paradoxes: A relational view. *Human Relations, 55*(5), 483–503.

De Rond, M., & Bouchikhi, H. (2004). On the dialectics of strategic alliances. *Organization Science, 15*(1), 56–69. https://doi.org/10.1287/orsc.1030.0037.

Eckstein, J., & Buck, J. (2018). *Company-wide agility with beyond budgeting, open space & sociocracy: Survive & thrive on disruption*. CreateSpace Independent Publishing Platform.

Gawer, A. (2014). Bridging differing perspectives on technological platforms: Toward an integrative framework. *Research Policy, 43*(7), 1239–1249. https://doi.org/10.1016/j.respol.2014.03.006.

Grund, M. (2015). Agile Softwareentwicklung als paradigmatisches Beispiel für eine neue Organisation von technischer Wissensarbeit. In T. Sattelberger, I. Welpe, & A. Boes (Eds.), *Das demokratische Unternehmen: Neue Arbeits- und Führungskulturen im Zeitalter digitaler Wirtschaft*. Haufe.

Huchler, N., & Sauer, S. (2015). Reflexive and experience-based trust and participatory research: Concept and methods to meet complexity and uncertainty in organisations. *International Journal of Action Research, 11*(1–2), 146–173.

Huchler, N., Weihrich, M., Porschen-Hueck, S., Monz, A., Schamann, S., & Böhle, F., et al. (2018). Dienstleistungen für Prävention im Altersübergang – die Idee kooperativer Dienstleistungsnetzwerke. In W. Schneider & S. Stadelbacher (Eds.), *Der Altersübergang als Neuarrangement von Arbeit und Leben* (pp. 115–150). Springer VS.

Jacobides, M., Cennamo, C., & Gawer, A. (2018). Towards a theory of ecosystems. *Strategic Management Journal, 39*, 2255–2276.

Komus, A. (2020). *Status Quo (scaled) agile*. https://www.hs-koblenz.de/bpm-labor/status-quo-scaled-agile-2020. Accessed 8 Nov 2020.

Laloux, F. (2014). *Reinventing organizations: A guide to creating organizations inspired by the next stage of human consciousness*. Nelson Parker.

Lansiti, M., & Levien, R. (2004). *The keystone advantage: What the new dynamics of business ecosystems mean for strategy, innovation, and sustainability*. Harvard Business School Press.

Leffingwell, D. (2007). *Scaling software agility: Best practices for large enterprises* (Agile Software Development) (Agile Software Development Series), Addison-Wesley Professional (Ed.), Boston.

Meyer, B. (2014). *Agile! the good, the hype and the ugly*. Springer International Publishing.

Moldaschl, M. (2005). Institutionelle Reflexivität: Zur Analyse von „Change" im Bermuda-Dreieck von Modernisierungs-, Organisations- und Interventionstheorie. In M. Faust, M. Funder, & M. Moldaschl (Eds.), *Die "Organisation" der Arbeit (Arbeit, Innovation undNachhaltigkeit, 1)* (pp. 355–382). Hampp. https://nbn-resolving.org/urn:nbn:de:0168-ssoar-324454.

Nazarenko, A. A., & Camarinha, L. M. (2019). Basis for an approach to design collaborative cyber-physical systems. In L. M. Camarinha, R. Almeida, & J. Oliveira (Eds.), *Technological innovation for industry and service systems* (pp. 193–205). Springer International Publishing.

Neef, A., & Burmeister, K. (2005). Die Schwarm-Organisation – Ein neues Paradigma für das e-Unternehmen der Zukunft. In B. Kuhlin & H. Thielmann (Eds.), *Real-time enterprise in der Praxis*. Springer.

Neumer, J., Porschen-Hueck, S., & Sauer, S. (2018). Reflexive scaling as a way towards agile organization. *Journal of International Management Studies, 18*(2), 27–38.

Oestereich, B., & Schröder, C. (2016). *Das kollegial geführte Unternehmen: Ideen und Praktiken für die agile Organisation von morgen*. Vahlen.

Peltoniemi, M., & Vuori, E. (2005). *Business ecosystem as the new approach to complex adaptive business environments*. Tempere University of Technology.

Porschen-Hueck, S., & Neumer, J. (2015). Participation in enterprises and research: The case of innovation work. *International Journal of Action Research, 1*(1–2), 174–194.

Provan, K. G., & Kenis, P. (2008). Modes of network governance: Structure, management, and effectiveness. *Journal of Public Administration Research and Theory, 18*(2), 229–252.

Radigan, D. (2016). *Agile Methoden. Ein Schritt weiter: Ausweiten agiler Methoden in großen Unternehmen*. https://de.atlassian.com/agile/ways-to-scale-agile. Accessed 11 Nov 2020.

Robertson, B. J. (2015). *Holacracy: The new management system for a rapidly changing world*. Henry Hold and Company.

Sauer, S. (2017). Partizipative Forschung und Gestaltung als Antwort auf empirische und forschungspolitische Herausforderungen? *Industrielle Beziehungen, 3*, 253–270.

Semolic, B. (2012). Global knowledge market and new business models. *PM World Journal, 1*(2). https://pmworldlibrary.net/wp-content/uploads/2013/01/PMWJ-Sep2012-SEMOLIC-GlobalKnowledgeMarket-FeaturedPaper.pdf . Accessed 03 June 2020.

Senge, P. M. (2011). *Die fünfte Disziplin: Kunst und Praxis der lernenden Organisation*. Klett-Cotta.

Shipilov, A., & Gawer, A. (2020). Integrating research on inter-organizational networks and ecosystems. *Academy of Management Annals, 14*(1). https://doi.org/10.5465/annals.2018.0121.

Spearman, S., & Dolman, R. (2016). *Agile scaling knowledgebase decision matrix*. Online access: http://www.agilescaling.org/ask-matrix.html.

Stettina, C. J., & Heijstek, W. (2011). Necessary and neglected? An empirical study of internal documentation in agile software development teams. *SIGDOC '11: Proceedings of the 29th ACM international conference on Design of communication*, 159–166. https://doi.org/10.1145/2038476.2038509.

Sydow, J., Schüßler, E., & Müller-Seitz, G. (2016). *Managing inter-organizational relations: Debates and cases*. Palgrave.

Uludag, Ö., Hefele, S., & Matthes, F. (2016). *Platform and ecosystem governance*. TUM.

Wareham, J., Fox, P. B., & Giner, J. L. C. (2014). Technology ecosystem governance. *Organization Science, 25*, 1195–1215.

Wilkinson, A., Dundon, T., & Marchington, M. (2013). Employee involvement and voice. In S. Bach & M. Edwards (Eds.), *Managing human resources* (pp. 268–288). Wiley.

Williamson, P. J., & De Meyer, A. (2012). Ecosystem advantage: How to successfully harness the power of partners. *California Management Review, 55*(1), 24–46.

Yin, R. E. (2013). *Case study research: Design and methods*. Sage.

Ziegler, A. (2020). *Der Aufstieg des Internet der Dinge: Wie sich Industrieunternehmen zu Tech-Unternehmen entwickeln*. Campus.

CHAPTER 6

# Design Thinking as an Agile Panacea? Towards a Symbiotic Understanding of Design Thinking and Organizational Culture

*Gordon Müller-Seitz and Werner Weiss*

## Statement of the Problem

Agile management approaches, such as Scrum or Kanban, are gaining increasing currency in managerial practice (e.g. Rubin, 2015; Sutherland, 2015) and scholarly debates (e.g. Sambamurthy et al., 2003; Tallon & Pinsonneault, 2011; Vázquez-Bustelo et al., 2007). Hence it seems as if being agile or striving to be agile is imperative these days (Beck et al., 2001a, 2001b; Müller-Seitz & Weiss, 2019) in order to master the challenges arising from phenomena such as the digital transformation (Brynjolfsson & McAfee, 2016; Lingnau et al., 2018). This observation holds particularly true for the agile management approach design thinking, an agile method or 'tool' with which to generate novel ideas

G. Müller-Seitz (✉)
Technische Universität Kaiserslautern, Kaiserslautern, Germany
e-mail: gms@wiwi.uni-kl.de

W. Weiss
Insiders Technologies, Kaiserslautern, Germany



S. Pfeiffer et al. (eds.), *The Agile Imperative*, Dynamics of Virtual Work,
https://doi.org/10.1007/978-3-030-73994-2_6

which is welcomed enthusiastically as a panacea for generating innovations (Plattner et al., 2009). One of the key strengths of design thinking—according to its advocates—is that it is deemed to be an isolated approach; to put it more bluntly: in the case of design thinking, one size (design thinking) fits all (types of organizations).

However, assuming that organizations exhibit idiosyncratic differences, it appears questionable to tout design thinking as a usable agile tool in organizations on a one-to-one basis. By nature, there are many characteristics that serve the purpose of distinguishing organizations from one another, e.g. the number of employees, the turnover, or the organizational field the organizations are operating in, etc. To this end, we suggest that organizational culture (Schein, 2004) is one particularly important characteristic to consider. Without an appropriate organizational culture, the organization is unlikely to benefit from design thinking adequately, as previous research has shown that generating innovations or adopting novel technologies or managerial tools depends heavily upon the organizational culture (Sarros et al., 2008). Building upon this observation, we posit that the 'one size fits all' premise is unlikely to hold true in managerial practice. Hence our objective in this chapter is to explore the role of organizational culture for employing design thinking as an agile management tool.

To come to terms with this objective, we draw on ongoing collaboration over four years (2016–2019) between the two authors of this study, an executive director (Werner) and a university researcher (Gordon). Aligning our perspectives allows us to substantiate our line of reasoning, making our interpretations comparatively robust for both managerial practice and research.

With our study, we make three primary contributions to the debates about design thinking as a tool for enabling disruptive innovations and also—in a broader sense—to the agile management discourse: first, we highlight the role of organizational culture as an important underlying success factor for the introduction and employment of design thinking. Second, we present potential benefits of employing design thinking and also elaborate on several challenges and how they can be overcome, since 'one size does *not* fit all'. Third, we critically reflect upon the alleged novelty of design thinking as a managerial tool.

The chapter is structured as follows: first, we elucidate the literature in which we anchor our study before presenting the research setting (Insiders Technologies) and the chosen case study approach, which is infused with elements from action research and ethnography. Our findings document how design thinking can be used successfully, and, moreover, we unearth the role of organizational culture as an underlying important aspect to consider. We then critically reflect upon our findings in light of present theorizing about design thinking as a prominent method from the managerial toolbox of agile management, before concluding a critical reflection and an outlook for future research.

## Quo Vadis? Design Thinking as an Agile Management Tool

To comprehend design thinking properly one needs to contextualize it against the backdrop of agile management. To this end, we briefly delineate the genesis of agile management approaches (section "Agile Management as the Source of Design Thinking") so as to introduce the key tenets of design thinking (section "Design Thinking as an Offshoot of Agile Management Approaches"), before reporting in a narrative way about how design thinking is put into practice at Insiders Technologies (sections "Research Setting and Methods" and "Design Thinking as a Participative Tool for Organizing Innovation and Nurturing Agility").

### *Agile Management as the Source of Design Thinking*

In our perception, the impetus for agile management approaches ensued from two key phenomena, the development of open-source software and an accompanying change in the zeitgeist. As for agile management approaches, they are heavily influenced by the way open- source software development took place in contrast to the way proprietary software is developed and distributed (here, and in the following, see Hilgers et al., 2010; Kaiser & Müller-Seitz, 2008; Müller-Seitz & Reger, 2009). According to Raymond (1999), proprietary software development is a cathedral in which software is developed within the organization in a hierarchical fashion with clear coordination and communication structures. The ambition behind this closed innovation approach (Chesbrough, 2003) is that the organization can make Schumpeterian gains by keeping the development in-house, and it is only after the final code lines have been refined that the customer base is offered the final software. Bearing this observation in mind, it becomes evident that developing such software aims to make a major innovative leap.

In contrast, open-source software resembles a bazaar (Raymond, 1999) in which self-organization is dominant and progress is made in innumerable minor steps; that is, developers are free to decide about their participation, self-selecting the tasks at hand with which they feel comfortable. Well-known examples such as Linux, Apache or Firefox epitomize open-source software development and are refined by a large number of volunteers. Being able to engage only with those tasks one feels comfortable with has been identified as a key driver for people's motivation (Bénabou & Tirole, 2003). Moreover, self-selection is only possible due to the modularity of tasks, as they can be broken down into individually manageable chunks which can be fitted together again afterwards (Benkler, 2002). Hence there is no fiat (Williamson, 2000) in place as in conventional organizational settings, and informal structures emerge from the engagement of the volunteering developers.

Second, and in line with the first observation, the zeitgeist of how to organize and innovate has changed. Hitherto, classical works of organizational studies and business administration were characterized by striving for clear hierarchical structures, efficiency-driven operations and predetermined paths (e.g. Fayol, 1949; Jacoby, 1984). Among other concepts, Taylor's (1911) idea of a scientific management was in line with the zeitgeist of the early to mid-twentieth century. However, today's zeitgeist displays different characteristics. Ever since the 1990s and the turn of the twentieth century, organizations have increasingly been characterized in organizational studies and business administration as becoming more fluid (Schreyögg & Sydow, 2010), hypercompetitive (D'Aveni, 1994), networked (Castells, 1996; Raab & Kenis, 2009), crowdsourced (Howe, 2006, 2008) and open (Chesbrough, 2003; for an overview of the debate about new organizational forms, see Puranam et al., 2014 and on coordination, Okhuysen & Bechky, 2009). This has influenced the way organizations coordinate their activities—not least how they organize their innovations (Morner, 1997). Whereas a closed innovation management mindset was best described in former times by striving for perfection in the course of in-house development and the subsequent aspiration to acquire Schumpeterian gains, today a more open innovation-oriented landscape can be observed (Chesbrough, 2003). Open innovation is characterized by collaborative and oftentimes dispersed efforts to generate innovations (Jeppesen & Lakhani, 2010; Sydow et al., 2016). To put it differently, the way open-source software development has challenged conventional, proprietary software development has been accompanied by managerial trends in the same vein.

As an interim summary, we submit that the development of open-source software with its bazaar-like character (Raymond, 1999) exhibits important features such as self-organization and accompanying decentralization, iterative ways of improving the software code etc. which represent key building blocks of what has become known as agile management and, moreover, is also ingrained in design thinking. Along similar lines, venturing beyond hierarchical and static conceptions of an organization towards flexible organizing—see also the contrast between organization and organizing proposed by Weick (1979)—calls for managerial conceptions that remain sensitive to one's environment, change and the unexpected (Müller-Seitz, 2014; Weick & Sutcliffe, 2015).

### *Design Thinking as an Offshoot of Agile Management Approaches*

Turning our attention to design thinking as a method, it is important to note that it is heavily influenced by agile management approaches and the aforementioned change in the managerial zeitgeist, insofar as it emphasizes an iterative way of organizing how to innovate. To avoid unnecessary repetition, we refer to our experiences (section "Design Thinking as a Participative Tool for Organizing Innovation and Nurturing Agility") to comprehend how design thinking is actually put into practice. Here, we simply wish to elucidate in what regard we deem design thinking to be rooted in agile management approaches.

Advocates of design thinking frequently use conventional innovation management frameworks as a strawman (e.g. Plattner et al., 2009). It is commonly argued that innovation management processes are too often conceptualized in a linear fashion. One (in)famous strawman in this regard is the stage-gate process model (Cooper, 1994), which assumes that ideas are ultimately turned into marketable and successful innovations through a course of different phases punctuated by intermediate milestones, Each and every phase is executed consecutively and once a milestone is positively evaluated, the next phase follows until the product or service is launched on the market.

In contrast, and in line with the way open-source software is developed, innovations generated by design thinking are developed in piecemeal fashion, in the form of iterative cycles that allow for small continuous improvements (Kelley & Kelley, 2015). These very inspirations initially stem from genuinely engaging with the respective target groups, be it customers or other target groups of interest (e.g. citizens with a specific need that should benefit from the introduction of a new public policy measure). Summing up, the roots of design thinking in agile management approaches are manifest in small iterative steps and a sensitivity to external impetus.

## Research Setting and Methods

Our insights are derived from Insiders Technologies, a small and medium-sized corporation in Kaiserslautern, a German city in southwestern Germany. After introducing the company (section "Insiders Technologies, a Hidden Champion of the Digital Transformation Embracing Agile Management"), we elaborate on data collection and analysis (section "Combining Insider and Outsider Perspectives at Insiders Technologies").

### *Insiders Technologies, a Hidden Champion of the Digital Transformation Embracing Agile Management*

Insiders Technologies was founded in 1998 as a spin-off from the German Research Centre for Artificial Intelligence. The company now has a staff of about 150 employees and a portfolio of approximately 1,500 customers.

Owing to its heritage, the company's product and service portfolio still revolves around omni-channel input management, which is driven by software solutions and supported by artificial intelligence. The portfolio offers solutions to identifying, processing and analyzing data in a holistic fashion, so as to allow customer-centric management of different communication channels and interfaces. Hence customer data can be managed, among other ways, in the form of e-mail correspondence, Facebook entries or apps.

Today, the core of Insiders Technologies portfolio is Ovation, software based on artificial intelligence. Among other things, the software allows users to scan documents (such as doctor's bills) using a smartphone or tablet and automatically transfer them to their insurance company, which in turn is able to instantaneously process the incoming information and immediately reimburse the customer for the invoice she or he submitted.

In addition, Insiders Technologies offers business intelligence solutions and cloud-based services that complete the product and service offerings. Another way to deal with customer needs is the introduction of chatbots (or bots for short). Chatbot is a portmanteau alluding to a 'chatting robot', which is usually put into place when it comes to communicating with customers, e.g. managing the first steps of a telephone hotline before a human agent takes over or guiding a customer through different web pages.

Insiders Technologies' innovativeness is underscored by frequently receiving awards as an innovative company from external evaluators and institutions. For instance, it is repeatedly ranked one of the most innovative small and medium-sized companies in Germany in the class of 50–250 employees, and was even ranked 'TOP innovator of the year' in 2015. In what follows, we will elucidate the underlying reasons for the company's innovativeness. As we will show, a critical success factor in this regard is the role of the organizational culture at Insiders Technologies, and design thinking as a managerial tool being consistent with this very organizational culture. As a side note, we would finally stress that both authors have professional experience with representatives of the Hasso-Plattner Institute, which researches and teaches design thinking and thus have profound insights into the genesis and execution of the conception beyond being trained in design thinking by the Hasso-Plattner Institute.

### *Combining Insider and Outsider Perspectives at Insiders Technologies*

We present experiences that both authors, as a managing director and a researcher, have gained in constant exchanges over the course of four years (2015–2019). This allows us to present findings that are corroborated from both spheres, managerial practice and research. While one author (Werner) is the executive director of a German small and medium-sized enterprise in the field of artificial intelligence, Insiders Technologies, the other (Gordon) is a management scholar. In doing so, we are able to reflect upon and align our perspectives as insiders (Werner) and outsiders (Gordon), as proposed by Gioia and Chittipeddi (1991).

As we will illustrate, design thinking can be implemented successfully so as to generate innovations in line with the ambitions laid out by design thinking advocates. However, design thinking needs to be aligned to the specific circumstances of the organizations employing this method and, as we will highlight, an organization's culture is critical for engaging with design thinking.

*Jours fixes* between both authors take place frequently and established cooperation has evolved over the years. To this end, we draw on insights not only from the perspective of the executive director but also from management research, as Gordon has also been involved in developing new ideas and design thinking processes. We thereby profit from triangulating these very perspectives and make use of experiences from design thinking processes at Insiders Technologies in collaboration with industry partners, predominantly from the insurance industry. For ethical and legal reasons, we refrain from reporting a single case study. However, given our insider–outsider triangulation and experience across cases, we are able to offer a more holistic picture. We deem this to be beneficial too, as we intend to critically reflect on the benefits and challenges arising from employing design thinking (section "To Be Agile or Not to Be Agile? Reflections and Recommendations").

Reflecting upon the traditional repertoire of explorative-qualitative research in the social sciences (for an overview, see Danner-Schröder & Müller-Seitz, 2017) we feel that a case study (Insiders Technologies being 'the case') is most likely the best label with which to qualify our research. However, given the insights from Werner, our insights are certainly infused with elements of autoethnography, as well as action research, given Werner's involvement and Gordon's engagement in closely exchanging ideas with him on how to further develop Insiders Technologies, and on the way digital transformation will unfold and affect virtually all organizations, not least via the use of agile management techniques such as design thinking.

## Design Thinking as a Participative Tool for Organizing Innovation and Nurturing Agility

In what follows, we report our observations and, later on in the discussion, interpretations of design thinking in light of organizational culture. We deem organizational culture to be a key feature that should be considered when it comes to engaging with design thinking and—in more general terms—agile management approaches. Against this backdrop, we start by introducing the key facets of the organizational culture at Insiders Technologies (section "Insiders Technologies' Organizational Culture as an Explanans") before we turn our attention to the way design thinking is employed at Insiders Technologies across innovation projects (section "A Sketch of How Design Thinking Is Employed at Insiders Technologies").

### *Insiders Technologies' Organizational Culture as an Explanans*

We submit that elucidating the organizational culture of Insiders Technologies is key to unearthing the reasons why design thinking as an agile management approach can be successfully employed. What is striking at first sight when engaging with the company—as it was for the first author, Gordon, at the turn of 2015/2016—is the vision to empower employees to come up with as many and as radical ideas as possible. A common mantra in this regard is the vision of every employee coming up with a new idea each and every day (see also Müller-Seitz & Weiss, 2019). This vision is not only radical and thus worth noting, but is also intriguing, insofar as it allows us to understand innovation not only as a top-down perspective put forward by the top management team, but also as a vision that is also lived bottom-up by each member of the organization. Other noteworthy aspects are the mutual trust and respect that constitute the precondition for empowering employees to become entrepreneurs within Insiders Technologies (for a detailed description in this regard, see Müller-Seitz & Weiss, 2019).

Relatedly, and also in line with agile management philosophies, there is the opportunity for self-organizing. This not only unfolds in light of common managerial measures, such as allowing home office. Instead, self-organization is ingrained in a number of agile management approaches, such as scrum or pair programming. Scrum is primarily employed to develop software in short, iterative cycles to satisfy customer needs and continuously strive for radical innovations. Daily stand-up meetings and other measures proposed by scrum advocates are successfully employed and serve to maintain an agile organizational mindset. It is critical to note that scrum can be viewed as a manifestation of self-organization at Insiders Technologies, insofar as the developer teams are able to constantly come up with radical solutions in close collaboration with customers without having to fear interventions from the top management team.

Along similar lines, pair programming is another agile management approach that lays emphasis on developing software in a tandem format. Two people collaborate, and while one of them develops the source code, the other is monitoring and reflecting upon the activities of the source code developer. Moreover, the tandems frequently change. This is beneficial for Insiders Technologies insofar as knowledge is dispersed throughout the company and established patterns are constantly in flux. Although such fluidity might also be detrimental (Schreyögg & Sydow, 2010), it is generally beneficial as practised at Insiders Technologies.

Both scrum and pair programming, and—as we will set forth later on—design thinking, rely upon the creative and proactive engagement of Insiders Technologies' employees. Without empowering employees and providing confidence in the activities of the employees, self-organization could not unfold within the organization. Hence, apart from empowering and trusting employees, an open mindset is also needed in order for the company to constantly remain sensitive to changes in the environment, customers' needs and the latest technological trends.

### *A Sketch of How Design Thinking Is Employed at Insiders Technologies*

We start by reporting the way design thinking is executed at Insiders Technologies. The process per se draws, by and large, on the existing framework as proposed by design thinking advocates from the Hasso-Plattner Institute and its affiliates (for popular images of how to conduct design thinking, see Kelley & Kelley, 2015; Plattner et al., 2009). In general, it can be presented along with six interconnected phases that mutually re-inform each other, namely understand, observe, point of view, ideate, prototype and test.

'Understand' is the very first phase, in which team members from Insiders Technologies try to comprehend the point of departure. To this end, the situation, challenge or objective is usually set out by the internal or external customer commissioning the design thinking process.

For instance, clients from the insurance industry approach Insiders Technologies to develop an innovation in interacting with customers. This might be an app that eases the interactions with final customers (e.g. in terms of handling doctor's bills). In this phase it is critical that Insiders Technologies' members start with an open mindset, so as to avoid premature conclusions that might hinder innovativeness.

Although a client from the insurance industry might strive to find a solution for 'the average customer'/'the mass market', design thinking is also decidedly conceptualized to come up with uncommon solutions—or, in managerial parlance: disruptive innovations. Hence it is not necessarily the case that Insiders Technologies tries to interact with an 'average' customer; often, the company engages with a decidedly unconventional or non-representative one. However, in any case it is important at this stage to try to capture the point of departure as accurately as possible.

The second phase, 'observe', builds upon the insights of the understand phase and its overarching aim is to come up with as many 'needs' (i.e. requirements or wishes) and 'pain points' (i.e. challenges or limitations) of the target group or customer as possible. To this end, it is critical to properly assess the target group or person to be observed. This in turn requires soft skills such as empathy or the ability to sensitively observe the person to be interacted with in detail.

For example, it might be of interest to better comprehend how customers actually handle doctor's bills. On the one hand, this might entail the need to observe the relevant customer. On the other hand, it might also necessitate interviewing the respective persons.

When it comes to interviewing, it is by no means just about asking for information and recording it properly in terms of what is aired content-wise. It is also about detecting latent needs, which requires socio-emotional competence besides mere content-related knowledge (Danner-Schröder & Müller-Seitz, 2017). In this spirit, it is critical to actually adopt the perspective of the respective person or group as much as possible. This is perhaps best illustrated by an example from a design thinking training session one of the authors participated in. In the course of this training, an instructor referred to generating innovations in hospital and adopting the perspective of the patients in a literal sense, implying using a camera on the patient's forehead. This helped the team members following the patients at the hospital to better comprehend what the situation 'looks like' if you are lying in a bed and staring at the ceiling. Looking at the ceiling later informed their process-related innovations, insofar as they ultimately arrived at the conclusion that the ceiling could bear words or pictograms so as to make the patient aware of where she or he actually is located or heading within the hospital (e.g. when being transferred from one ward to another).

In the 'point of view' phase, one tries to adopt the fictitiously interpreted perspective of a specific person or a few persons. This implies that one needs to narrow down the number of potential person(s) one wants to deal with. The input is generated from the previous 'observe' phase.

For the sake of argument, think of a female hipster in her mid-twenties who works for a start-up in Berlin, Germany. Members of Insiders Technologies might have been in touch with her, since Insiders Technologies also has a branch in Berlin, and they want to come up with software-related innovations, employing design thinking by means of exchange with her. Building upon interviews with her and observing the way she engages with her insurance company, the team members try to come up with a holistic profile of this person. By its very nature, some information might be missing. However, this is no limitation per se, as the design thinking method certainly allows room for creativity in this particular phase. Hence interpreting her information and blending it with inspirations from the observing team represents a welcome measure.

To this end, emotions are a key aspect to consider in order to comprehend the needs and pain points of the person in question. From a methodological perspective, storytelling might be a viable path. Storytelling can be conducted by completing the following sentences:

- Basic information about the person: We met … [name of the person].
- Insights: We were surprised to discover that … [surprising insight to be documented in as much detail as possible].
- Need: A solution from the viewpoint of the person in question first and foremost targets … [elaborate on the potential solution to the key challenge mentioned by the respondent].

In summary, by painting a colourful picture of the respective person, we attempt to better comprehend the underlying ambitions of that very person and what his or her genuine needs and pain points look like.

In the course of the 'ideate' phase, established creativity techniques are put into practice: brainwriting or brainstorming, for instance. By employing these creativity techniques, the solution space is opened up and as many ideas as possible are sought. In this phase, at first quantity intentionally dominates over quality in terms of the ideas being generated. Later on, and in preparation for the subsequent prototyping phase, ideas are evaluated and narrowed down to a manageable set of solutions.

By means of an illustration, think about the challenge of how to improve the design of an app that helps people process their doctor's bills. Ideas to improve the design might stem from a broad range of settings, be it related experiences from the person at stake (e.g. the woman might have been laying emphasis on mass-customizing the app surface/interface), apps (e.g. one person might come up with ideas from competitors or service providers in different industries), IT-based service offerings in general terms (e.g. contributing ideas from intuitively accessible services or products from Apple Inc., personal experiences of the Insiders Technologies' team members (e.g. reporting ideas generated from what works or does not work in the case of handling doctor's bills in former times by snail mail), etc.

Subsequently, the 'prototyping' phase is deemed to turn ideas into practice, or rather, reality. Hence the ideas are transformed into a physical mock-up or prototype if possible, a mock-up being the 'predecessor' of a prototype, merely for presentational purposes. In the process, it also becomes evident why design thinking is called *design thinking*, as ideas (thinking) are turned into physical objects that need to be designed. To this end, it is common to make use of a large number of materials, that is, Lego bricks, pieces of wood, paper, modelling clay, etc. in addition to pencils, scissors, post-it notes and the like. Tinkering with the mock-ups or prototypes is an integral part of the process insofar as usage can be better envisaged when one is dealing with a physical artefact.

For illustrative purposes, think of a paper-based mock-up of an app or a digital prototype on a smartphone. The basic ideas can be sketched and documented or programmed so as to offer solutions for the 'needs' and 'pain points' that the young woman faces. Keeping the point of view of the person at stake in mind is critical if the development is to actually address what the person needs.

Finally, the 'testing' phase is geared towards engaging with potential or real persons or groups of users/customers. It is in this phase that the previously designed mock-ups or prototypes are tried out. Remaining open to change—here in the form of feedback—is a critical component of every design thinking process. This holds particularly true for this particular phase, as feedback is immediately used to refine and redesign the mock-up or prototypes in question.

For instance, the design of the app for handling the doctor's bill might be refined on the basis of customer feedback from a young female hipster. For the sake of argument, she might be used to handling documents in other apps in a different fashion to the present app she uses to handle the doctor's bills. This might then be the critical point at which to intervene, so as to integrate her feedback into the insurance app.

In summary, design thinking is a combination of existing methods in the social sciences and in the field of innovation management (Corsten et al., 2016), which is intelligently geared to fostering the identification of radical innovations in iterative steps. However, a word of caution is needed. As we will argue in the following, it is crucial to bear in mind the organizational culture if design thinking is to be implemented properly.

## To Be Agile or Not to Be Agile? Reflections and Recommendations

The design thinking process put forward might appear quite straightforward and easily applicable at first sight. Towards this end, we will first sketch the benefits that can be derived from employing design thinking to generate radical innovations (section "Benefits of Employing Design Thinking as an Agile Tool"). However, we submit that it is not as easy to implement design thinking in an organization as it might initially appear. Hence we must also advance critical reflection on the boundary conditions of what needs to be considered and what potential limitations might be encountered (section "All That Glitters Is Not Gold—Challenges and Limitations of Design Thinking").

### *Benefits of Employing Design Thinking as an Agile Tool*

First and foremost, design thinking is an approach that allows us to generate radical innovations and enable the service of customer- or user-centric needs. This certainly merits attention, insofar as generating radical innovations is one of the holy grails to which every innovative organization strives to aspire (Corsten et al., 2016).

In line with other agile management approaches such as scrum, pair or extreme programming, this also allows iterative developments in contrast to conventional waterfall organizing. Hence being flexible and remaining sensitive to changes can be deemed further key strengths of design thinking.

However, far more than the mere economic value of turning ideas into profitable outcomes, design thinking also enables participation and self-organization. This facet should not be underestimated. To put it another way, design thinking should be conceived of not only as a managerial tool for innovation purposes, but also as a human resource management tool, fostering the development of self-organization efforts, empowering and motivating employees. Similar to the possibility to self-select (modular) tasks in the case of voluntarily developing open-source software (Bénabou & Tirole, 2003; Hilgers et al., 2010; Raymond, 1999) or even proprietary software (Kaiser & Müller-Seitz, 2008), employees are likely to be more motivated when they are allowed a certain leeway within the daily operations of the organization.

Moreover, the possibility to self-organize can also be deemed a capability or precondition for self-transforming an organization as put forward by Etzioni (1968) and later by management scholars (Gomez & Probst, 1989; Kirsch, 1997). Viewed from this perspective, self-organization contrasts with intentionally planned actions and is rather spontaneous (Hayek, 1976). It also represents the foundation for successful adaptation to changing organizational and environmental demands in the future (along similar lines, cf. the discussion about organizational resilience; for an overview, see Müller-Seitz, 2014).

Finally, we submit that design thinking with its opportunities to organize for self-organization has the potential to reduce complexity. Self-organization as part of organizational culture reduces complexity, insofar as members of the organization share a common understanding on which they can rely (Luhmann, 1984). This common understanding fosters trust and eases communication and coordination processes—even in the absence of a strict hierarchy and coordinating authority, owing to the empowerment and encouragement to self-organize.

### *All That Glitters Is Not Gold—Challenges and Limitations of Design Thinking*

We would like to avoid the impression that we are uncritical advocates of introducing design thinking to organizations. Based on our experiences at Insiders Technologies and from our professional activities, we would like to caution those considering the introduction of design thinking to their organizations to reflect upon the challenges and hurdles set out below, namely the issue of adequate organizational culture and leadership, the danger of a dialectic, the resources required, the need for mass-customized implementations, failure tolerance and context specifics.

First and foremost, design thinking demands an organizational culture and leadership that allows the empowerment of employees. This is certainly easy to demand, but is difficult to put into practice. Empowering employees to engage with each other in a self-organized fashion is certainly overdue timely and might help unleash employees' intrinsic motivations (Müller-Seitz & Weiss, 2019). Similar to the observations made in the fields of open-source software (e.g. Bénabou & Tirole, 2003; Benkler, 2002) and beyond (e.g. Hilgers et al., 2010; Müller-Seitz & Reger, 2009), it can be expected that self-organizing teams might have a positive impact on employees if the organizational culture and leadership are supportive of this.

However, this does not imply that unstructured chaos should reign, with every person or team working towards their own aspirations in an unstructured fashion. Instead, certain framework conditions should be defined and adhered to. To illustrate our idea, think of design thinking as not being a measure for everyone in the organization and for every kind of task. From our perspective, it does not appear meaningful for everyone to try to be innovative and self-organize their actions. This does not seem plausible for two simple reasons: first, not everyone in the organization is keen on self-organizing their own activities—though they can nevertheless be very successful when it comes to contributing to the organization's activities. Second, some activities are unlikely to benefit from constant refinements, close interactions with customers and the aspiration to seek radical innovations; for instance, consider employees working in the controlling department or those dealing with legislative issues.

In summary, we feel that areas such as those where interactions with customers take place or those that are research- and development-intensive can benefit from the introduction of design thinking if the organizational culture and leadership correspond to these needs. A potential countermeasure to mitigate the aforementioned challenges might be tight control of the framework conditions and the actual execution of the design thinking process. Similar to a scrum master who oversees the scrum process, a person should be clearly assigned to monitoring the overall design thinking activity in question.

As a second challenge, we would like to draw attention to a dialectic of design thinking or—in more general terms—agile management (cf. also Zidulka & Mitchell, 2018). To this end, we assume that organizations oftentimes run the risk of employing design thinking and in doing so, divide the organization into those that are allegedly 'good' employees deemed innovative due to their employment design thinking, and those that are 'bad', that is, not deemed innovative since they do not use such state-of-the-art innovation methods as design thinking. We feel that this represents a dark side to innovation management activities in general, but it holds particularly true for design thinking, as it is not suitable for all managerial tasks, as noted above (e.g. controlling or legislative activities).

One potential countermeasure to this thorny issue might be to avoid championing design thinking too much in the organization. To put it the other way round: also highlighting the value of every department or team within the organization for overarching success might help avoid this challenge.

Another challenge is the resources needed to employ design thinking. First of all, time resources might be scarce, as plenty of time is certainly needed if design thinking is to be employed in line with the approach set out above. Take, for instance, data collection in the form of participant observations and interviews that need to be arranged in advance, let alone data analysis afterwards. Additionally, financial resources are needed to arrange for a proper, stimulating workspace. For example, at Insiders Technologies' Berlin office, mobile furniture has been customized and unique furniture has even been built for purpose. Depending upon the importance of the innovation-related activity, we see no alternative to properly investing time and financial resources in the design thinking process as a countermeasure to this rather mundane, but nonetheless pressing challenge.

Moreover, the need for mass-customized implementations of design thinking in the organization is critical. Although rough ideas exist on how to conduct design thinking as proposed by the initiators (Kelley & Kelley, 2015; Plattner et al., 2009), modifications to an organization's specific needs appear unavoidable. Although this is not a problem per se, we feel that those responsible for introducing design thinking to the organization should reflect critically on the circumstances of its actual introduction. For instance, the number of potential feedback cycles between the prototyping and testing phases are likely to be contingent upon the organization's time and financial resources and the customers or other persons to be engaged with. While some customers might offer the respective amount of resources (e.g. as many feedback cycles with its employees as demanded by the company that employs design thinking), others might be more critical and reduce the number of feedback cycles.

Another, related critical issue that needs to be considered is the legal framework. Design thinking advocates call for the adoption of the method while neglecting such aspects. Nonetheless, deciding on who owns the intellectual property or what is being developed from it is certainly critical when conducting design thinking in business-to-business settings.

Along similar lines, it is noteworthy that the context specifics need to be taken into account, which we presume to be critical along with three levels of analysis, namely a micro-, meso- and macro-level of analysis. On a micro-level, we presume that both individual dispositions and team-related circumstances are likely to play a critical role, e.g. if the positive affect impacts on the activities (Amabile et al., 2005). Generalizing from this observation, it might be no surprise to argue that on the meso-level of departments or even the entire organization, an organizational cultural influence (Schein, 2004) might be observable, which impacts on the success of innovation-management-related activities (Sarros et al., 2008) such as design thinking. Finally, the macro-level, which we conceive of as the organizational field (DiMaggio & Powell, 1983) in which the organization is operating, might have an influence on the successful introduction and execution of design thinking activities. Bearing this observation in mind, we presume that some organizational fields such as that of software development, in which Insiders Technologies operates, are comparatively open to collaborating in the course of design thinking activities in order to come up with radical innovations. Although this certainly also owes, in the case of Insiders Technologies, to the innovative culture and genesis of the corporation (Heinlein & Weiss, 2017; Müller-Seitz & Weiss, 2019), it is also a consequence of operating in the field of software development, whence agile management ideas emanated, due to their inspiration from the field of open-source software.

In contrast, one should consider strongly regulated organizational fields such as that of defence or legal counselling, where different cultures are likely to be observable. Engaging in collaborations to generate radical innovations in these particular settings is most likely more difficult, and professional norms and identities might be a further hindrance (see along similar lines for the case of the NASA organization: Lifshitz-Assaf, 2018).

Finally, yet importantly, the organizational culture needs to be failure tolerant. This represents a common challenge for innovation management (Corsten et al., 2016). As research in the field of high reliability organizations (e.g. Weick & Sutcliffe, 2015) and knowledge management and organizational learning (e.g. Müller-Seitz, Macpherson, 2014) have shown, paying attention to what does not work can be of tremendous importance. Preventing stigmatization of those who are failing with their efforts in organizations thus seems to be a key managerial task.

## Concluding Observations

In this chapter, we sought to explore the role of organizational culture for employing design thinking as an agile management tool and reflect upon the benefits and challenges in doing so. Altogether, we feel that the most difficult underlying task for successful design thinking is organizing for self-organization. Design thinking cannot be employed successfully if the organizational culture does not allow for such an agile management approach. Furthermore, we would even tentatively submit that this assertion is at least partially generalizable, allowing the presumption that other agile management approaches might also be dependent upon a fit with the respective organizational culture. Take, for instance, scrum with its emphasis on self-organization and rapid iterative improvements. Such a managerial approach is also highly likely to be contingent on a suitable organizational culture.

Despite these insights, some limitations warrant attention. First, from a theoretical perspective it appears necessary to gain a better understanding of where to delineate what kind of work is deemed suited or subject to design thinking activities—or in more general terms: agile management—and what kind of work should preferably be pursued by means of conventional managerial techniques. Alternatively, drawing a line between types of activities suited to design thinking or agile management might not be possible at all. Nonetheless, this might result in the question whether or not there are boundary conditions that foster the introduction and execution of such approaches.

Second, to a certain extent design thinking is old wine in new bottles (Corsten et al., 2016). This can be justified by the observation that in effect, design thinking represents an amalgamation of established methods from the social sciences, particularly qualitative-explorative measures. This does not limit its attractiveness per se for a discussion in light of agile management approaches, but should be kept in mind in more general terms, especially from a method-related perspective.

Third and as already reflected on above, empirically speaking we might be in the lucky position that Insiders Technologies itself exhibits many features deemed critical for the employment of agile management approaches such as design thinking (e.g. it is an organization operating in the organizational field of software development, the organization is research- and development-driven, heavily emphasizing agile management approaches while having top management support etc.). Experiences from organizations with a different history, operating in different organizational fields etc. might be informative in order to complement our insights.

Bearing these limitations in mind, we submit that future research and managerial practice might benefit, among other things, from offering insights from large-scale organizations. Whereas Insiders Technologies, as a small and medium-sized enterprise, is comparatively easy to steer and develop strategically, managing change in large organizations is considered more difficult. Hence the ongoing efforts to make large corporations more agile, as evidenced in a number of settings (e.g. at TUI, XING or Sipgate; Häusling, 2018; Mois, 2018), might offer different perspectives to those we have outlined here.

## References

Amabile, T. M., Barsade, S. G., Mueller, J. S., & Staw, B. M. (2005). Affect and creativity at work. *Administrative Science Quarterly, 50*(3), 367–403.

Beck, K., Beedle, M., van Bennekum, A., Cockburn, A., Cunningham, W., Fowler, M., et al. (2001a). *Manifest für Agile Softwareentwicklung*. http://agilemanifesto.org/iso/de/manifesto.html. Accessed 31 Aug 2018.

Beck, K., Beedle, M., van Bennekum, A., Cockburn, A., Cunningham, W., Fowler, M., et al. (2001b). *Prinzipien hinter dem Agilen Manifest*. http://agilemanifesto.org/iso/de/principles.html. Accessed 31 Aug 2018.

Bénabou, R., & Tirole, J. (2003). Intrinsic and extrinsic motivation. *The Review of Economic Studies, 70*(3), 489–520.

Benkler, Y. (2002). Coase's Penguin, or, Linux and the nature of the firm. *The Yale Law Journal, 112*(3), 369–446.

Brynjolfsson, E., & McAfee, A. (2016). *The second machine age*. Norton.

Castells, M. (1996). *The rise of the network society*. Wiley-Blackwell.

Chesbrough, H. W. (2003). *Open innovation: The new imperative for creating and profiting from technology*. Harvard Business School Press.

Cooper, R. G. (1994). Perspective: Third-generation new product processes. *The Journal of Product Innovation Management, 11*(1), 3–14.

Corsten, H., Gössinger, R., Müller-Seitz, G., & Schneider, H. (2016). *Grundlagen des Technologie- und Innovationsmanagement*. Vahlen.

D'Aveni, R. A. (1994). *Hyper-Competition*. Free Press.

Danner-Schröder, A., & Müller-Seitz, G. (2017). Qualitative Methoden in der Organisations- und Managementforschung: Ein anwendungsorientierter Leitfaden für Datensammlung und -analyse. Vahlen.

DiMaggio, P. J., & Powell, W. W. (1983). The iron cage revisited: Institutional isomorphism and collective rationality in organizational fields. *American Sociological Review, 48*(2), 147–160.

Etzioni, A. (1968). *The active society: A theory of societal and political processes*. Free Press.

Fayol, H. (1949). *General and industrial management*. Pitman Publishing Company.

Gioia, D. A., & Chittipeddi, K. (1991). Sensemaking and sensegiving in strategic change initiation. *Strategic Management Journal, 12*(6), 433–448.

Gomez, P., & Probst, G. J. B. (1989). Organizational closure in management: A complementary view to contingency approaches. *Cybernetics and Systems: An International Journal, 20*(4), 311–320.

Hayek, F. A. v. (1976). *Individualismus und wirtschaftliche Ordnung*. Neugebauer.

Häusling, A. (2018). *Agile organisationen: Transformationen erfolgreich gestalten—Beispiele agiler Pioniere*. Haufe Lexware.

Heinlein, K., & Weiss, W. (2017). Innovationskultur von Morgen – Zukunft gestalten im Zeitalter des digitalen Wandels. In V. Lingnau, G. Müller-Seitz, & S. Roth (Eds.), *Management der digitalen Transformation* (pp. 245–258). Vahlen.

Hilgers, D., Müller-Seitz, G., & Piller, F. (2010). *Benkler revisited—Venturing beyond the open source software arena?* ICIS 2010 Proceedings Paper 97. St. Louis.

Howe, J. (2006). *The rise of crowdsourcing*. https://www.wired.com/2006/06/crowds/. Accessed 5 Sept 2018.

Howe, J. (2008). *Crowdsourcing: Why the power of the crowd is driving the future of business*. Crown Business.

Jacoby, S. M. (1984). *Employing bureaucracy: Managers, unions and the transformation of work in the 20th century*. Lawrence Erlbaum.

Jeppesen, L. B., & Lakhani, K. R. (2010). Marginality and problem-solving effectiveness in broadcast search. *Organization Science, 21*(5), 1016–1033.

Kaiser, S., & Müller-Seitz, G. (2008). Leveraging lead user knowledge in software development: The case of weblog technology economics of open-source collaboration. *Industry & Innovation, 15*(2), 199–221.

Kelley, D., & Kelley, T. (2015). *Creative confidence: Unleashing the creative potential within us all*. Harper Collins.

Kirsch, W. (1997). *Kommunikatives Handeln, Autopoiese, Rationalität: Kritische Aneignungen im Hinblick auf eine evolutionäre Organisationstheorie*. Kirsch.

Lifshitz-Assaf, H. (2018). Dismantling knowledge boundaries at NASA: The critical role of professional identity in open innovation. *Administrative Science Quarterly, 63*(4), 746–782.

Lingnau, V., Müller-Seitz, G., & Roth, S. (2018). *Management der digitalen Transformation: Interdisziplinäre theoretische Perspektiven und praktische Ansätze*. Vahlen.

Luhmann, N. (1984). *Soziale Systeme: Grundriss einer allgemeinen Theorie*. Suhrkamp.

Mois, T. (2018). Im besten Fall werde ich ignoriert. *Harvard Business Manager, 8*(4), 64–70.

Morner, M. (1997). *Organisation der Innovation im Konzern: Gestaltung von Konzernstrukturen zur Hervorbringung von Produktinnovationen*. Gabler.

Müller-Seitz, G. (2014). Von Risiko zu Resilienz: Zum Umgang mit Unerwartetem aus Organisationsperspektive. *ZfbF, 66*(68), 102–122.

Müller-Seitz, G., & Reger, G. (2009). Is open source software living up to its promises? Insights for open innovation management from two open source software-inspired projects. *R&D Management, 39*(4), 372–381.

Müller-Seitz, G., & Weiss, W. (2019). *Strategien zum Umgang mit der digitalen Transformation…aus der Sicht eines mittelständischen „Hidden Champions"*. Vahlen.

Okhuysen, G. A., & Bechky, B. A. (2009). Coordination in organizations: An integrative perspective. *Academy of Management Annals, 3*(1), 463–502.

Plattner, H., Meinel, C., & Weinberg, U. (2009). *Design-thinking*. Munich: mi-Wirtschaftsbuch.

Puranam, P., Alexy, O., & Reitzig, M. (2014). What's "New" about new forms of organizing? *Academy of Management Review, 39*(2), 162–180.

Raab, J., & Kenis, P. (2009). Heading toward a society of networks: Empirical developments and theoretical challenges. *Journal of Management Inquiry, 18*(3), 198–210.

Raymond, E. (1999). *The cathedral & the bazaar: Musings on Linux and open source by an accidental revolutionary*. O'Reilly.

Rubin, K. S. (2015). *Essential scrum: A practical guide to the most popular Agile process*. Pearson.

Sambamurthy, V., Bharadwaj, A. S., & Grover, V. (2003). Shaping agility through digital options: Reconceptualizing the role of information technology in contemporary firms. *MIS Quarterly, 27*(2), 237–263.

Sarros, J. C., Cooper, B. K., & Santora, J. C. (2008). Building a climate for innovation through transformational leadership and organization culture. *Journal of Leadership and Organizational Studies, 15*(2), 145–158.

Schein, E. H. (2004). *Organizational culture and leadership*. Jossey-Bass.

Schreyögg, G., & Sydow, J. (2010). Organizing for fluidity? Dilemmas of new organizational forms. *Organization Science, 21*(6), 1251–1262.

Sutherland, J. (2015). *Scrum: The art of doing twice the work in half the time*. Random House.

Sydow, J., Schüßler, E., & Müller-Seitz, G. (2016). *Managing inter-organizational relations: Debates and cases*. Palgrave.

Tallon, P. P., & Pinsonneault, A. (2011). Competing perspectives on the link between strategic information technology alignment and organizational agility: Insights from a mediation model. *MIS Quarterly, 35*(2), 463–484.

Taylor, F. W. (1911). *The principles of scientific management*. Harper & Brothers.

Vázquez-Bustelo, D., Avella, L., & Fernández, E. (2007). Agility drivers, enablers and outcomes: Empirical test of an integrated agile manufacturing model. *International Journal of Operations & Production Management, 27*(12), 1303–1332.

Weick, K. E. (1979). *The social psychology of organizing*. Addison Wesley.

Weick, K. E., & Sutcliffe, K. M. (2015). *Managing the unexpected: Sustained performance in a complex world* (3rd ed.). Wiley.

Williamson, O. E. (2000). The new institutional economics: Taking stock, looking ahead. *Journal of Economic Literature, 38*(3), 595–613.

Zidulka, A., & Mitchell, I. K. (2018). Creativity or cooptation? Thinking beyond instrumentalism when teaching design thinking. *Journal of Management Education, 42*(6), 749–760. https://doi.org/10.1177/1052562918799797.

CHAPTER 7

# Strategility—A Challenging Alliance

*Kerstin Pichel and Andrea Müller*

## Purpose

The following paper aims to encourage a discussion about strategility, a new strategic practice of agile strategic decision-making. We wish to share our research questions and initial findings about the practices and praxis of strategility and outline further research steps.

## Researching Agile Strategy-Making as Practice

In the following sections, we first review extant research. Recent strategy research has been exploring new ways to develop and realize a strategy that transcends the linear, rational process of strategic management (for an overview, see Golsorkhi et al., 2015: 6). The challenges of an environment characterized by volatility, uncertainty, complexity, and ambiguity (a VUCA world as proposed by Bennett and Lemoine [2014]) have created a new phenomenon: agile strategy-making, also known as strategility. Strategility is defined as strategy-making with iteration loops for assessing information and defining strategic details, allowing companies

K. Pichel (✉) · A. Müller
Zurich University of Applied Sciences, Winterthur, Switzerland
e-mail: piet@zhaw.ch



S. Pfeiffer et al. (eds.), *The Agile Imperative*, Dynamics of Virtual Work,
https://doi.org/10.1007/978-3-030-73994-2_7

to further develop and refine their strategy gradually according to the facts it generates.

Digitalization offers potential for new products and markets that are, however, complex and difficult to fully analyse strategically.

Iterative loops for analysing and defining strategic issues seem helpful for making the right strategic decisions about how to attract customers, relevant product characteristics, or effective business partnerships for new, unproven business ideas. Agility is required in making strategic decisions (De Smet & Gagnon, 2018), and related concepts such as scrum (an agile way to manage projects, usually software development) have been introduced to strategic management (Cervone, 2014; Lyngso, 2017; Process Management Consulting, 2015). As a result, strategic decisions can be developed in iterative sequences or time slots called scrum sprints.

While companies are asking for strategility and managers are experimenting with this new practice, little systematic research appears to have been conducted. In the context of reviewing the existing literature, we have a number of questions concerning strategility:

- Williams et al. (2013: 4) recommended a shared mission statement and a business model that provides orientation as clear strategic intent—especially in agile strategies. Our question is: how can a clear strategic intent and agile strategy-making be combined? Is strategic alignment possible, even when you realize agile strategy-making?
- Strategility research mainly uses case studies to illustrate certain design aspects (e.g. Doz et al., 2008; Williams et al., 2013). Questions: how is strategility implemented in practice? Can patterns be found for agile strategy processes for companies of similar size, age, or industry, or with similar strategic challenges?
- Lyngso (2017) described a sophisticated set up for agile strategy implementation which differentiates functions and activities. Our question is: what functions and activities exist in large enterprises compared to small and medium-sized enterprises?
- Sibony et al. (2017: 8–11) distinguished three types of strategic decision processes: investment, resource allocation, and blue-sky (involving ideas that are yet to have practical uses). While the outcome of resource allocation processes reflects the degree of agility, the outcome of blue-sky processes (with open-ended strategy questions, high uncertainty, and ill-defined problems) is the degree of innovation. Our question is: is strategility linked to blue-sky

strategic decision processes and can it be promoted by allocating strategic resources?

- Holbeche (2018: 75) described the balance of strategic control and autonomy in agile strategizing. Our question is: does strategility change the responsibilities for strategic decision-making?

For our strategility research, we transformed the questions posed above into three main research questions:

1. What types of agile strategy-making praxis are there and what are successful practices in that context?
2. What value-adding roles can be found in agile strategy-making?
3. For what kinds of strategic topics does it make sense to practise agile strategy-making?

These research questions cover the three main areas of strategy as practice research (Jarzabkowski & Spee, 2009: 70)—which is why the working title of our study is "Strategility as Practice".

## An Example of Strategility

To investigate strategility practice, we started by conducting field research and explorative interviews.

First, we facilitated an agile strategy process in an IT company. The company was planning to diversify by entering a new digital market just opening up involving IT solutions for retail customers that connect augmented reality devices with order and checkout systems. Our focus was on using information loops to support fact-based strategy development, even though strategic analysis could not be finalized without customers and existing markets. We therefore designed a strategy process with iterative loops for information-gathering and refining the strategic decision. Each loop was designed as a kind of strategic Sprint: for a period of two to four weeks, teams of two to four people tested the development of a strategic element. For instance, product specifications were examined in co-creation with customers and contract specifications with potential business partners. The iteration loops between analysing and refining are illustrated in Fig. 7.1 (for a detailed description, see Pichel & Müller, 2018).

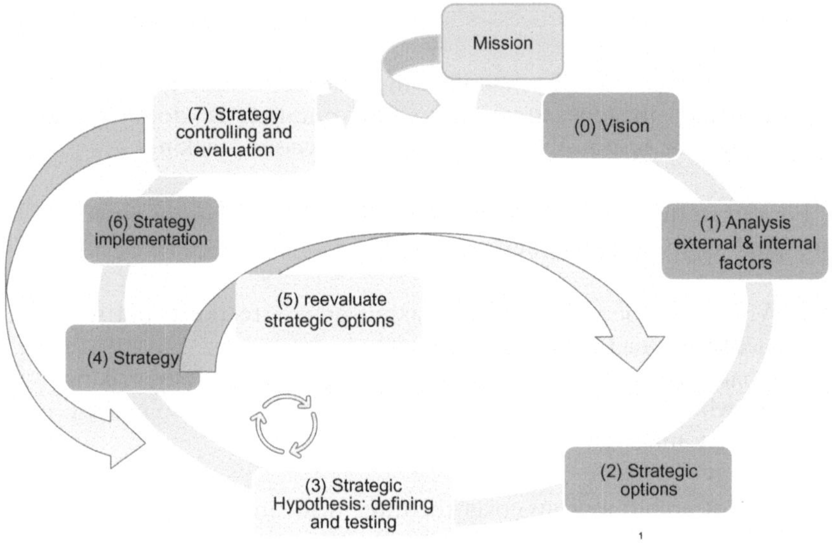


**Fig. 7.1** Agile strategy process with iterative loops

During this field experiment, we identified some challenges of agile strategy processes, described in the findings below.

To determine how other companies and consultancies deal with these challenges, we conducted explorative interviews on strategility practice. Subjects included:

- three large international insurance groups, one of which involved two areas—one (A) on the group level and one (Ö) on the division level—while the other one (M) involved the group level only;
- two small national IT companies (DC and D);
- two small national consulting companies (L and P); and
- one large national retail company (G).

We used a semi-standardized questionnaire asking subjects for their definition of strategy and the strategy process as well as about participants in strategy processes and how they deal with typical challenges.

## Heterogeneous Features of Strategility

The strategy process we had designed and facilitated enabled us to derive some challenges and questions about an agile strategic practice.

1. The iteration between the analysis and refinement of a strategic option is never completed. In our case, the strategy team never felt it had enough analytical background information to decide on the strategic direction of the company. This gave rise to the question as to the analytical information needed for a strategy team to decide on the company's direction.
2. Because of the continuous feedback loops, a strategic decision can always be optimized and adjusted. At the same time, strategic projects need some stability in order to be staffed and to develop. The questions thus arose as to which elements of a strategy should be defined and remain in place, and which ones should be constantly adapted, as well as what level of abstraction an agile strategy can and must have.
3. The iteration between analysing and refining strategic options included activities to be considered as strategy implementation, such as bargaining about product-price specifications. While the strategic overall decision had not been made yet, negotiations were already underway. The question is, therefore, whether an agile mixture of implementation and decision-making is also appropriate for the fundamental strategic decisions of a company.
4. When an agile strategy team uses iteration loops to work on a strategic initiative, it needs to have the authorization to take financial decisions or negotiate specific contractual provisions. The question is who is responsible for the strategic decisions to be made?

We contacted eight companies claiming to work with agile strategy processes and interviewed them about their experiences with strategility. After familiarizing ourselves with what they do, we found a heterogeneous understanding of strategility, including the strategy-making process and the strategy content. To characterize these heterogeneous activities, we divided their activities into clusters, proposing the hypothesis that these clusters might describe a continuum of maturity (see Fig. 7.2).

The two axes of the graph in Fig. 7.2 indicate the maturity of an agile strategy process and the strategy content.

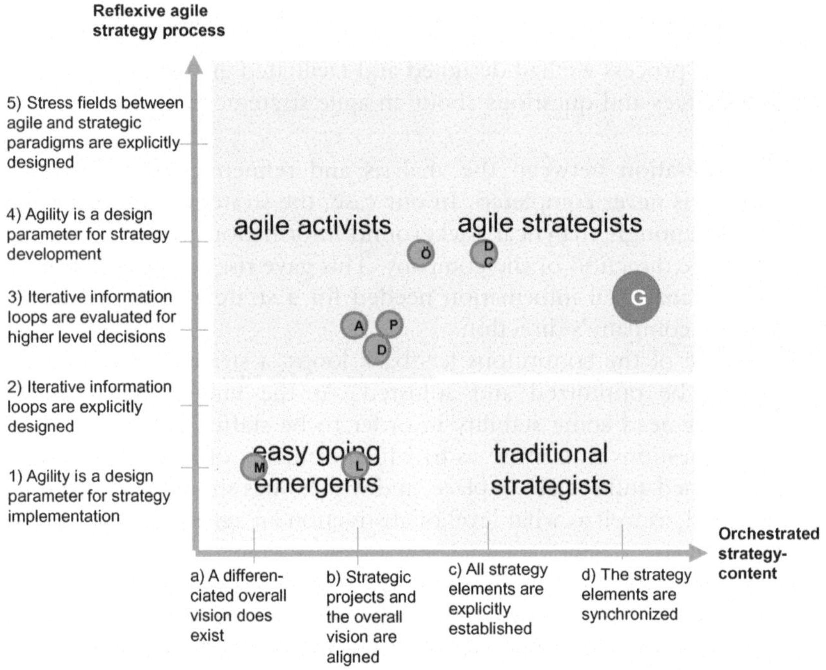


**Fig. 7.2** Maturity cluster for agile strategies

For a mature agile strategy process, strategic decision-making should be reflective and take into account the relevant information about the situation.

1. The starting point for an agile strategy process is often the integration of agile principles into the strategy implementation. Strategic projects are managed with the help of agile development principles, for example, iterative, evidence-based, or collaborative decision-making (Davidson & Klemme, 2016).
2. The next step towards a reflexive agile strategy process is to design information loops for strategic know-how generated in strategy implementation projects—for example, by defining objectives and key results (OKRs) or key performance indicators (KPIs) (Hao &

Yu-Ling, 2018) that help those involved understand how value-creating strategic projects are. Insurance Company M, for example, realizes multiple agile projects in IT or marketing to analyse customer response to new offerings. The information gathered in these projects is used to optimize the performance of the projects and achieve a high project value.

3. In a third step, the information of implementation projects in cross-project evaluations are considered. This includes the question as to what can be learned from implementation projects overall about customers, product needs, or the economic logic of the company. This overall evaluation needs to go hand in hand with a structure or a person who has an overview of the company's strategic development. Consulting Company P, for example, uses a balanced scorecard (Kaplan & Norton, 1996) to conduct a continuous review of activities and the success of strategic projects. In quarterly strategy reviews, all strategic projects are evaluated according to the overall strategic plan, and the lessons learned are discussed to determine if the underlying strategic logic still holds.
4. The fourth step includes agility in the strategy development itself. Not only are implementation projects realized in an agile way, but the analysis and definition of the strategic position of a company are also conducted in iterative loops in which information-gathering and the adjustment of strategic elements alternate (for example, see Pichel & Müller, 2018). Insurance Company Division Ö is working on a diversification project to enter a new market with new products. The analysis and definition of the products, customers, prices, partners, and other strategic elements are realized in an agile way using co-creation (Ranjan & Read, 2016), involving prototyping and constant adjustment of strategic decisions.
5. Finally, a mature agile strategy process integrates both the agile and the strategic paradigms. To resolve the conflicts that this creates, the seven levers proposed by Sibony et al. (2017) for designing strategic processes might prove helpful. Activities might include creating incentives in strategy workshops to reflect on given information or to come to a conscious decision (Pichel & Luethi, 2015: 181–186, 243–246).

Mature strategy content can be defined as the concentration of different strategic steering methods.

A. As the first strategic steering method, a company should define an overall vision. To provide helpful strategic guidance, this vision should include a hypothesis about the company's future market development and market positions.
B. The second strategic steering method is an alignment of the company's vision and strategic projects. The allocation of resources should take into account the overall vision. Consultancy L, for example, has developed a sophisticated project management system with designated roles such as Strategy Governance Teams, which ensure that projects reflect the overall vision.
C. The third strategic steering method is the explicit definition of relevant strategy elements. As a helpful overview of strategy elements, we refer to the structure of the five elements of strategy proposed by Hambrick and Fredrickson (2005), which distinguishes, for example:

   - strategic arenas in which a company is active, such as product categories, market segments, or value creation stages;
   - vehicles a company uses to be present in these arenas, such as organic development or joint ventures; and
   - differentiators a company creates to take a winning position among competitors, such as image, style, or product reliability.

   These elements need to be defined to enable managers to know what kinds of market or customer to target. The insurance company's Division Ö is entering a new market and is thus redefining its services, customers, prices, partners, and other strategic elements.

D. The final step in coordinating strategic steering means is to synchronize the strategic elements defined in Step C. Especially customers, products, differentiation, and economic logic have to be aligned to stay successful (Hambrick & Fredrickson, 2005).

Retail Company G is heading towards diversification and is, therefore, investigating which customers have specific needs the retailer can meet at reasonable prices, realizing a differentiation that still fits its image.

## Strategility Using the Example of G

Online trading by companies such as Zalando and Amazon has become a threat for the business model of Swiss consumer Retail Company G (G), especially in view of the strong Swiss franc. To counteract this development, G decided to develop new, lucrative business segments.

After a traditional strategy development process yielded no results, two years ago the CEO of G decided to implement a new approach of strategic decision-making based on the company's experience with agile project management to develop a new cash desk programme. Iterative decision-making and techniques for activating collective intelligence and transparent decision-making, such as big room planning (all stakeholders coming together (in a "big room") to coordinate and collaborate towards a shared understanding of how to achieve business goals over a period of time (usually the next quarter) (Jepsen, 2018), seemed attractive possibilities for addressing the strategic issue of developing new business segments.

Three consultants of Rocket Consulting AG—a consulting firm—and three G employees form a core team for an agile strategy project. Together, they represent a heterogeneous range of expert knowledge in the field of strategy, software development, product design, branding, marketing, and project management. In addition, they are able to draw on the knowledge of point of sales employees whenever necessary.

The core team was tasked with assessing new business segments and testing hypotheses about a new business model in terms of relevant customers, products, and business logic. The main hypothesis was that the concept of the "sharing economy" (i.e. collaborative consumption and crowd-based capitalism) (Botsman & Rogers, 2011) had the potential to provide a new business segment for G.

The consulting firm designed an agile strategy process within four main sequences:

- The first sequence was to test the business model to establish which customer segments would be interested in renting what kind of products at a reasonable price.
- The second sequence was to set up marketing and communication.
- The third sequence was to design processes.
- The fourth sequence was to design IT and technology.

Using a combination of lean start-up, design thinking, and scrum management, the core team defined activities and expected outcomes, experimented with the activities, and reviewed the results before moving to the next sprint:

- The core team set up a trial store for two weeks renting out consumer durables.
- The core team analysed the lessons learned about the business model and went on to the next experience sprint: a pop-up store with a limited product range for a smaller customer segment: renting fashion items to young women in a trendy downtown area.
- After analyzing its experiences with the pop-up store, the core team started the next sprint: five online stores for the rental of segment-specific products such as luxury handbags.

In a customer survey, customers were asked whether they were interested in renting rather than buying consumer products and what types of products these would be. Their feedback was reported directly to the CEO of G, enabling him and the project manager to make forecasts concerning the number of potential customers, products, and expected revenues in preparation for the next iteration (e.g. prototyping).

## Strategility Challenges

We found that some of the companies we interviewed did not implement all the steps identified to complete a reflective agile strategy process. IT Company D, for instance, generated products and customers over time without ever defining them explicitly. Only when further growth proved impossible did they start analyzing their customer groups and identifying possible new target groups.

At the same time, we wondered whether there is a reason these steps are missing. The paradigms of strategic management and agility are oppositional in some respects (see Fig. 7.3).

Strategic management relies on the idea of rational decision-making by legitimate strategists in a logical, linear process (Johnson et al., 2008: 30 et seq.). Careful analysis of complex influencing factors provides a basis for predicting developments and appropriate strategic positions. Decisions about strategy content come first and are cascaded down through

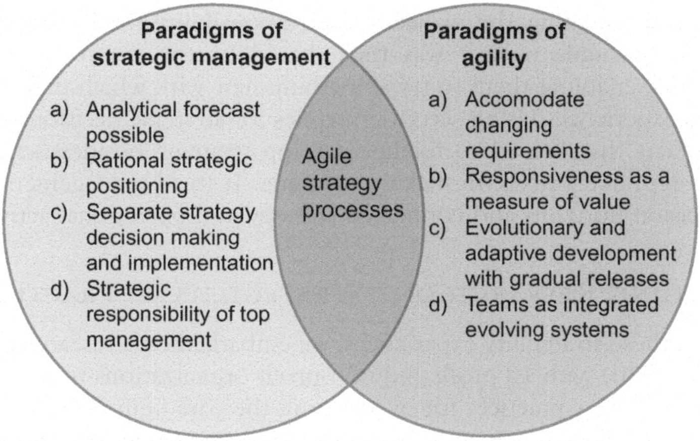


**Fig. 7.3** Oppositional paradigms of strategic management and agility

the organization to put strategic decisions into action. The company's senior management is thus responsible for the strategic development of a company.

Agility emphasizes elements such as speed and flexibility to respond to changes and uncertainty (Thiry, 2015: 3). Customer needs define what must be done. Practitioners need to be part of agile teams to realize and test quick prototypes.

Before launching the trial store, the senior management of G had been tempted to implement the usual decision-making procedures: appoint an expert team to analyse potential customer segments, needs, and reactions and to design a sophisticated concept. This would have minimized the risk of failure while providing good reasons why setting up a trial store was worth the risk. However, the paradigm of rational analysis and decision-making by responsible managers often prevents companies from overcoming possible biases and finding out what they need to know about prospective new business segments. Detailed analysis concerning the rental of products such as kitchen equipment or furniture for one-person households might indicate that a trial store would not be feasible. The chances of finding out whether women might be interested in renting handbags would, therefore, have been slim.

The expertise and proactive commitment demonstrated by Rocket Consulting's agile consultants resulted in a relationship of trust that was helpful in completing the project. The responsibility for the success or failure of the agile project was thus shared by the company and the consultants, enabling them to try something new with which they had no previous experience. Using scrum principles for strategic decision-making created facts that helped to further develop strategic business segments step by step, like a decision-making machine. It freed management from epic decision horizons and connected strategy and operational activities.

## Ongoing Research on "Strategility as Practice"

Based on these strategility experiences, we embarked on a research project (ZHAW, 2020) with 10 profit and non-profit organizations to investigate helpful strategility practices for overcoming the paradigm dilemma.

To date we have conducted three interviews and three workshops with all 10 organizations. This enables us to extract sense-making steps for the strategy process and important principles for agile strategy-making (see Fig. 7.4).

| STRATEGILITY PRINCIPLES / STRATEGILITY PROCESS-STEPS | **A) ALIGNMENT** of strategic decision with higher ranking targets | **B) EVIDENCE-BASED:** explicit usage of best information | **C) ITERATIVE:** Switching between information gathering and decision concretizing | **D) COLLA-BORATIVE:** strategic discourse with bearer of knowledge | **E) AUTO-NOMOUS:** strategy work in self organizing teams |
|---|---|---|---|---|---|
| 1. Analysis external and internal factors | | | | | |
| 2. Defining strategic options | | | | | |
| 3. Defining and testing of strat. Hypothesis | | | | | |
| 4. Strategy definition | | | | | |
| 5. Reevaluate strategic options | | | | | |
| 6. Strategy Implementation | | | | | |
| 7. Strategy evaluation | | | | | |

**Fig. 7.4** Strategility matrix

By combining these steps and principles, one of the things we discovered was a helpful practice for agile strategy development: making strategic hypotheses (see Process Step 3).

Strategic hypotheses are assumptions about promising strategy elements, such as lucrative customer clusters or helpful cooperation partners. When they are carefully combined with the strategility principles, they can help overcome the oppositional strategic and agile paradigms a, b, and c (Fig. 7.3).

In workshops with our research partners, we extracted helpful configurations of strategic hypotheses combined with strategility principles, transferred for this book chapter and explained and illustrated in the following using the previous example of Company G:

Strategic hypotheses

- must be derived from the strategic option (Field 3A in Fig. 7.4). Company G selected the strategic option to start renting out rather than selling products to its customers. One main strategic hypothesis derived from this option was that there is sufficient demand for renting out products.
- should define specific aspects which are tested in real business settings (Field 3B in Fig. 7.4). Company G specified the hypothesis about sufficient demand by clustering the demands geographically: "The demand for renting products is bigger in cities than in the country". The test activities are described in the section "Strategility using the example of G" above.
- should be modified by changing one aspect after the other to make sure that the right strategic decision is made (Field 3C in Fig. 7.4). When Company G realized that rental activities in a city were not sufficient, they modified the city areas. The iterative switch between gathering information and decision-making made the strategy team aware of the necessity to specify customer clusters and geographic areas rather than giving up on the hypothesis of sufficient demand in cities.
- should be developed and analysed in a collaborative discourse between decision-makers and bearers of knowledge (Field 3D in Fig. 7.4). The sales team of Company G had implicit information about their customers' reactions, demographic characteristics, and graduation of reactions. Only in a dialogue with the strategy team could this information be made explicit, consolidated, and used.

- should be delegated to strategy teams with the freedom to test and modify them autonomously (Field 3E in Fig. 7.4). In Company G, the core team could iterate tests and hypothesis specifications according to their ongoing findings, which made them fast and accurate.

In our ongoing research, we focus on further strategility practices, such as constant strategy derivation from ongoing test information.

At the same time, we will take a closer look at the strategility praxis, especially strategility implications for management functions. The first interview results let us hypothesize that in most organizations senior management still makes the final strategic decision. Nevertheless, autonomy of strategy teams and a real discourse between strategy teams and senior management are important for value-adding iterations of a strategic hypothesis. This implies a kind of paradoxical leadership, combining participative and directive behaviours (Alfes & Langner, 2017: 97 et seq.).

These initial "strategility-as-a-practice" insights lead us to the third research question for our project: strategility seems to be a complex and time-consuming way to make strategic decisions. Which strategic options should be developed further using strategility, and for which strategies would a traditional approach be more effective and efficient?

On the basis of our initial findings, we propose the following hypotheses about the new practice of agile strategy-making:

1. Strategility is mainly used for strategy implementation and emergent competitive strategies. It is seldom used for corporate strategy development, and, if so, only parts of agile decision-making are integrated. Strategility is, therefore, a typical approach of entrepreneurial companies and strategic reorientations. In larger companies, an ambidextrous combination of linear and agile strategy processes occurs.
2. Strategility leads to new strategic steering methods: agile strategy-making uses the five strategy elements of Hambrick and Fredrickson (2005) only as a framework without defining them in detail. Instead, a differentiated vision with sophisticated aims for business segments guides agile strategic approaches that develop in stages.

3. Senior management will be considered capable and successful if they manage to realize paradoxical strategic leadership.
4. Strategility demands tolerance for strategic decisions, which may be left pending for some time. It challenges neutral analysis and evaluation of management teams, even if they have been involved in agile projects for some time. Methods that help an agile strategy team run through a conscious process of co-sensing and co-creation (Scharmer, 2009: 19 et seq.) promote an unbiased agile strategy.
5. Strategility challenges paradigms of long-term strategic management. In other words, strategility appears to be especially useful for medium-term decisions with strong, unknown influencing factors.

To test these hypotheses, we will conduct further interviews with companies and consultancies that use strategility. In addition, we will try to deduce recommendations for the design of roles and processes of strategility. Hopefully, that will allow us to contribute to a better understanding of this new practice of strategizing.

## References

Alfes, K., & Langner, N. (2017). Paradoxical leadership. *Organizational Dynamics, 2*(46), 96–103.

Bennett, N., & Lemoine, G. J. (2014). What a difference a word makes: Understanding threats to performance in a VUCA world. *Business Horizons, 57*(3), 311–317.

Botsman, R., & Rogers, R. (2011). *What's mine is yours: How collaborative consumption is changing the way we live* (Vol. 5). Collins.

Cervone, H. F. (2014). Improving strategic planning by adapting agile methods to the planning process. *Journal of Library Administration, 54*(2), 155–168.

Davidson, A., & Klemme, L. (2016). Why a CEO should think like a Scrum Master. *Strategy & Leadership, 44*(1), 36–40.

De Smet A., & Gagnon, C. (2018). Organizing for the age of urgency. *Mc Kinsey Quarterly*. https://www.mckinsey.com/business-functions/organization/our-insights/organizing-for-the-age-of-urgency. Accessed 23 Mar 2018.

Doz, Y., Doz, Y. L., & Kosonen, M. (2008). *Fast strategy: How strategic agility will help you stay ahead of the game*. Pearson Education.

Golsorkhi, D., Rouleau, L., Seidl, D., & Vaara, E. (2015). *Cambridge handbook of strategy as practice* (2nd ed.). Cambridge University Press.

Hambrick, D. C., & Fredrickson, J. W. (2005). Are you sure you have a strategy? *Academy of Management Perspectives, 19*(4), 51–62.

Hao, Z. H. O. U., & Yu-Ling, H. E. (2018). Comparative study of OKR and KPI. *DEStech Transactions on Economics, Business and Management, (eced).*

Holbeche, L. (2018). *The agile organization: How to build an engaged, innovative and resilient business*. Kogan Page Publishers.

Jarzabkowski, P., & Spee, P. A. (2009). Strategy-as-practice: A review and future directions for the field. *International Journal of Management Reviews, 11*(1), 69–95.

Jepsen, O. (2018). *Scaling agile—Big room planning*. https://www.infoq.com/articles/making-scaling-agile-work-4. Accessed 7 Mar 2019.

Johnson, G., Scholes, K., & Whittington, R. (2008). *Exploring corporate strategy: Text & cases*. Pearson Education.

Kaplan, R. S., & Norton, D. P. (1996). *The balanced scorecard: Translating strategy into action*. Harvard Business Press.

Lyngso, S. (2017). *Agile strategy management: Techniques for continuous alignment and improvement*. CRC Press.

Pichel, K., & Luethi, E. (2015). *Strategie und Diversitaet* (2nd ed.). Haupt Verlag.

Pichel, K., & Müller, A. (2018). Strategility: Agility in strategic decisions. *International Journal of Strategic Management, 18*(1), 81–88.

Process Management Consulting. (2015). *Agiler Strategieprozess, Sonderheft aspect 2/15*. München.

Ranjan, K. R., & Read, S. (2016). Value co-creation: Concept and measurement. *Journal of the Academy of Marketing Science, 44*(3), 290–315.

Scharmer, C. O. (2009). *Theory U: Learning from the future as it emerges*. Berrett-Koehler Publishers.

Sibony, O., Lovallo, D., & Powell, T. C. (2017). Behavioral strategy and the strategic decision architecture of the firm. *California Management Review, 59*(3), 5–21.

Thiry, M. (2015). *Agility is not just for projects: Crafting the agile organisation*. Paper presented at PMI® Global Congress 2015—EMEA, London.

Williams, T., Worley, C. G., & Lawler III, E. E. (2013). The agility factor. *Strategy + Business, 15*(4), 1–9.

ZHAW. (2020). *Strategility*. https://www.zhaw.ch/de/sml/institutezentren/zue/forschung/strategility/.

CHAPTER 8

# The Implementation of the 'Agile' Method in a Start-Up Company: A New Way of Controlling Work?

*Marion Flécher*

## Introduction

Over the past two decades, industries of the 'new economy' have been portrayed as trail-blazers in building competitive advantage in a challenging world of global competition and rapid technological change. Among advocates of the 'new economy', unprecedented attention has been paid to the role of start-up companies as standard-bearers in the development of innovative products and services. These companies are often seen as a driving force behind new work and management practices, based on empowering, flexible and knowledge-based production systems, akin to the 'liberated firm' model (Carney & Getz, 2009; Peters, 1992). From a sociological point of view, these companies are valuable laboratories for observing the changes affecting the world of work and organizations, since their founders often seek to go against the grain of

M. Flécher (✉)
Paris-Dauphine University, Paris, France
e-mail: marion.flecher@dauphine.psl.eu



S. Pfeiffer et al. (eds.), *The Agile Imperative*, Dynamics of Virtual Work,
https://doi.org/10.1007/978-3-030-73994-2_8

traditional organizations. In common with companies from the creative industries (Hodgson & Briand, 2013), start-up firms 'stand as an implicit rebuke to the failure of the traditional machine bureaucracy and inflexible Fordist production processes' (Hodgson & Briand, 2013: 309). Yet their claims to promote liberated and emancipatory work must be empirically and critically examined (Hodgson & Cicmil, 2006).

Literature dealing with the issues of the 'new economy' often points out that innovative companies commonly adopt a 'management by project' approach. Hiring 'knowledge workers' searching for autonomy and 'emancipatory' ways of working, these innovative organizations often require the abandonment of the traditional and hierarchical structures of industrial society (Thompson et al., 2009) as well as the adoption of alternative project management methodologies and team structures (Beirne, 2008; Harley, 2001). In management science, this type of organization is often uncritically lauded and extolled as offering 'emancipatory' possibilities that move beyond hierarchical control towards empowering and fulfilling work that could reap the fruits of workers' creativity (Peters, 1992; Roy & Audet, 2003). For their proponents, the project-based organizational forms epitomize the desire to break with the bureaucratic tendency to control with a modernist vision of management based on horizontality, autonomy, and worker empowerment. With a more critical perspective, other authors (Clegg & Courpasson, 2004; Hodgson, 2004; Hodgson & Briand, 2013) show, rather, that the project-based organizational form serves as an alternative mechanism of workplace control built upon project management technologies and professional self-discipline. They emphasize the importance of empirically examining the nature of project-based organization and critically question these purported 'post-bureaucratic' methods which claim to offer more flexible and empowering alternatives (Hodgson & Briand, 2013). These developments echo the recent debates on teamwork, which was also associated with a rhetoric of empowerment (Harley, 2001; Knights & McCabe, 2000), yet identified by others as an operator of 'concertive control' (Barker, 2005) and peer or self-monitoring (Sewell, 1998) strengthening managerial control.

This contribution aims to bring an empirical approach to this debate by critical scrutiny of the adoption of the agile project management technique in a French start-up company. As new entrants to an established online marketplace selling electronic devices, the founders' objectives were to develop an operational website, but also to continuously integrate new functions to capture and build additional market-share while ensuring retention of their merchants and customers. The single largest group within their workforce were the software engineers/programmers charged with the technical development of the website, but the firm also employed sales staff to look for new merchants and convince them to sell their products on the platform, marketing staff to promote the website and attract customers, a customer service team to manage the relationship between customers and merchants, and specialists responsible for operations and human resources. Given the challenge of adapting quickly to their market, the chief technology officer (CTO)[1] of the company decided to set up an 'Agile' organization within the software engineering department. The other departments were also using project-based management methods and tools, but this contribution will focus on the case of these purportedly 'emancipatory' post-bureaucratic 'Agile' methods, which were only implemented within the software engineering department. What were the objectives of the adoption of such a form of project-based management?

Examining how work was structured, allocated, and monitored following the adoption of 'Agile' project management, this chapter aims to show that this method is still under-mined by persistent hierarchical divisions, both in the decision-making process and in day-to-day interactions. The agile method aims to flatten the hierarchical levels while increasing individual commitment at work, using management technologies and rituals to produce self- and peer control while encouraging employees to invest and immerse themselves in their work. This analysis will examine the consequences of the agile project management method, not only for the effectiveness of the organization structure but also for the outputs achieved. How is it planned and implemented in start-up companies? What does it change in terms of management and workplace monitoring? How does it affect professional and power relationships? To what extent does it bring more meaning and autonomy at work? The main research question of this contribution will be to understand how this organization reshapes the way employees are controlled. My hypothesis is that agile frameworks are a new way to manufacture consent (Burawoy, 1979) among employees that makes them willing to deliver faster and better.

[1] In a start-up company, the chief technology officer (CTO), is often one of the co-founders and has the technical vision for the product.

## Methodology

This research focused on the empirical case of a start-up company created in 2014 by three co-founders and developing a marketplace for electronic products. Like most start-up companies, they had to start with very little in the way of financial and human resources before attracting their first customers and beginning to raise funds. The company really started to grow in the autumn of 2015, when they raised 7 million euros. From October 2015 to October 2017, the staff increased from 7 to 45. Six months later, they raised another 40 million euros, and the workforce grew rapidly to reach 130 employees by the end of 2018. As the staff grew, the organization of work became more structured and rationalized. This case of a 'hyper-growing' start-up company thus raises the question concerning maintaining the autonomy and flexibility at work that the agile model claims to offer: to what extent does the agile method help protect the organization from over-bureaucratization?

This fieldwork is part of broader research studying the world of start-ups in a comparative approach between France and the United States and can be considered an ideal case study of a start-up company. It is also an ideal empirical case via which to observe and analyse the changes induced by growth. Data collection was based on participant observation and semi-structured interviews. Over a four-month period, I worked as a project manager in the human resources department, where I led the analysis of a survey that had been administered to all employees. I also conducted interviews on corporate culture, to replace an employee who was on sick leave. As I was a full-time worker in the company, but introduced as a Ph.D. candidate in Sociology, I was able to take notes on the daily life of the company while having time to bond with employees. During these four months, I conducted 45 interviews with employees of different hierarchical levels (non-executives, executives, managers, and heads of departments), employment status (interns, freelancers, permanent employees, and partners), and specializations (engineering, marketing, sales, quality, customer satisfaction, operations, and human resources). Interviews lasted from one to two hours, and were tape-recorded and fully transcribed. The agile management method was an unexpected but fascinating subject that emerged in the course of the investigation. In the first week of my fieldwork, I was invited to attend an off-site training day that presented the agile method to the software developers. I then discovered a broad new professional world, with its specific vocabulary, methods, and ways of working, which I would later understand.

Based on this ethnographic material, this work aims to analyse the conditions and the consequences of the implementation of the agile project-based organization. What are the managerial goals of such an organization and how are they being pursued? What are the conditions and the obstacles to its implementation? To what extent do they improve the working conditions of workers? Do they flatten hierarchical levels and bring more freedom, flexibility, and autonomy at work?

## What Does the Agile Method Do to Work Organization?

### *The Agile Method: The Lean Production Method of the Digital Sector*

The emergence of agility and new project management methodologies relied on a set of principles described in the *Agile Manifesto*. This text was written in 2001 by seventeen software engineers who were opposed to the micro-management of projects. The *Agile Manifesto* set up the ideology and the theory of the agile methodology, supporting the idea that the best way to uncover new ways of developing software was by helping each other and sharing knowledge. The principles thus valued 'individuals and interactions over processes and tools', 'working software over comprehensive documentation', 'customer collaboration over contract negotiation', and 'responding to change over following a plan' (Agile Alliance, 2012). In many senses, the agile methodology represented 'the most serious attempt to integrate the principles of modern teamwork with project management' (Hodgson & Briand, 2013), referring to projects built on reliance on trust, internal communication, dialogue, and adjustment.

Various methodologies emerged following this Manifesto, attempting to find concrete ways of applying these guidelines in practice. One of the most influential ways which has spread to most software companies is the 'Scrum' methodology (Schwaber & Beedle, 2002). This method organizes the development of software features through repeated and iterative cycles, called 'sprints'. This cyclic organization aims to adapt quickly and responsively to the evolving needs of the clients, relying on an 'empowered' team structure. Self-organization is thus seen as a way to deal efficiently with complexity (see Chapter 2 by Nicklich et al.). Beyond software companies, digital companies have been inspired by these methods to set up a flexible organization capable of adapting to the needs of their market. Among them, start-up firms are consistently evolving their business model, and must be able to make changes that adapt to market feedback. Scrum and Agile methodologies are then often implemented to encourage self-organization and increase the speed of execution.

Beyond the managerial rhetoric associating agile methods with principles of collaboration and employees' empowerment, these methods seek to increase teams' productivity and companies' revenues. Their proponents argue that agile methodologies enable employees to deliver more efficient results, through the flexibility and commitment of self-organized teams (Agile Alliance, 2012). During my fieldwork, the head of product even assumed that the move to the agile method would effectively create value for the company.

> The goal is to create value for the company, to make money, in the most objective way possible, and based on all the data that we can get. So my role is to manage the optimization of the product, considering the propositions that come from the different departments and professions, which have very clear ideas on what they want to do, and you also have the customers' feedback. And the goal is to mix all of that, and to implement it.[2]
>
> Leo,[3] 30 years old, head of product.

Indeed, the agile method is a way to increase teams' programming pace and enable them to integrate clients' requests into the cycles of development. This kind of organization becomes particularly useful above a certain threshold of employee numbers. When the number of web developers exceeded twenty, the head of product proposed switching to the agile project-based organization, arguing that such a switch would help solve the issues caused by their previous form of organization:

> Here is the thing: the atmosphere was getting shitty, they were all competing against each other, we were not able to produce like we used to, and they forgot that the cool thing about a start-up was to deliver quickly. So we had to change this. And that's why I said we had to go agile. [...] The model we had before was called 'Small Batch/Big Batch'.

[2] Verbatim statements are translated from French. Every attempt is made to reflect the original spirit.

[3] The names of the interviewees have been changed to ensure anonymity.

> The principle is that you make a Big Batch team and a Small Batch team. The Big Batch team goes to work on a feature for six weeks, and they have six weeks to kill it. So you have three people to do a subject from A to Z. The Small Batches, their objective is to ship as many subjects as possible, but small features. [...] So it started with a small number of people. That's what made it work. But it started to be a real mess as soon as there were more and more developers. I think it was still working until 12/13 devs, but with the big arrival this summer, when we went up to 25/30 people or so, it was not possible anymore.
>
> Leo, 30 years old, head of product.

The goal of such a move to the agile method was to reduce the 'time to market', which is the time between the ideation of the feature and its integration on the website. To pilot this change of organization, the CTO organized an off-site training day in order to present the principles of this new organization to his team. '*The goal*', he said, '*is to go from a technology-centred organization to a product-centered organization. We split the final product – in our case, the website – into small products, which will correspond to functional divisions of the general product. So each feature team will work within a specific perimeter in autonomy*'. This new organization thus aims to produce more efficiently, using multi-skilled teams, capable of working autonomously within a specific and defined perimeter. But what are the workings of such an organization in 'feature teams'? How are they supposed to increase employees' productivity?

### *A Team-Based Organization*

Within the technology department, 35 engineers were working with different specializations. First, the role of product owners is to define the new features of the product. They collect the needs of each of the other departments (marketing, sales, customer service) and gather them in a list of features called the 'backlog'. Next, they write the 'user story' of each feature to explain what their benefits for users would be. For instance, the user story of a search and navigation feature would be: 'as a user, I would like to be able to search a specific product in the navigation'. They then prepare the 'ticket': they list all the steps and the tasks needed to create a new feature, before passing it off to the developers. Product owners then make sure that developers always have something to work on thanks to a project management tool (see Chapter 4 by A. Mordi) called Jira.

> As a product owner, I'm a bit of a conductor. I'm a bit like a wall between the developers and the other employees, who are always asking to implement new features on the website. [...] When someone in the company asks me something, the first thing I do is I put it in the backlog. The backlog is a kind of wish list, it's not really a to-do-list, because it's not really prioritized. But it's kind of a wish list of all the bugs to fix and the things to do. So once I collected everything, I need to prioritize the tickets, so I move them in the 'Need Spec' section, which means that I'll have to think about it. And once I've thought about it, I move it to the 'Need Refinement' section. And this is when I give them to the devs.
>
> Jess, 25 years old, product owner.

There are two types of software developers: the back-end developers, who are responsible for the technical aspects of the website, and the front-end developers, who are in charge of the visible parts of the website (buttons, architecture, tabs). Both types of them work along with UX designers, product owners, and team leaders. Team leaders and engineering managers are responsible for coordinating their activities and helping the product owners list the tasks and set priorities within the 'backlog'.

With the agile methodology, teams are not divided by expertise but by functional perimeter. Each 'feature team' is an autonomous squad organized around a user-centred functionality called a 'feature' (payment, product pages). Each feature intends to provide functional value to the website. For instance, in Boomerang, the 'Customer Satisfaction Team' was in charge of all the interfaces linked to the after-sales service and all the tools to follow up customer satisfaction (after-sales service template, automatic messaging, customer notifications, 'My account/my orders' page, email management). The 'Bucks and Shipping Team' was responsible for all the features related to payment options and delivery methods (invoicing, reimbursement, fraud, coupon codes, funnel management, basket pages, confirmation or failure of payment pages). The 'Offer and Navigation Team' was in charge of all the product-related issues (product pages, search and landing pages, homepage and navigation pages, back-office catalogue tools).

Within a defined functional perimeter, teams consisted of all the skills required to produce a feature in autonomy: a product owner, a UX designer, a lead developer, a lead tech, a DevOps, a front-end developer, a back-end developer, and a Q/A analyst. This type of organization thus relies on a specific division of labour. As Jess explains, some developers work more on feature design and task prioritization issues, while others are more focused on execution:

> For example, in my team, there's one front-end developer and two back-end developers. And one of the two back-end developers is a lead developer. I work very closely with him on the questions of prioritization because he has a technical eye on the global product, so he prioritizes with me. The other back-end developer, he's more in execution. We don't bother him, he's got to deliver. With the lead dev, we're a bit of a duo. He also develops, but he's more [involved in working] on complex subjects. They work hand in hand, they advise each other, but he's the referee when they have to take decisions.
>
> Jess, 25 years old, product owner.

Based on a combination of skills, these co-located teams are supposed to improve their expertise but also their production rate. By creating small and self-organized teams responsible for a specific area, this type of organization aims to increase the speed of development of new features and to adjust to the needs of the market just in time, while ensuring the daily maintenance of the website.

### *An Endless Production Cycle*

Following the Scrum methodology, the project's timetable of the feature teams is divided into two-week sprints. Each Sprint followed the same pattern: 'sprint planning', 'refinement meeting', and the 'demo' (see Fig. 8.1).

> So first you have the 'sprint planning', where you basically give the tickets. So what we put in 'Ready To Dev' are tickets which have already been refined. We take them, and we decide what we're going to work on for the next few weeks. So basically, I put all the 'ready to dev' tickets into the sprint that's about to begin. And then, once we have the to-do-list for the sprint, the sprint begins. And so [...] while they work on this, I get other needs from the other departments, I take them, I classify them, I prioritize them [...] So once we've agreed on the needs to be processed, I'm busy making them 'ready to dev' for the next sprint. So the next 'sprint planning' is going to start here (he shows me the end of the current sprint), and we're going to work on launching the stuff that will have been refined during this sprint (he shows me the previous sprint).
>
> Jess, 25 years old, product owner.

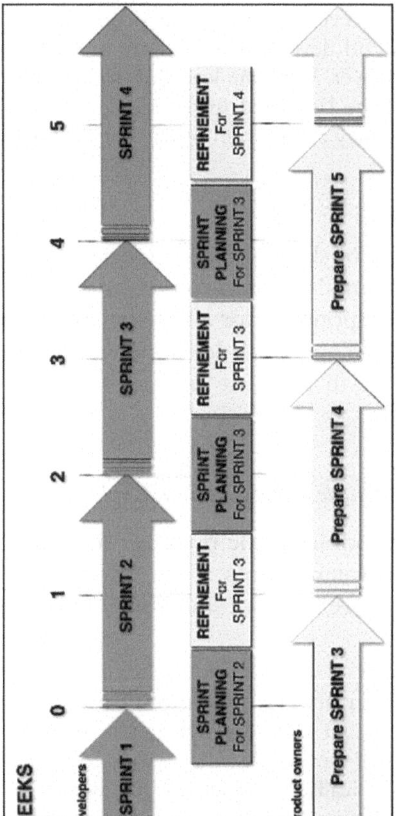


**Fig. 8.1** Diagram of four two-week sprints

During the refinements, the product owners present to the developers the 'tickets' that they have selected from the backlog for the next sprint. The tickets are prepared in advance by the product owners during the 'sprint planning'.

> During the refinement meeting, I present the tickets that I've prepared to the devs and I say "well here are the specs that we'd like to do", and then potentially the dev can say "ok perfect, the ticket is clear, we can put it in 'Ready To Dev'", and then it's ready to go to the next sprint. And then we do the scoring system.
>
> Jess, 25 years old, product owner.

The refinement meetings are also an opportunity for team members to estimate the working time needed for each ticket by using a scoring system. Using the Fibonacci sequence (2, 3, 5, or 8), every team members attributes a number to the tickets as an estimate of its complexity. These numbers, called 'story points', help the product owners define the number of developers needed to complete the tickets. When they plan a sprint, product owners add up all these numbers and make sure it does not exceed 15 story points per developer, which has been fixed as the limit for a two-week sprint. This method encourages developers to do their best to meet deadlines, even when tickets turn out to be more complex than expected. It is also a means of quantifying a type of work that is usually hard to measure:

> The goal is to be able to figure out exactly how long it's going to take for a feature to be released. And there are lots of ways to do that, but, depending on the developer, and on lots of other things, it's not going to take the same number of days. So we need to take a completely abstract notion, which doesn't mean anything in itself. But basically, you give it a value, the 'story points', and at the end, in your sprint, you add up all the 'story points' from all your tickets, and you have to get 15 points, but you must not exceed 15 points because we can't do more than that. So sometimes you have to say "we can't put it in this sprint. We'll have to put it in the next sprint". Developers also often reevaluate their story points while they're developing and they're doing it.
>
> Tom, 25 years old, product owner.

Once the product owners have selected the tickets and assigned them a labour value, they meet with the developers to give them the tickets they will be responsible for during the next sprint. While the developers are working on them, product owners will start to plan the next sprint. The 'Scrum' methodology thus consists of an endless workflow in which the production of tickets never ends the development process.

Many businesses adopt 'rituals' to embed these methods into their organizational culture and, in doing so, build support and effectiveness (see Chapter 6 by G. Müller-Seitz and W. Weiss). Daily meetings—called 'stand-up meetings'—are held every morning within each feature team. Team members stand in a circle and take turns giving a brief account of how their work is progressing, what was done the day before, and what still needs to be done. These stand-up meetings do not last more than 15 minutes and aim to foster communication and support coordination between trades.

Beyond the managerial discourse that highlights the goals of such project-based management methods (empowering employees, better coordination, flat working relations, flowing communication), this kind of organization also tends to expand individual accountability and increase productivity standards. Emphasizing projects instead of individuals, Scrum and agile managerial methods draw their impetus from a purported flat organization valuing autonomy and empowering workers while they serve management purposes. A critical analysis shows that the effectiveness of these methods precisely derives from the fact that they create new and invisible forms of constraints, which push workers to over-invest at work.

## The Nuts and Bolts of the Agile Project Management

Managers and start-up founders often present the adoption of the agile project management method as a way to enhance collaboration and creativity at work. What they don't say is that such a method aims to increase engineers' productivity without the need to closely control and monitor it. In practice, how does this method improve productivity?

### *Empower to Deliver Faster*

In keeping with the affirmations of the flat and democratic culture of these methods, the CTO and the head of product hold the view that there is no hierarchical authority in an agile organization, arguing that this is a 'matrix system' where 'no one has the final word'. Dismantling the idea of a flat organization involves moving beyond the managerial discourse and identifying the rational underpinnings of such an organization.

Implementing a flat organizational structure can be a powerful way of encouraging developers to work harder and faster because it engenders a belief that they are working for themselves and their team, and not for hierarchical superiors. Product owners, who give the work to developers, monitor the progress of projects, and review performance when developers don't achieve their goals, don't see themselves as managers but as members of a team:

> I'm not a manager. But in the same time, there's a requirement for leadership, which is different from managing people, which is, in my opinion, to set an example, to show the direction the team must go in. So my job is kind of an 'in-between job', between the lead devs and the CTO, and I tell them [the developers] things like "well, we didn't reach our objectives on the sprint, if it happens again it won't work".
>
> Tom, 25 years old, product owner.

As far as 'lead developers' are concerned, their view tends to prevail over that of the other programmers during refinement and sprint planning sessions (Hodgson & Briand, 2013). Yet they do not feel like they are their superiors either, because they do not assign the tasks. They even express a loathing of hierarchies and rather see their position as that of counsellors or mentors who mostly give technical advice.

> I don't distribute the tasks, that's the job of the product owner. But my job is to ensure technical consistency. I'm not going to come in and tell them, "Listen, that's the way it has to be done", or anything like that. [...] The lead dev, he's more mentoring people, trying to help people learn from each other. The lead tech, he will have more of a voice in decision-making, saying things like "We should go this way or that way" or "Don't do that, I don't think that's the right decision."
>
> Ted, 33 years old, lead developer.

The analysis of the hierarchical structure in an 'Agile' organization is further complicated by the complex distribution of power that gives great responsibilities and autonomy to programmers. That is precisely the purpose of such a collegial system: as Leo, the head of product, argues, people are less willing to work a lot when they are responding to a hierarchical order than when they are doing it for themselves and their team. Since orders do not come from hierarchical superiors but product owners, in the suggestion mode, they are made more acceptable.

> When you do things in a formal way, it's a pain in the ass. Because if you say, "You're going to do this, you're going to do that", it's a pain in the ass. That's why all the organizational aspects, the rituals, etc., play a key role. Because you're not a guy who gives tasks anymore, you're a guy who works with them, just as they do, and that's the key.
>
> Leo, 30 years old, Head of Product.

Agile management thus departs from the rationalist principles of traditional organizations, which follow a clear 'plan-monitor-deliver' format and exercise control with performance measurement tools and a pyramidal hierarchical structure. This method offers a distinctive mode of management where control is enacted via employees' empowerment. The emphasis is put on autonomy, initiative, and individual responsibility rather than hierarchical supervision, but it still aims to motivate developers to work on projects as if they were their own:

> So the advantage of doing things this way is that everyone will be motivated to do the best possible thing for your product. [...] So it develops their expertise, but also their will to go further in everything they do [...] because they understood that the goal of the game is to cherish their baby and make it as clean as possible.
>
> Leo, 30 years old, head of product.

The strength of this model thus lies in the fact that, in the daily experience of work, employees feel more concerned and involved in their work. Therefore, these 'knowledge workers' who yearn for varied work and substantial autonomy in their roles (Benson & Brown, 2007) embrace this project-based organization:

> I have a lot of autonomy. And I know it was a bit of a *sine qua non* condition, because some people need more autonomy than others, and I know that I wouldn't have liked to have a guy coming to check on me and my work all the time. And I don't think that's how you get the best out of people, because if you're on their backs too much, you turn them into robots rather than really intelligent people.

Tom, 25 years old, product owner.

By fostering autonomy and empowering engineers, such project-based management methods give them the feeling of being trusted in their expertise and of having a considerable impact on the decision-making process. In doing so, engineers feel valued and develop a sense of ownership of their projects. While strategic decisions are still taken upstream by those at the top of the hierarchy, one explanation for the neglect of the hierarchical structure is in part due to the perceptions of workers themselves, which tend to obscure or dismiss the existence of power relationships.

### *A System That Enhances Self- and Social Control*

While engineers feel less controlled and more autonomous in their work, agile project management creates new types of constraints. First, control is produced by the agile system itself, which increases productivity through just-in-time project workflows. The project management systems and technologies of the 'Scrum' approach also encourage developers to keep a steady and sustained delivery rhythm. The backlog and the story point systems make it possible to keep track of developers' coding speed. They are then often doing unpaid extra hours, working from home in the evenings or on the weekends. Additionally, the scoring system relies on productivity standards that continuously prompt engineers to increase their pace of development. When they prove that they can deliver faster, it then can become the new standard. This way, developers are encouraged to work more and more to improve the speed and quality of their code.

> The first two sprints we had were over a month long, and they were very intense. We rushed so much to deliver. But we can't hold this pace in the long run. You can't say that this level of requirement is a standard, it's not possible. A standard, it must be an average. We had to deliver a sprint of 120 story points, whereas normally a standard sprint is 50/60 maximum.[4] So we have to go back down a bit to be realistic over time.
>
> Tom, 25 years old, product owner.

[4] He is talking about the sum of its feature team developers' story points. A total of 120 story points delivered by four developers means that each of them has delivered 30 story points, on average, instead of the usual limit of 15.

Such an organization in small teams also favours peer control. The rituals, the meetings, and the project management tools create the conditions of mutual observation and peer monitoring. Furthermore, in such feature teams in which all functions are interdependent, any slow or delayed delivery can penalize the whole team. This type of structure thus creates a type of organic solidarity that leads people to do their best for their team.

This project-based organization also relies on a set of values reminiscent of those of the 'projective city' described by Luc Boltanski and Eve Chiapello (2007). In such a project-centred organization, the behaviour that is rewarded is to show commitment to a project and become fully involved in it. Employees have to be adaptable, autonomous, active, flexible, versatile, and enthusiastic in their way of working. They also have to act as leaders with ideas, talent, and intuition, capable of taking risks. In such a context of functional interdependence and mutual observation, a lack of enthusiasm, motivation, or engagement in working situations can thus lead to social sanctions, ranging from a bad reputation to dismissal.

## Conclusion

Start-up companies are often hailed as presenting a liberating model for the future of work that epitomizes the virtue of distinctive mode management emphasizing flexibility, empowerment, and autonomy at work instead of vertical and quantified control. The adoption of these purportedly 'emancipatory' and 'post-bureaucratic' agile project management practices has the same purpose as the rational principles underpinning traditional companies, which is to make people work more efficiently. The fundamental difference between the two management approaches is not the objective, but the means deployed to achieve it.

Instead of resting on vertical and constrained forms of control, this type of method draws its impetus from the trust and the autonomy given to workers. By giving them more room for initiative and creativity, empowering them with technical or managerial responsibilities, and enhancing their accountability, this system makes employees feel valued, trusted, and more engaged in their work. The autonomy allowed by self-organization nevertheless relies on strong social control. The flattened distribution of power combined with the functional interdependence of team members reinforces peer and self-control that prompt all the engineers to provide evidence of their effectiveness.

This system thus completely reverses the logic of power and domination operating in traditional companies. Instead of being asked to work more, staff are encouraged to work better and faster, as proof of their self-worth, without their employers having to compel them.

## References


Agile Alliance. (2012). *The Agile Manifesto*. www.agilealliance.org. Accessed 25 September 2012.

Barker, J. R. (2005). Toward a philosophical orientation on control. *Organization, 12*(5), 787–797.

Beirne, M. (2008). Idealism and the applied relevance of research on employee participation. *Work, Employment and Society, 22*(4), 675–693.

Benson, J., & Brown, M. (2007). Knowledge workers: What keeps them committed; what turns them away. *Work, Employment and Society, 21*(1), 121–141.

Boltanski, L., & Chiapello, E. (2007). *The New Spirit of Capitalism*. Verso.

Burawoy, M. (1979). *Manufacturing consent: Changes in the labor process under monopoly capitalism*. University of Chicago Press.

Carney, B. M., & Getz, I. (2009). *Freedom, Inc.: Free your employees and let them lead your business to higher productivity, profits, and growth*. Crown Business.

Clegg, S., & Courpasson, D. (2004). Political hybrids: Tocquevillean views on project organizations. *Journal of Management Studies, 41*(4), 525–547.

Harley, B. (2001). Team membership and the experience of work in Britain: An analysis of the WERS98 data. *Work, Employment and Society, 15*(4), 721–742.

Hodgson, D. E. (2004). Project work: The legacy of bureaucratic control in the post-bureaucratic organization. *Organization, 11*(1), 81–100.

Hodgson, D., & Briand, L. (2013). Controlling the uncontrollable: 'Agile' teams and illusions of autonomy in creative work. *Work, Employment and Society, 27*(2), 308–325. https://doi.org/10.1177/0950017012460315.

Hodgson, D. E., & Cicmil, S. (2006). *Making projects critical*. Palgrave Macmillan.

Knights, D., & McCabe, D. (2000). 'Bewitched, bothered and bewildered': The meaning and experience of teamworking in an automobile company. *Human Relations, 53*(11), 1481–1507.

Peters, T. (1992). *Liberation management*. Pan.

Roy, M., & Audet, M. (2003). La transformation vers de nouvelles formes d'organisation plus flexibles: Une cadre de référence. *Gestion, 27*(4), 43–49.

Schwaber, K., & Beedle, M. (2002). *Agile Software Development with Scrum*. Prentice Hall.

Sewell, G. (1998). The discipline of teams: The control of team-based industrial work through electronic and peer surveillance. *Administrative Science Quarterly, 43*(2), 397–429.

Thompson, P., Jones, M., & Warhurst, C. (2009). From conception to consumption: Creativity and the managerial missing link. In A. McKinlay & C. Smith (Eds.), *Creative labour: Working in the creative industries* (pp. 51–71). Palgrave.

PART III

# Agility on the Societal Level

CHAPTER 9

# Travelling Management Ideas: Agility in Japan

*Takahiro Endo, Masatoshi Fujiwara, and Yuki Tsuboyama*

## Introduction

This chapter focuses on travelling management ideas. We use this term to refer to dynamics surrounding the adoption of management ideas which are created, implemented and (sometimes) translated from one context to another. In our view, such dynamics include both vertical and horizontal contexts. Here, vertical indicates long-term development of ideas, while horizontal cross-national interactions concerns management ideas.

Empirically, this chapter sheds light on the adoption of agile methodologies in Japan. Endo et al. (2015), by systematically examining academic articles published in business and management journals over several decades, illustrate the changing academic discourse concerning Japan and Japanese management. Up to the early 1990s, Japan and Japanese management tended to be associated with 'best practice' in various subcategories of management, including human resource management, organizational culture, inter-firm networking, corporate strategy and new product development. For the majority of these sub-categories, academic discourse has departed from 'best practice' since the mid-1990s,

T. Endo (✉) · M. Fujiwara · Y. Tsuboyama
Hitotsubashi University, Kunitachi, Japan
e-mail: endo.takahiro@r.hit-u.ac.jp



S. Pfeiffer et al. (eds.), *The Agile Imperative*, Dynamics of Virtual Work,
https://doi.org/10.1007/978-3-030-73994-2_9

probably because of the impact of the bubble economy burst in the early 1990s and the economic stagnation that followed, sometimes known as the 'lost decade(s)'. In contrast to the overall trend, the subcategory of new product development has witnessed consistent treatment. This is because, according to Endo et al. (2015), Japanese automakers, particularly Toyota, continued to sustain strong economic performance.

In this chapter, we aim to examine the adoption of agile methodologies in Japan by considering both horizontal and vertical contexts. In terms of these contexts, we focus on long-term evolution with respect to Toyota Production System (TPS), originating from the car manufacturer Toyota based in Japan, and agile methodologies, originating from Silicon Valley. In other words, we examine the meaning attached to these two management ideas over time. While agile methodologies have increasingly been considered to be 'best practice' not only regarding software development but also in various other industrial sectors (Dingsøyr et al., 2018; Ghobakhloo & Azar, 2018 ), TPS also provides prescriptions widely adopted in new product development (Tortorella et al., 2016). In a way, agile methodologies and TPS provide competing prescriptions and it would thus be interesting to examine the interaction in the origins of TPS with respect to the adoption of agile methodologies. In particular, we show how the 'reference points' concerning new product development have conditioned the adoption of agile methodologies in Japan.

In what follows, we first examine some insights derived from the existing literature concerning TPS and agile methodologies. Our emphasis will be on briefly outlining the historical development of both ideas in order to provide a basis for contextualizing the adoption of agile methodologies in Japan. There then follows a methods section that explicates our overall research project focussing on the adoption of agile methodologies in Japan as well as the specific focus of this chapter, which sheds light on the ebb and flow of articles in a leading economic newspaper in Japan discussing agile methodologies as a new management idea brought from 'outside' as well as TPS, inherent 'within' the economy. The findings section illustrates key changes and continuity concerning the adoption of TPS and agile methodologies. Finally, we discuss the implications for workers by referring, where relevant, to insights derived from our ongoing research project examining the adoption of agile methodologies in Japan.

## Ebb and Flow of 'new Management Ideas'

### *TPS*

Taiichi Ohno started his career as an engineer and later became the vice president of Toyota. His book on TPS, first published in Japanese and then translated into many other languages, including in English in the late 1980s, has been widely recognized as a first systematic attempt to explain TPS (Womack & Jones, 1997). According to Ohno (1988), TPS aims to reduce 'waste, inconsistencies, and excess' (p. 77) and entails the two main pillars of 'autonomation' and 'just-in-time'. As is widely known, Toyota has its roots in a weaving machine producer. One of the pillars, *autonomation*, is closely associated with looming. In looming factories, the entire process, including inspection, needs to be *autonomated*. Importantly, this goes beyond mere factory automation in the way that it achieves a high degree of autonomy. Machines with 'built-in' workers' knowledge intelligently stop by themselves as soon as they find a problem, which tends to be known as 'poka-yoke'. The other pillar, 'just-in-time', Ohno (1988) argues, originated from the spirit of Japanese automakers in competition with their US counterparts. Although the US automakers enjoyed scale merit largely due to the enormous size of the country, the Japanese manufacturers could not adopt the same path given the geographical constraints. 'Just-in-time', by providing the exact number of components at the right time, enables automakers in a small country to be free from restrictions derived from size. In achieving 'just-in-time', *Kanban* tends to be utilized. The Japanese word, Kanban, literally meaning signboard, may be used to visualize the name and quantity of components necessary for each production process.

If TPS is applied to the new product development, the main characteristics typically lie in the primary emphasis on the satisfaction of customer needs, which will be addressed by leveraging 'surplus' resources generated by the ultimate and continuous elimination of waste. Such an application of TPS to product development is commonly known as lean product development (Liker & Morgan, 2006). Towards the primary objective of customer satisfaction, relevant actors in the firm adopting lean product development engage in collaboration with various departments, which includes not only product development divisions but also other related ones such as testing, purchasing, suppliers, manufacturing, inspection and sales (Monden, 2011). Furthermore, such collaborative involvement may not be confined to a single company but can embrace wider supply chain networks (Takeishi, 2001). In those cases, relevant actors both within and outside the firm develop products in collaboration.

### *Agile Methodologies*

Now we turn briefly to the existing literature concerning agile methodologies, commonly known as Scrum, eXtreme Programming (XP), and Feature-Driven Development (FDD). (See Chapter 1 of this book for more detailed discussion of the development of agile methodology). The emergence of agile methodologies dates back to sometime around 1990. It was around 1990 when the importance of flexibility became increasingly recognized, since both the complexity and speed of changes were increasing in business environments, in particular in the field of software development (Thomke & Reinertsen, 1998). Such increasing complexity and change typically result in unstable customer needs, which posed new types of challenges for many software developers. In this environment in software development, the role of agility became increasingly important. Against this background, predecessors of Scrum, EX and FDD began to be implemented around 1990 and came to deliver successful outcomes (Highsmith & Cockburn, 2002). Along these lines, agile methodologies were officially declared an established approach to software development in the brief document known as the *Agile Manifesto* (formally known as the *Manifesto for Agile Software Development*) published in 2001 (Kettunen, 2009).

Agile methodologies tend to be juxtaposed with mass production (Burgess, 1994), which is also the case with TPS. Indeed, research indicates that Toyota's approach to new product development, often embraced by the umbrella concept of TPS, certainly influenced the emergence and development of the idea (as well as the practice) of agile methodologies (Putnik et al., 2012), in particular removing waste to a maximum extent in any process of product development (Poppendieck & Poppendieck, 2003). Agile methodologies may include significant variations depending on authors and application sites, so it may be worthwhile concentrating on agile principles represented in the *Agile Manifesto* (Dingsøyr et al., 2012). As seen in Table 9.1, agile principles can be characterized in terms of key focus, deliverable, customer relations and flow. With respect to key focus, agile principles emphasize the attention to people and their interactions, rather than non-human processes and tools.

**Table 9.1** Key summary of Agile manifesto

| | *Agile principle* | *Non-agile principle* |
|---|---|---|
| Key focus | Individuals and interactions | Processes and tools |
| Deliverable | Working software | Comprehensive documentation |
| Customer relations | Customer collaboration | Contract negotiation |
| Flow | Responding to change | Following a plan |

*Source* Adapted from Agile Manifesto (https://agilemanifesto.org)

Regarding deliverables, agile principles prioritize working software rather than comprehensive documentation. Customer relations under agile principles stress the importance of collaboration rather than confrontation. Moreover, the flow of work, under agile principles, aims to be flexible and thus responsive to changes.

## Japan and Agility Project

In 2018, we launched a research project, 'Japan and agility', examining the adoption of agile methodologies in Japan. The project is ongoing, and to date we have interviewed 30 informants who (have) played important roles in the adoption of agile methodologies in Japan. Our underlying motivation is to examine the adoption of agile methodologies by adequately considering the role of Japanese contexts that, historically, favoured TPS (Tsuboyama et al., 2020).

In this chapter, we consider the role of contextual factors revealed in mass media. To this end, we focus on textual data derived from Nikkei Telecom Database. This database enables us to trace the articles of one of the leading economic newspapers, *Nikkei Sangyo Shimbun*, from the past 40 years.

The Nikkei Sangyo Shimbun, in particular, focuses on industrial issues. Since our focus lies in contextualizing the adoption of agile methodologies in TPS-favoured environments, we decided to use keywords related to agile methodologies and TPS. While there were several hundred articles containing the term 'agile methodologies', there were several thousand hits for 'TPS'. Hence we felt the necessity to combine these keywords with something that specifies our analytical direction. Since our primary focus in the overall research project is related to the transition of *product development*, we decided to combine these two keywords (TPS and agile methodologies) with 'product development'.

After much trial and error, we decided to perform a keyword search with 'product development and TPS' (33 articles) and 'product development and agile' (41 articles). After removing irrelevant articles such as those referring to specific product/service names such as 'Agile PLM', 'Agile Eye' and 'Agile Falcon', we examined the relevant articles.

Our analysis was developed in three stages. First, we carefully read these articles and understood the content. Then, in a second step, we grouped relevant articles together in terms of overall focus. In this process, we developed Tables 9.2 and 9.3. We summarized the premise of each article within two bullet points before grouping relevant articles together. Consequently, we developed the following three categories: Improvement; Application; Diffusion. Improvement indicates either technological/technical or organizational improvement in terms of either TPS or agile methodologies. The application indicates the adoption of TPS/agile methodologies. While TPS originated from car manufacturing, the agile concept came from software development. Their application was considered here both with the origin (i.e. car manufacturing for TPS and software development for agile methodologies) and beyond the origin. Diffusion here means accelerating forces contributing to the diffusion of these two management ideas. It should be noted that some articles were found to be relevant to more than one category. Finally, we interpreted the adoption of agile methodologies in Japan by referring to contextual factors derived from the literature as well as from the newspaper articles. In what follows, the findings section shows the analysis of our textual data. This will be further analyzed mainly by referring to our other empirical data collected from relevant respondents from the field of Japanese software development.

## Strong Persistence of TPS as a Condition for Adopting Agility

Figure 9.1 shows the ebb and flow of relevant articles. While TPS continued to appear during the analytical period, agile methodologies came to be seen after the mid-2000s. Moreover, in terms of qualitative

**Table 9.2** TPS in development

| *Date* | *Summary* | *Category* |
|---|---|---|
| 1982, January | • Mitsui Engineering & Shipbuilding company<br>• Cost reduction efforts by adopting the kanban system amid the rise of Korean shipbuilding companies | Application |
| 1982, April | • Japan Management Association<br>• New award program due to the increasing attention to Japanese management practice represented by kanban system | Diffusion |
| 1985, May | • Toyota<br>• Machine manufacturers' robots and numerical control machines contribute to factory autonomation | Improvement |
| 1985, October | • Suppliers in the auto industry have to keep their supplying components in their inventories due to the diffusion of the kanban system<br>• Rust prevention technique would be more and more important | Improvement |
| 1987, March | • Zeon corporation<br>• Develops so-called 'expert system', which enables sales prediction necessary for Kanban system | Improvement |
| 1987, December | • Hitachi's Introduction of 'software kanban system'<br>• Under this system, a bug is recorded and visualized at 'software kanban', which all software developers can see until a proper measure is found for the bug | Application |
| 1987, December | • Olympus<br>• Reduces waste amid the appreciation of Japanese Yen by adopting the kanban system | Application |
| 1888, June | • Bar code has enabled not only retailers but also manufacturers to accurately trace the flow of goods<br>• With bar code, the kanban system has significantly enhanced its efficiency | Improvement |
| 1988, December | • Mineta company (located in Yamagata prefecture)<br>• First knitted fabric manufacturer to introduce TPS and enabled the firm to be a competent player amid the emergence of knitted fabric manufacturers in newly industrialized economies | Application |

(continued)

**Table 9.2** (continued)

| *Date* | *Summary* | *Category* |
|---|---|---|
| 1989, February | • Japanese carmakers together with major suppliers now have factories in the US<br>• Not all the components and machines are available there; 'just in time' delivery from Japan by Yusen Air Service's air cargo rapidly expanded the delivery volume | Application |
| 1989, November | • Nippon Tungsten company<br>• Adequately responded to the appreciation of the Japanese Yen by adopting the kanban system and reducing a significant amount of waste | Application |
| 1990, January | • Computer Integrated Manufacturing is emerging in Asian economies such as South Korea<br>• Related to this, Hyundai Motors actively adopted and developed the kanban system | Application |
| 1991, September | • Allen-Bradley, owned by Rockwell Automation specializes in factory automation<br>• Adopt both just-in-time and kanban system in technology development, which enables them to manufacture a product in less than an hour after receiving an order | Application |
| 1995, July | • US origin product development technique, known as concurrent engineering<br>• By combining concurrent engineering and TPS, Japanese car manufacturers further shorten product development and manufacturing time | Improvement |
| 1999, July | • Domestic suppliers are still enjoying an advantage by TPS, but modularization pressure gets stronger<br>• Kansei and Calsonic merged and aim to produce modularized components | Improvement |
| 2001, May | • TPS is now combined with ICT technology<br>• E-kanban system leverages know-how derived from Toyota's kanban experience and ICT technology | Improvement |
| 2001, September | • Toyota asked its first-tier supplier Denso to develop a system enabling it to handle kanban information online<br>• Denso developed QR code (Quick Response code) | Improvement |
| 2001, September | • Sony's factory recently liaised with product development teams in the US<br>• The lead time was drastically shortened | Improvement |

(continued)

**Table 9.2** (continued)

| *Date* | *Summary* | *Category* |
|---|---|---|
| 2001, October | • E-Kanban system now becomes a standard for Toyota and other manufacturers<br>• The E-Kanban system reduced inventory volume and cost drastically | Improvement |
| 2002, December | • NEC's consolidation of technology development divisions and initiatives to deal only with suppliers adequately handling the Kanban system | Improvement |
| 2004, September | • In Thailand, Toyota and Denso have enabled production of core components there<br>• They encourage Thai workers to learn and internalize TPS | Application |
| 2005, July | • Fujitsu develops software by adopting TPS<br>• They now regard software under development as inventory and put emphasis on reducing inventory | Application |
| 2005, November | • Semiconductor manufacturing equipment manufacturers are increasingly needed to enhance technological development capacities by recruiting highly skilled engineers<br>• They utilize the kanban system and reduce waste in the production process, which is used for recruitment | Application |
| 2006, June | • Fujitsu deploys a specialist team helping software divisions utilize TPS<br>• The team will help software developers to visualize waste related to software development | Application |
| 2007, October | • Ricoh<br>• Develops a new cost-saving printer that can be used for operating the Kanban system at engineering management sites | Improvement |
| 2009, December | • Toyota Industries Corporation [the origin of Toyota Auto-manufacturer]<br>• Changed its organizational structure and increased its capacity to provide human resources capable of improving TPS and utilizing ICT technologies | Improvement |
| 2010, May | • Toyota invests 50 million dollars in Tesla and jointly develops EV<br>• Toyota also provides know-how related to TPS | Application |

(continued)

**Table 9.2** (continued)

| *Date* | *Summary* | *Category* |
|---|---|---|
| 2010, June | • Toyota assists Tesla's new EV development by providing know-how concerning TPS<br>• Two parties have agreed to use Toyota's existing car models combined with a lithium-ion battery | Application |
| 2012, March | • Toyota plans to increase the number of expatriates in China<br>• They take care of localization, including diffusion of TPS in their factories | Application |
| 2013, March | • Kanban system is increasingly combined with new product development and designing functions<br>• Employees across the globe share a basic understanding of such core concepts, in order to maintain quality of operations | Improvement |
| 2014, March | • Daihen Corporation, taking care of electric power transmission and distribution products<br>• Recovered from sharp sales decline due to the global financial crisis by improving workflow | Application |
| 2015, January | • Denso introduced "energy JIT"<br>• Visualized necessary energy use at every process | Application |
| 2018, May | • Toyota explained its investment in autonomous cars<br>• TPS is not enough to compete with Google and Apple | Application |

characteristics, overall, both TPS and agile methodologies were referred to as an important source of competitive advantage.

### *TPS*

Table 9.2 summarizes relevant articles that touched on TPS and development. The first article that appeared in our data set was from 1982. The majority of the articles emphasized TPS, particularly the Kanban system's cost reduction functions. Commonalities and variations were found regarding the articles related to TPS. In terms of commonalities, all the articles shared an assumption that TPS works as a source of competitive advantage. The majority of the articles indicate that since TPS significantly reduces the production costs and/or time, companies can allocate more resources to product and technology development.

**Table 9.3** Agile in development

| *Date* | *Summary* | *Category* |
|---|---|---|
| 2007, December | • Japan Oracle introduce PLM (product lifecycle management) software<br>• By leveraging agile methodologies, the company improves the software | Application |
| 2008, September | • Ulsystems provides consultancy services for software and system development<br>• They adopt and promote agile methodologies | Diffusion |
| 2008, December | • IBM Japan starts to provide services assisting the adopting of agile methodologies<br>• New service can be used for large scale teams | Diffusion |
| 2009, December | • Japan Oracle<br>• By adopting agile methodologies, they developed software for food and beverage industry | Application |
| 2010, January | • Hitachi Systems and Services<br>• Utilizes agile methodologies in developing systems | Application |
| 2011, February | • Fujitsu started to provide cloud services for corporations as a vendor<br>• Used agile methodologies for the first time in taking care of this service | Diffusion |
| 2012, January | • Digital Garage, an ICT company, acquire two American companies<br>• Both are well known for agile methodologies | Application |
| 2012, March | • SCSK, a Japanese ICT and software-related service provider, acquired a US-based company<br>• The newly acquired firm has strength in agile methodologies | Application |
| 2012, May | • Waterfall method has been dominant in the Japanese software development industry<br>• But large Japanese firms started to adopt agile methodologies | Application |

(continued)

**Table 9.3** (continued)

| *Date* | *Summary* | *Category* |
|---|---|---|
| 2012, October | • NTT Data open training centers focussing on agile methodologies in the coming years<br>• The first center just opened in India | Diffusion |
| 2012, November | • NTT Data and Rakuten are going to collaborate<br>• In training PO (Product Owners) | Diffusion |
| 2012, November | • Nihon Housing switched the software developer from a waterfall-based one to an agile-based one<br>• They develop a necessary component in two weeks | Application |
| 2013, January | • NTT Data regards Malaysian subsidiary as a software development hub in Asia<br>• Malaysian subsidiary's engineers learned agile methodologies earlier than those in the headquarters in Japan | Improvement |
| 2013, April | • GE Healthcare launched software development for medical professionals<br>• They adopt agile methodologies | Application |
| 2013, May | • Software AG's Japanese subsidiary starts to provide cloud software development service<br>• Assist agile methodologies | Improvement |
| 2013, May | • NTT Data and its Indian subsidiary started to provide educational services for university students and system engineers<br>• Emphasis on acquiring skills necessary to practice agile methodologies | Diffusion |
| 2013, June | • NTT Data, NEC, Yahoo, and Bandai Namco collaborate in sharing know-how concerning agile methodologies | Diffusion |

(continued)

**Table 9.3** (continued)

| *Date* | *Summary* | *Category* |
|---|---|---|
| 2014, September | • Hitachi Solutions starts to provide cloud software development service as a vendor<br>• Suitable for those planning to adopt agile methodologies | Improvement |
| 2015, June | • Pivotal Lab plans to open Tokyo subsidiary<br>• Aims to spread agile methodologies | Diffusion |
| 2015, September | • CTC starts to provide new services known as a hackathon<br>• CTC sends their software developer(s) to clients to facilitate idea generation | Diffusion |
| 2015, October | • Intech, by collaborating with Pivotal, aims to deliver services for the financial sector | Application Diffusion |
| 2015, October | • Nihon Unisys is ICT services provider<br>• Established purpose-built division specializing in agile methodologies | Improvement |
| 2015, December | • NTT Data and Pivotal agreed to collaboratively develop software for Japanese financial companies | Application Diffusion |
| 2016, February | • CTC developed software that can predict when elderly people living in nursing homes go to the toilet<br>• In their agile methodologies, clients used the prototype and gave feedback to CTC | Application |
| 2016, May | • Agile methodologies came to be widely adopted in Japanese software development<br>• The market for assistive software is steadily growing | Application |
| 2016, May | • Fujitsu created a new division specializing in agile methodologies | Improvement |
| 2016, August | • Red Hat consultancy subsidiary in Japan started to provide new service<br>• Optimizing not only the usage of agile methodologies in the software development division but integrated operation across divisions | Diffusion |

(continued)

**Table 9.3** (continued)

| *Date* | *Summary* | *Category* |
|---|---|---|
| 2017, January | • Pivotal emphasizes the importance of corporate culture and team building to make agile methodologies work<br>• They ask client firms to send their engineers to Pivotal's workplaces and spend as much time as possible | Diffusion |
| 2017, May | • NTT Data promotes the interaction between Japanese headquarters and international subsidiaries<br>• Japanese headquarters need to learn know-how concerning agile methodologies | Improvement |
| 2017, September | • CEO of Pivotal plans to provide more services in Japan<br>• US big businesses changed their mindset and recognized the necessity of in-house software development as early as the early 2000s | Diffusion |
| 2017, December | • KDDI, a Japanese telecom operator, used to emphasize waterfall method<br>• Since 2016, the firm has started to put more emphasis on agile methodologies by recruiting ex-Google manager | Application |
| 2018, May | • Fujitsu receive consultancy services from Pivotal<br>• Fujitsu will establish agile laboratories and start to provide Pivotal's services to their client firms | Diffusion |
| 2018, September | • CTC now allocates 200 engineers exclusively to projects utilizing agile methodologies<br>• CTC indicates that the waterfall method may take more time for software development and often faces a communication difficulty | Improvement |
| 2018, October | • Fujitsu opened an agile laboratory<br>• Agile methodologies are now applied to various fields | Improvement |

(continued)

Table 9.3 (continued)

| *Date* | *Summary* | *Category* |
|---|---|---|
| 2018, October | • Eiwa System Management, the Japanese software developer, opened a purpose-built studio<br>• It will be exclusively used for agile methodologies in a long-distance setting | Improvement |
| 2018, November | • ISID (Information Services International Dentsu), is a Japanese system developer<br>• They introduced cloud-based software development services for their engineers | Improvement |
| 2019, March | • Scrum Inc Japan was established<br>• 51% of the stake is owned by KDDI, 44% Scrum Inc (US) and 5% Eiwa System management | Diffusion |
| 2019, June | • NTT Comware, a systems integrator, put more emphasis on agile methodologies<br>• Opened a purpose-built studio for engineers specializing in agile methodologies | App Improvement |
| 2019, July | • IHI Corporation, machine industry company, opened a purpose-built building, specializing in agile methodologies<br>• Spent 10 billion Japanese Yen to complete this building and aims to find new business opportunities | Improvement |
| 2019, July | • Mizuho Bank developed a new core banking system, called MINORI by investing 400 billion Japanese Yen<br>• Basically adopted waterfall method, but, where relevant, combined agile methodologies | Application Improvement |
| 2019, November | • Kao, a cosmetics manufacturer, came to utilize agile methodologies in these 2 years<br>• Agile methodologies would be useful to accommodate such diverse needs | Application |

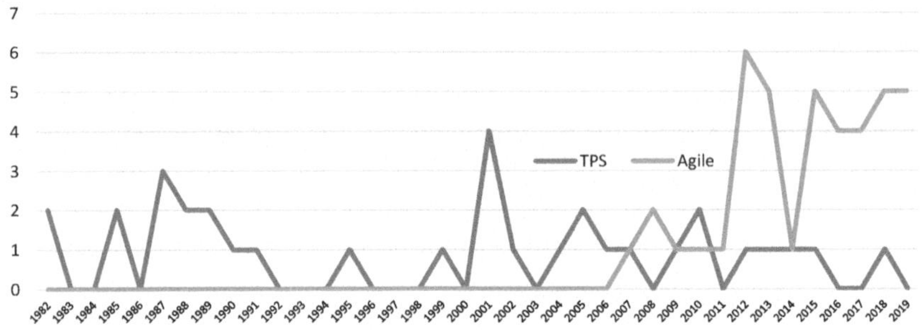


**Fig. 9.1** Number of articles (TPS, Agile)

Within these commonalities, there have been, roughly, three variations: the application of TPS; improvements in TPS and accelerators of TPS diffusion.

*Application of TPS Within and Beyond Car Manufacturing.*
The application of TPS was found to vary. The term itself originated from a specific Japanese company in car manufacturing. As seen elsewhere in this book, agile methodologies originated from software development, and were later applied to various managerial issues. Such a wider application of popular management ideas beyond the original focus was not just limited to agile methodologies. In fact, our data set concerning TPS also witnessed the application of the idea within and beyond car manufacturing.

Application within auto manufacturing may include geographical expansion as well as 'perceptual' expansion. In terms of geographical expansion, TPS was applied to car manufacturing beyond Japan. One article (2012, Mar) reports that Toyota plans to increase the number of expatriates in China. They intend to give autonomy to the Chinese subsidiary in terms of the development of new cars and components procurement as well as diffusion of TPS in related factories there.

In terms of 'perceptual' expansion, TPS was applied beyond the existing perception of car manufacturing, namely to EVs (electronic vehicles) as well as autonomous cars and energy use. Articles (2010, May, Jun) reported collaborations between Toyota and Tesla, including the application of TPS to Tesla. With respect to autonomous cars, an article (2018, May) illustrates Toyota's plans for autonomous cars. At the financial results briefing in 2018, Toyota explained their record high investment in new technology development including autonomous cars. Toyota says their strength certainly lies in their know-how concerning TPS. However, they report they are behind ICT giants such as Google and Apple, which have spent more money on new technology including autonomous cars. Moreover, it was reported that Denso, known as a first-tier supplier to Toyota, introduced a just-in-time system for the usage of electricity in their factories known as 'energy JIT' (2015, Jan), visualizing necessary energy use at every process. For example, because of this visualization, they only use the exact amount of compressed air to clean shavings.

Beyond auto-manufacturing applications, articles include not only application to other manufacturing industries (e.g. 2005, Nov 2014, Mar) but also software development (e.g., 1987, Dec 2006, Jan). Although the application of TPS to other manufacturing industries has commonly been seen across the globe, one article reports an exceptional manufacturer in electronic power transmission products (2014, Mar). Daihen Corporation, dealing in electric power transmission and distribution products, dispersed power systems, welding machines and industrial robots, recovered from a sharp sales decrease due to the global financial crisis in 2008. They had not adopted TPS before and considered adopting it as a measure to recover from the crisis. However, they thought better of it and reached the conclusion that it was not a good fit for them, since their products such as power transmission products were far heavier and were produced in far smaller batches compared to automobiles. Instead, they reviewed their production line and found some improvements, such as the deployment of production machines and workers.

In terms of the application to software development, Fujitsu developed software by adopting TPS (2005, July). In their software development business, they did not have a standardized workflow or the concept of waste. Last year, they introduced the PDCA (plan, do, check, act) cycle as standard workflow and also introduced objectives to reduce waste. Consequently, they now regard software under development as inventory and put emphasis on reducing inventory. For example, they often have to wait for specific responses from clients or subcontractors: that waiting time was not previously considered waste. Now, it is considered waste and they try to remove it by, for example, shortening and clarifying instructions for subcontractors and only asking for yes/no responses.

*Improvement in TPS*

Another type of variation concerned improvements in TPS, including both technological (2001, Sept, Oct 2007, Oct) and organizational improvement. The technological improvement includes electronic Kanban and QR (Quick Response) code. The Electric Kanban system replaces the printed form of Kanban with electronic data. According to the article, such replacement contributed to further reductions in costs for handling (printed) data (2001, Oct). QR codes can be considered a further improvement to electronic Kanban. It was reported that Toyota asked Denso to develop a better system for handling Kanban information than a bar code. While the bar code electronically replaced physical Kanban, it could not load much information. Denso, after much trial and error, developed the QR code, which can load more information than a bar code (2001, Sept).

Organizational improvement concerning TPS can be typically represented in an article dealing with Sony's factory. Their factory in Ishikawa prefecture produces a circuit board for PlayStation. They recently improved the Kanban system by intentionally liaising with product development teams in the US. The lead time was drastically shortened (from 40 days to under 20 days) and they can now integrate their circuit board into the final assembled product in a more rapid manner (2001, Sept). Similarly, NEC actively implements cost reduction activities, including the consolidation of technology development divisions and initiatives for dealing only with suppliers adequately handling the Kanban system (2002, Dec).

### *Accelerators of Diffusion*

The final variation is related to the diffusion of TPS. Although there are many consultancy firms and learning networks concerning TPS, such activities were not included in our data set. Instead, an article (1982, Apr) was found illustrating the diffusion of TPS and related ideas in the Japanese management field. The Japan Management Association was established in the early 1940s and engaged in research and developmental activities, such as publishing relevant books and providing seminars for practitioners. According to the article, the association launched a new award program due to the increasing attention to Japanese management practice represented by the Kanban system. It was reported that such an award program would encourage practitioners to adopt widely recognized management practices such as TPS.

### *Agile Methodologies*

Table 9.3 briefly summarizes articles concerning agile methodologies and development. The adoption of agile methodologies in Japan is illustrated in an article from May 2012 noting that waterfall methodologies were dominant in the Japanese software development industry. However, as global competition intensified, even large software developers were considering adopting agile methodologies. Also, users of software in Japan needed to change their mindsets, since they traditionally left it to software developers and did not specify their needs. Instead, under agile methodologies, users had to clarify their needs and communicate with developers.

In terms of overall tendencies, similar to TPS, there are commonalities and variations regarding agile methodologies and development. In terms of commonalities, all the data indicated that agile methodologies enable the adopters to be able to shorten product development time. In this sense, unlike TPS, the relationship between agile methodologies and development is explicit and direct. Variations observed include applications within and beyond software development, improvements to agile methodologies and diffusion of agile methodologies.

#### *Application Within and Beyond Software Development*

The application was first seen in software development industries. In the later years of our analysis, non-software-related companies (Kao) also practised agile methodologies. Regarding software development, an article reported that Hitachi Systems and Services extended the usage of agile methodologies to developing systems (2010, Jan), observing that in the Japanese market, waterfall methodologies were widespread. But, since agile methodologies can focus on and develop separated functions, efficiency and cost-saving concerning software development would be drastically improved. That said, the complete replacement of waterfall methodologies by agile methodologies was not seen in our data. Mizuho Bank developed a new core banking system called MINORI by investing 400 billion Japanese Yen. Mizuho Bank adopted the waterfall method, but, where relevant, combined agile methodologies. One example of this is the exchange reservation system. The initial design was based on waterfall, but this was divided into smaller functions and agile methodologies were applied. Such 'patchwork' was helpful for Mizuho's engineers, who were familiar with the waterfall method, allowing them to learn and utilize agile methodologies (2019, July).

The application of agile methodologies within software development could be achieved by acquiring those companies that had made advancements in agile methodologies. For example, SCSK, a Japanese ICT and software-related service provider acquired a US-based company specializing in database software development. The newly acquired company's agile methodologies flexibly improved the software by adding or deleting items, thus enabling Big Data to be dealt with (2012, Mar). Similarly, the application might have been performed by forming new contractual relations. Nihon Housing switched the software developer from a waterfall-based one to an agile-based one. The agile-based software developer, ITF (IT Frontier), separated several important functions and developed each of these in approximately two weeks (2012, Nov).

Beyond the application of software development, Kao, a cosmetics manufacturer, came to utilize agile methodologies during these two years. They allocated five people to a purpose-built team. Those five people had previously dealt with different products, but they specialized in marketing. The company started to sell a new 'quick and easy' hair colouring product developed by this team, having spent less than a year working on it, amounting to approximately 40% of the usual product development time. The company says the mass market products are developed long-term, but the needs of consumers are increasingly diversifying and agile methodologies would be useful to accommodate them (2019, Nov).

*Improvements to Agile Methodologies*

Similar to TPS, this included both technological and organizational improvements. Technological improvements can be typically seen in the introduction of cloud-based assistance, while the organization's one purpose was to build divisions or laboratories. With respect to the former, Software AG's Japanese subsidiary started to provide cloud software development services to assist companies aiming to leverage agile methodologies. Such cloud services enable engineers to easily find necessary functions and tools, which ultimately reduces the time required for software development (2013, May).

Another improvement was related to organizational arrangements, in particular establishing purpose-built agile divisions or laboratories. For example, according to one article (2018, Sept), CTC, a Japanese software developer, started to allocate 200 engineers exclusively to projects utilizing agile methodologies. Similarly, Fujitsu created a new division specializing in agile methodologies. The firm had 30,000 system engineers and 500 of them were to be allocated to that division (2016, May). In terms of purpose-built laboratories, IHI Corporation, a machine industry company, for example, opened a purpose-built building specializing in agile methodologies. The company spent 10 billion Japanese Yen completing this building and aimed to find new business opportunities (2019, July).

*Accelerators of Diffusion*

Regarding accelerators of diffusion, different pathways were identified, including training centres and consultancy firms. In terms of the training centre, NTT Data decided to open training centres focussing on agile methodologies in the years ahead. The first centre was opened in India, with one instructor teaching five to ten trainees. This service targeted for university students and system engineers (2013, May). The emphasis was placed on actual software development rather than classroom lectures. Furthermore, inter-firm networks also formed in such training centres (2012, Oct). NTT Data and Rakuten announced that they were going to collaborate in training PO (Product Owners), an important role in deciding prioritized functions to be developed in Scrum. The first year would involve training 30 POs, while 90 POs would be trained from the second year on (2012, Nov).

Another pathway for diffusion accelerators was consultancy firms. These included both Japanese and foreign (in particular, US-based) firms. Japanese ICT consultancy firm Ulsystems adopted and promoted agile methodologies which divided development processes into small ones. Ulsystems claimed agile methodologies prevented software and system developers from being overdue and from overspending, which may be a common tendency for waterfall methodologies, which inevitably lead to delay and overspending if the initial design does not work during the testing phase (2007, Dec). Foreign consultancy firms, for example, included Pivotal and Red Hat. Pivotal argued that the Japanese market was important and planned to provide more services there. They indicated that US big businesses changed their mindset and recognized the importance of in-house software development as early as the early 2000s. However, in Japan, it was said in-house software development was not important, but, over time, the situation changed, marking a departure from the past (2017, Sept). Moreover, according to an article (2016, Aug), Red Hat consultancy subsidiary in Japan started to provide new consulting services to Japanese clients. The service aims to optimize not only the usage of agile in the software development division but also integrated operation across divisions.

## Japan and Agility: A Saviour or Old Wine in New Bottles?

As we have seen, our textual data indicates that companies in Japan, particularly large established ones, continue to adhere to TPS throughout the analytical period. Such adherence to TPS can be understood as the widespread adoption of lean product development, reducing costs and allocating 'surplus' resources for product and technology development (Liker & Morgan, 2006). Importantly, this adherence was not confined to the auto and other manufacturing sectors. It was also seen in software development sectors in Japan. Perhaps because of this widespread adherence, many Japanese companies did not show a strong interest in them until around 2010. Globally speaking, there has been a craze for the adoption of agile methodologies since the early 2000s, which has resulted in various versions of agile methodologies across industrial sectors (Dingsøyr et al., 2012). Such multiple versions of agile methodologies only came to be seen in Japan at the very end of our analysis period, for instance in the cosmetic company's application of agile methodologies.

Although the significant adoption of agile methodologies was not seen until the early 2010s, according to our ongoing research project involving interviews with respondents in Japanese software development, there has been a grassroots approach to permeating the idea since the early 2000s. The main actors here were software engineers working at the 'bottom' of the software industry structure. In the Japanese software development sector, as the findings demonstrate, waterfall methodologies continued to be dominant. Similar to the adoption of TPS in Japanese manufacturing, software development in Japan involved various 'suppliers'. Software developers upstream received orders from client firms. Most importantly, such upstream software developers usually did not take care of significant aspects of software development. Instead, they tended to outsource actual development to multiple subcontractors. Moreover, such a subcontractingstructure sometimes involved several layers. Those upstream software developers tended to impose unfair terms and conditions on those operating in downstream layers (Minetaki & Motohashi, 2009). In particular, those working at the 'bottom' had motivations to change the status quo and agile methodologies were considered to provide a possible 'solution' for them.

The emergence of agile methodologies in Japan's software industry can be traced back to 2000, when some software engineers at the 'bottom' read Ken Beck's Extreme Programming Explained (Beck, 2000) and were motivated to generate engineer communities for promoting XP. Such communities particularly attracted engineers working at the 'bottom' of the software development structure in Japan. Extreme Programming was appealing, since the dominant mode of software development in Japan was waterfall methodologies, lacking flexibility at all layers of software development. In particular, at the 'bottom' of the subcontracting structure, 'last resort' ordering was not so common. That is, at the 'bottom', software developers basically had to accept any kind of modifications from the upper stream, which sometimes forced them to put in 'extreme' overtime. Therefore, for those software engineers at the 'bottom', Beck's (2000) idea, which aims to make software development more efficient and effective, was particularly appealing and many of them agreed to promote XP.

The first such community generated was 'XP-jp' in 2000. This community utilized an email list for disseminating information about XP. The primary organizer of this community was Kenji Hiranabe, a software engineer working for Eiwa System Management, which, at a later stage, contributed to the establishment of an agile methodologies consulting company, Scrum Inc. Japan (2019, Mar). The number of subscribers to 'XP-jp' reached 884 within one year. A series of discussions in the virtual community in XP-jp led to the upgrading of the community and consequently to the establishment of the XP Japanese User Group (XPJUG) in 2003, which started to run an annual event called the XP Festival. Such events attracted engineers, especially those working at the 'bottom' of the software development structure.

According to our respondents, in contrast to such 'fever' at the 'bottom', those upper stream software development companies, typically prime contractors of commissioned software development projects, were, not interested in agile methodologies. This is because they were not necessarily dissatisfied with the status quo. Hence they argued that agile methodologies seemed unreliable and dubious from their perspectives, having long been accustomed to waterfall methodologies. Thus this lack interest in agile methodologies on the part of upstream companies did not result in industry-wide adoption. However, our respondents pointed out that software engineers, not only at the 'bottom' but also upstream, began to show interest in agile methodologies, which had not 'exploded' at this early stage. In reality, even though Hiranabe was the main advocate of EX in Japan, his software development company at the 'bottom' could not utilize agile methodologies in their daily operations. Again, this is because their roles were either subcontractor or sub-subcontractor of commissioned development projects with a precise budget and specification based on the waterfall-based contract at the upper stream and thus they did not have any authority to 'insert' agile methodologies.

In response to the situation in which the adoption of agile methodologies had not made much headway, those active promoters of agile methodologies at the 'bottom' started to shift their grassroots activities, which were rather confined to these communities at the 'bottom'. They began to focus on *managers in upstream companies* and considered ways to encourage them to adopt agile methodologies. In the mid-2000s, for example, Hiranabe and pro-agile communities at the 'bottom' launched a Project Facilitation initiative. This initiative picked up some practices of agile methodologies and translated their *English names* into Japanese ones *a la TPS*. For example, 'sprint' in Scrum was intentionally associated with one of the TPS components, 'kaizen' (continuous improvement) when the term was translated into Japanese. As outlined above, our textual data indicated that TPS was influential even in software development in the 2000s. By creatively translating agile names into Japanese, they hoped that upper stream managers would realize that there was room for *kaizen* in the process of software development.

Such a shift from grassroots to upstream led to some 'tailwind'. That is, the leading Japanese business press, including the *Nikkei Sangyo Shimbun* newspaper examined in this chapter, started featuring articles on agile methodologies. To add further momentum to the trend, those key actors in communities at the 'bottom' created new agile events aiming to bridge between engineers and non-engineers. For example, with support from the Agile Alliance, those key actors at the 'bottom' began to organize Agile Japan, first held in 2009. Along the lines of TPS translation of agile methodologies, in 2009 Agile Japan invited Mary Poppendieck and

Satoshi Kuroiwa as keynote speakers. While Mary Poppendieck argued for the acceptance of the influence of TPS on agile methodologies (e.g., Poppendieck & Poppendieck, 2003), Satoshi Kuroiwa was a well-known IT expert who, importantly, had worked at Toyota. As the organizers of Agile Japan anticipated, both talked about the affinity between agile and TPS. Similarly, at the second Agile Japan, held in 2010, Ikujiro Nonaka, a management guru, was a keynote speaker. Nonaka, observing new product development processes across leading Japanese companies, developed the concept of Scrum, which implied a cross-divisional and continuous commitment to new product development in the same way a scrum is formed in rugby football (Nonaka & Takeuchi, 1995; Takeuchi & Nonaka, 1986). Nonaka indicated that this leading methodology had its roots in Nonaka's theory and that there was a strong connection between Scrum in agile methodologies and methods of product development seen in leading Japanese companies. Against this background, since around 2010, large traditional Japanese companies such as Fujitsu and Hitachi have started to adopt agile methodologies in their software development, as the findings demonstrate.

In conclusion, this chapter has revealed that the strong emphasis on and adherence to a single management idea conditions the adoption of a new management idea. Management ideas travel not only horizontally from one economy to another but also from one past to another future within the economy. The Japanese adoption of agile methodologies may be a typical example of strong vertical conditioning. While in the Japanese context agile methodologies may emancipate engineers downstream, this may need to be carefully examined in a long-term perspective, given the usage of agile methodologies in various different contexts included in this book.

## References

Beck, K. (2000). *Extreme programming explained: Embrace change*. Addison-Wesley Professional.

Burgess, T. F. (1994). Making the leap to agility: Defining and achieving agile manufacturing through business process redesign and business network redesign. *International Journal of Operations & Production Management, 14*(11), 23–34.

Dingsøyr, T., Moe, N. B., Fægri, T. E., & Seim, E. A. (2018). Exploring software development at the very large-scale: A revelatory case study and research agenda for agile methodologies adaptation. *Empirical Software Engineering, 23*(1), 490–520.

Dingsøyr, T., Nerur, S., Balijepally, V., & Moe, N. B. (2012). A decade of agile methodologies: Towards explaining agile software development. *Journal of Systems and Software, 85*(6), 1213–1221.

Endo, T., Delbridge, R., & Morris, J. (2015). Does Japan still matter? Past tendencies and future opportunities in the study of Japanese firms. *International Journal of Management Reviews, 17*(1), 101–123.

Ghobakhloo, M., & Azar, A. (2018). Business excellence via advanced manufacturing technology and lean-agile manufacturing. *Journal of Manufacturing Technology Management.*

Highsmith, J., & Cockburn, A. (2002). What is agile software development? *The Journal of Defense Software Engineering, 15*(10), 4–9.

Kettunen, P. (2009). Adopting key lessons from agile manufacturing to agile software product development—A comparative study. *Technovation, 29*(6–7), 408–422.

Liker, J. K., & Morgan, J. M. (2006). The Toyota way in services: The case of lean product development. *Academy of Management Perspectives, 20*(2), 5–20.

Minetaki, K., & Motohashi, K. (2009). Subcontracting structure and productivity in the Japanese software industry. *The Review of Socionetwork Strategies, 3*(2), 51–65.

Monden, Y. (2011). *Toyota production system: An integrated approach to just-in-time.* CRC Press.

Nonaka, I., & Takeuchi, H. (1995). *The knowledge-creating company: How Japanese companies create the dynamics of innovation.* Oxford University Press.

Ohno, T. (1988). *Toyota production system: Beyond large-scale production.* Productivity Press.

Poppendieck, M., & Poppendieck, T. (2003). *Lean software development: An agile toolkit.* Addison-Wesley.

Putnik, G. D., Alves, A. C., Dinis-Carvalho, J., & Sousa, R. M. (2012). Lean production as promoter of thinkers to achieve companies' agility. *The Learning Organization, 19*(3), 219–237.

Takeishi, A. (2001). Bridging inter-and intra-firm boundaries: Management of supplier involvement in automobile product development. *Strategic Management Journal, 22*(5), 403–433.

Takeuchi, H., & Nonaka, I. (1986). The new product development game. *Harvard Business Review, 64*(1), 137–146.

Thomke, S., & Reinertsen, D. (1998). Agile product development: Managing development flexibility in uncertain environments. *California Management Review, 41*(1), 8–30.

Tortorella, G. L., Marodin, G. A., Fettermann, D. D. C., & Fogliatto, F. S. (2016). Relationships between lean product development enablers and problems. *International Journal of Production Research, 54*(10), 2837–2855.

Tsuboyama, Y., Fujiwara, M., Wakairo, J., & Endo, T. (2020). Eiwa system management: Agile software development and software developer communities. *Hitotsubashi Business Review, 68*(1), 126–143.

Womack, J. P., & Jones, D. T. (1997). Lean thinking—banish waste and create wealth in your corporation. *Journal of the Operational Research Society, 48*(11), 1148–1148.

CHAPTER 10

# What Do Workers Get Out of Agility? Examining Workers' Capability for Democratic Self-Government of Work

*Olivier Jégou and Fyriel Souayah*

## A Slippery Notion: Agility as a Management Doctrine

Writing about agility raises some conceptual problems. Analyzing the scientific literature on agility, Charbonnier-Voirin (2011) shows that there are many controversies surrounding what it means. In the last 30 years, a small but diversified group of academics have operationalized agility and given it some analytical content, producing a plurality of models: agile manufacturing (Nagel & Dove, 1991), organizational agility (Dyer & Shafer, 2003) or workforce agility (Olak & Szopa, 2018), to cite but a few examples. This modelization has also decoupled the conceptualization of agility from its actual practice, leading some to simply subsume agility under the contingency theory, holding that agility stands for "adapting to contingencies" rather than planning or controlling the organization's

O. Jégou (✉) · F. Souayah
UCLouvain, Louvain-La-Neuve, Belgium
e-mail: olivier.jegou@uclouvain.be



S. Pfeiffer et al. (eds.), *The Agile Imperative*, Dynamics of Virtual Work,
https://doi.org/10.1007/978-3-030-73994-2_10

environment (Donaldson, 2001; Hatch, 1997; Vecchio, 2006, cited by Sherehiy et al., 2007).

A second difficulty comes from the association of agility with software development methods. The *Manifesto for Agile Software Development* (Beck et al., 2001) was a major industry-led contribution to the theorization of agility. The *Manifesto* lists four values that make work agile: humans over formalized processes; easy-to-use products; collaboration with clients and adapting instead of planning. Written by leading software engineers who pioneered different methods of software development (like Scrum) at the beginning of the century, the *Manifesto* identified key common principles with respect to their methods. Success stories of agile tech companies (like Spotify) inspired firms accelerating into strategies of digitalization (Clegg et al., 2011) to adopt agility—as was the case at the bank presented in this chapter.

This problem is not only conceptual, but also has repercussions for actors. While recent polling in Belgium shows that "becoming agile" is one of the top ten priorities for HR directors,[1] most cannot define what agility actually means in terms of work arrangements (Hudson & Vlerick Business School, 2019).

We suggest that conceptualization difficulties are due to a misunderstanding of the nature of agility. Conceptually, we understand agility as a doctrine of management (Le Texier, 2016), a prescriptive theory for governing work: it prescribes a set of principles, not a specific method. Moreover, agility is not a descriptive concept or an explanatory theory.

Guided by the data gathered in our ethnographic fieldwork at Selecta Bank and the debates in the literature, we understand agility in this chapter as a management doctrine promoting decentralized autonomous teamwork with short and iterative work sequences, involving some level of end-user feedback throughout the entire development process.

## A Critical Pessimistic Assessment of Agility

Considered as such, agility may seem a promising workplace government reform program for critical scholars interested in building knowledge on ways to extend democracy in the economic sphere (Habermas, 1971).

[1] The Hudson-Vlerick Business School HR barometer polls HR directors from Belgium's largest CAC40 public corporations.

We understand the project of a democratic society as the advancement of individual and collective emancipation rooted in the principle of equality (Castoriadis, 1998; Charles & Ferreras, 2017). Ideally, the project of a democratic society envisions the abolition of alien sources of authority—heteronomy—that does not emanate from the governed people themselves. Following this logic, workers are the ones governed in the workplace (Archer, 1996; Dahl, 1985) and their autonomy depends on them being the constitutive authority of workplace government (Ellerman, 1999; Ferreras, 2017)—which we will refer to as the democratic self-government of work. Therefore, by promoting autonomy and decentralization with greater power for workers in the decision-making process, agility would tick many of the boxes.

However, we believe it is necessary to curb this enthusiasm, because of agility's inherent limit: it does not challenge the fulcrum of the employment relations. We posit the capitalist firm as a political institution promoting the shareholders' domination over the use of resources and the government of work (Ferreras, 2017). By signing an incomplete employment contract (Hart, 1995), workers rent their labour and place themselves at the command of the shareholders (Ellerman, 1992, 1999). Shareholders and their representatives rule over the firms as their own private government (Anderson, 2017) and workers are legally subordinated to them. However *soft* or *liberal* the exercise of subordination may be, the firm remains a project of domination of the shareholders (Courpasson, 2000).

As promising as agility might appear, it will inextricably unfold within the confines of the employment relationship. But this is not only a theoretical limit, as Hodgson and Briand (Hodgson & Briand, 2013) show in their case study of agility in the creative industry:

> Although agile and Scrum emphasize collegiality, mutual adjustment and rational democracy, the study indicates how this is undermined by regular interventions from senior management and also by the persistence of an emphatically hierarchical division of decision-making power within the team and by micro-political actions to influence decision-making and engineer decisions on the part of senior management within the team. (Hodgson & Briand, 2013)

Implementations of agility thus reveal an important paradox: management appears unable to engineer an environment in which workers are fully able to enact their autonomy without doing away with themselves and the shareholders. This is one of many reasons to be pessimistic about agility.

However, as Coutrot (2018) explains, even if management consultants' and scholars' proposals for reorganizing work on less hierarchical and antiauthoritarian grounds such as agility are a fool's errand, they should still be acknowledged. They constitute rare real-life examples of achieving something approaching the democratization of working life that we can learn from. Between the ideal of democratic self-government of work and the totalitarian manipulation of workers by management (Chassagnon, 2013; Willmott, 1993), there is room for critical nuance.[2]

This chapter aims to describe and analyze an empirical manifestation of agility without letting pessimism cloud what workers may get out of it. The case study we present below explores agility's consequences for the democratization of the working experience. Using the capability approach, we show that agility has developed some features that can contribute to the ideal of democratic self-government of work.

### *Evaluating the Development of Capabilities*

Amartya Sen's capability approach is concerned with real freedom, the idea that people should be free "to lead the kind of lives they value – and have reason to value" (Sen, 1999). In a capitalist society, having resources is a condition of many liberties and lacking resources means that some may have access to fewer opportunities. Instead of defending an equalization of resources, Sen argued that different individual, social and environmental factors (dispositions, characteristics, capacities, etc.) allow individuals and groups to convert these resources into more freedom than others. Rather than equalizing resources, the idea is to look at "what people can do and be (their capabilities) and what they are actually achieving in terms of beings and doings (their functionings)" (Robeyns, 2017: 9). The capability approach is interesting from both a descriptive and a normative point of view because it forces us to take into account

[2] For instance, applied to the organizational context, Sherry Arnstein's (1969) classical ladder of participation allows us to qualify different intensities of workers' power in workplace decision-making processes. It is necessary to avoid the pitfall of calling whatever may not be fully fledged democratic self-government of work manipulation (Charles et al., 2018).

the many possible conditions that allow for a certain freedom to truly be accessible to people.

Applied to the organizational context, this approach has inspired scholars to evaluate, among other things, the way policies and practices of management may foster human development (Cameron & Eyeson, 2012; Kuchinke, 2014; Subramanian & Zimmermann, 2013). Critical studies have also evaluated the capability-enhancing potential of some employment regulations and institutional features of the system of employment relations, specifically concerning the development of workers' capabilities to have a voice (Bonvin, 2012; De Munck & Ferreras, 2013).[3]

In a logic of discovery and following a series of abductions (Corbin & Strauss, 2008; Reichertz, 2007) between our fieldwork and the literature, we asked what the necessary conditions (resources, social and individual factors) could be for workers to have a capability for the democratic self-government of work and how agility may contribute to developing them. There is no textbook definition of what is and what could be needed for a capability for democratic self-government of work as such. In our findings, we have highlighted what could be considered conditions for a capability for democratic self-government of work that agility may reinforce.

The fieldwork supporting the case study of Selecta Bank was conducted from September 2018 to February 2019. A researcher worked inside the bank on a five-month internship in the human resources department. In addition to the analysis of the observation journal, interviews were conducted with inside and outside agility consultants in Belgium and their conception of agility was reconstructed. This study was completed by the analysis of semi-structured interviews conducted with 16 back office workers working with agility and key actors of the introduction of the concept at Selecta Bank. We will now describe relevant features of agility in the empirical setting of Selecta Bank.

[3] Voice is understood in the sense of Hirschman (1970) tryptic *Exit, Voice, Loyalty*, where voice corresponds to the opportunity for individual and social actors to express their concerns and be heard. Workers' voice captures most aspects of what we described earlier as workers' participation.

## Agility at Selecta Bank

Selecta Bank is the Belgian office of a well-known international bank established in many places across the globe. In 2016, Selecta Bank restructured and reorganized work in line with the principle of agility inspired by Spotify. Their doctrine of agility, *One Agile Way of Working*—henceforth "Agile"—prescribes the specific practices and structures of work at Selecta Bank. To understand the workers' reaction to the new conception of work, it seems relevant to present the reasons behind this change and the way agility is supposed to be put into practice.

Before Agile, Selecta Bank used a sequential method of project management. For a long time, the bank evolved slowly in a stable environment until it experienced various disruptions. As explained by Selecta's management, the banking industry is facing three challenges on the part of its customer base: the dissolution of loyalty to the bank, the demand for better flexibility in time and places for banking services, and the evolution of needs towards more digitalized banking products.

FinTech—small financial firms concentrated in niche markets—answered this challenge by providing specialized and relatively cheap products, thus becoming a serious threat to traditional banks. Consequently, implementing Agile came as a strategic decision to replace the sequential method of project management, which was deemed unsatisfactory due to its lack of reactivity and the scant innovation it generated. Agile was expected to increase both the frequency and the quality of services, but also the bank's reactivity, allowing it to adapt quickly and qualitatively to the clients' needs.

But Agile is also considered a way to give workers more responsibility and autonomy in their work. For a senior officer in charge of the implementation of Agile,

> It is also the way, I believe, to increase the happiness of staff by allowing them to operate much more from their strengths, from a sense of empowerment, a sense of deciding what to do and when, [...] really applying the people skills and competencies where they need to be, rather than having someone telling them what to do and how to do it. [...] It has been proven one way or another that it actually does improve the happiness of staff or the engagement of staff. [...]. (Director Agile Coach)

By giving workers more autonomy and inviting them to work in a job that exploits their strengths, Selecta Bank hopes to increase their happiness and level of commitment. Top management's perception of Agility is also that it best meets the needs of the new generations of workers in their quest for their job to have a better impact on the company.

## How Does Selecta Bank Go About It?

The introduction of Agile meant a significant change in culture and moved Selecta Bank to rebrand many roles and institutions of work coordination along with the use of a new language. To understand Agile at Selecta Bank, one also has to master its language. In this section, we highlight the structures and roles created to conform to Agile and we identify the key principles behind it.

### *Structure and Roles*

The ambition of the Agile structure was to move from hierarchical department-based coordination to decentralized team-based coordination. Largely inspired by Spotify's organization, they adopted a three-level structure of coordination with peculiar nomenclature: Squads, Tribes and Chapters. Agile also prescribes specific coordination roles within these groups: the Product owner; the Agile coach; the Tribe lead and the Chapter lead (see Fig. 10.1).

A *Squad* is a multidisciplinary team entrusted with the mission to deliver a product or a project from its conception to its concrete execution, thanks to the diverse expertise of its members. The multidisciplinary feature of Squads is based on two types of profile: Business and IT. IT profiles are specialized in the implementation of technological solutions for products or projects, whereas Business profiles manage projects and products and are referred to as Customer Journey Experts (CJE). The latter encompasses specialists in domains like marketing, sales and product management. The number of members and the variety of the profiles depend on the Squad's project. Although a Squad should theoretically have all the expertise it needs to achieve its goals, it is not always the case in practice. Some Squads rely on the expertise of other Squads' members to function, creating interdependencies that can cost time and make the prioritization of work more difficult.

When introducing Agile and composing the Squads, the HR department assigned one specific role to a member of each Squad: the *Product Owner* (PO). Being either a CJE or an IT profile, the Product Owner

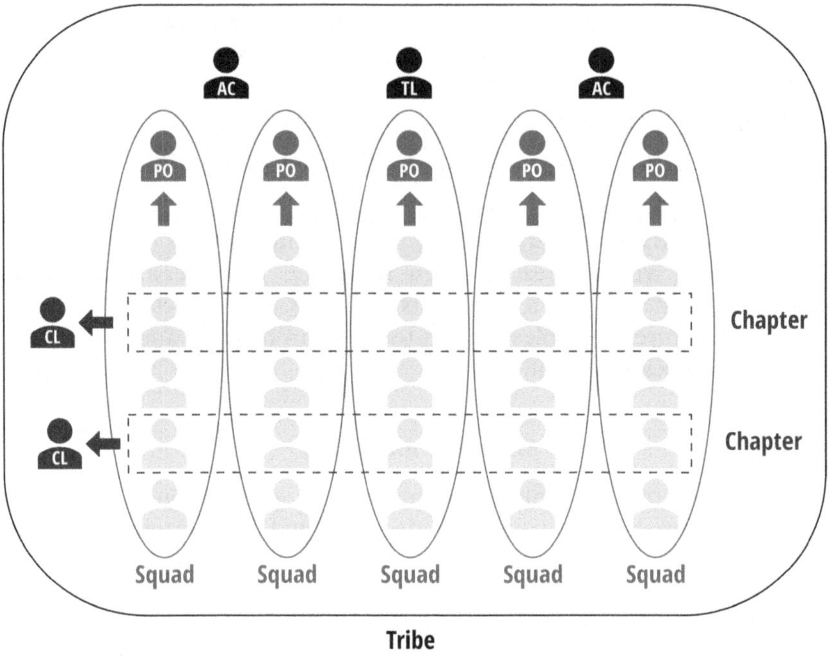


**Fig. 10.1** Structure and roles at Selecta Bank

holds several additional responsibilities, including the prioritization of tasks and ensuring the alignment with the strategic hierarchy and stakeholders. During a bimonthly meeting called a "Sprint Review", the PO is in contact with the hierarchy[4] (Tribe lead or representatives) and stakeholders (an internal or external client[5] concerned with the specific projects the Squad is currently working on). The PO's role is to communicate with these actors to understand their expectations and gather the feedback they need to adapt and prioritize the workload of the Squad.

A *Tribe* is a group of Squads that coordinate with each other for at least two to three years in the pursuit of a common goal. Tribes

[4] The Tribe lead and representatives are the functional hierarchy of the Squad members, defining their work content in alignment with the global strategy of the organization.

[5] Whereas "external clients" refers to actual clients of the firm, "internal clients" denotes any entity within Selecta Bank that stands to benefit from the Squad's specific project.

were intended to simplify Selecta Bank's structure by avoiding departmental structures. In the bank's opinion, departments create silos causing a slowdown in operations and therefore raising the cost of coordination between departments. The introduction of Tribes came as a solution to these obstacles, by bringing together Squads, conceived as autonomous entities aligned around a common goal. Each Tribe should be able to manage its mission independently of other Tribes in the organization. However, the complexity of the bank makes most Tribes interdependent on one another. The *Tribe lead* sets the Tribe's general strategy and breaks it down into concrete operational objectives for the Squads making up the Tribe. The role of the Tribe lead is to be the motor of the Squad's work content, guiding the PO on priorities during Sprint Reviews, either in person or through a representative. *Agile coaches* are the theoretical experts of Agile within a Tribe. Their role is to guide the Squads in the implementation of the new way of working in workers' daily practices. The Agile coach defends the Agile mindset within the Squad, develops the autonomy of the Squad, and coaches the members on the operational aspects of the Agile methodology.

The *Chapter* is the hierarchical line of the members of the Squads, with a Chapter lead as a line manager. Composed of 8–10 people from the same profile who are not always part of the same Squad, the Chapters organize personal development and skills training within a Tribe. The Chapter lead, specialized either in Business or in IT, is the direct supervisor of the members of the Chapter he or she manages. Specifically, this role involves the evaluation and professional development of the members, making sure they have the right skills and sufficient resources to handle their objectives in their Squad. However, Chapter leads are not involved in the content of the operational work of their members; they are mainly responsible for general people management.

### *The Fundamentals of Agile*

#### *Aligned Autonomy*

Squads should theoretically be able to work autonomously on a product or a project from conception to its launch. The multidisciplinary expertise of Squad members should indeed be sufficient to handle the entire process without external help. Still, this autonomy has to be aligned. Alignment concretely happens during the Sprint Reviews and through the communication between the PO, the hierarchy and the stakeholders.

The principle of aligned autonomy then suggests that the Squads should understand *what* to focus their work on by consulting their strategic hierarchy and stakeholders ("aligned") and decide autonomously on *how* they want to deliver it ("autonomy"). It is autonomy over the means rather than autonomy over the ends. With regard to work content (what you should work on), alignment still implies following objectives defined by the tribe lead, who in turn receives strategic lines to follow. Finally, squad members are not involved in the formulation of the strategy; they must implement it.

Moreover, as pointed out above, considering the many interdependencies inside the bank between the squads and outside the tribe, squads do not always gather all the expertise needed in-house, reducing the potential to handle end-to-end projects on their own.

*An Incremental and Iterative Process*

Within the Squads, work is to be organized according to an incremental and iterative process. The iterative dimension refers to the requirement that Squads have to create something within a short period of two weeks, called a *Sprint*. Sprints are continuous and regular intervals within which Squads commit to deliver for the hierarchy and the stakeholders. This is where the incremental dimension of the process comes into play. A squad cannot complete a project in one Sprint due to its complexity. To respect the two-week timeframe, projects are cut into self-sustaining deliverables called *User Stories*.

At the end of each Sprint, the Squad collects stakeholders' feedback on the user stories during the Sprint Review. The meeting allows the project to be improved and priorities to be defined for the next Sprint. This is the iterative part of the process. It is cyclical and allows work to stay grounded in the stakeholders' demands. In comparison, the sequential method traditionally used at Selecta Bank was to set a longer cycle, with the risk of having a finished project that ended up being abandoned because of its irrelevance to the stakeholders.

However, the bank struggles to respect this way of working. When Agile was introduced as the main method of project management, top executives at the bank decided to go through another transformation that we will refer to as "Unity". The main objective of Unity was to create a platform of financial services common to Belgium and the home country through a two-year project. It included various milestones, cross-country cooperation and inter-Tribe coordination.

Since the project had great complexity and was long-term in its planning, Agile was hardly adapted to handle it. As one CJE explains:

> [...] I just think that it's a very, very difficult combination of going Agile while doing Unity, with such strict deadlines. [...] If in the end, everybody needs to get to a finish line at the same moment, you need someone to do the planning and to set intermediate deadlines. But then you lose the value of Agile completely. For me, it's quite an impossible combination, doing such a big program [...] together with implementing Agile. (CJE 01)

This double transformation made workers wary and darkened their perception of Agile. Certain workers perceive it as a contradiction: on the one hand, management calls for autonomy and dismisses sequential project management, but on the other hand, it imposes a long-term sequential project and asks workers to practise Agile.

*Agile Ceremonies*

The Agile ceremonies are meetings that pace the work of the Squad during a Sprint. We have already mentioned *Sprint Reviews*, where Squads receive feedback from the strategic hierarchy and stakeholders. To begin a new Sprint, a Squad organizes *Sprint Planning* to determine what User Stories they want to prioritize during the next two weeks. Squad members have a certain freedom to organize their work, but the PO holds the responsibility for ensuring negotiated priorities with the stakeholders are met.

Every day, Squad members gather for a *Daily Stand-up*, a daily ceremony lasting 10–15 min during which Squad members communicate on the progress of their User Stories. This meeting allows members to ask for help on some issues they are facing, to reflect on how to overcome potential obstacles, identify opportunities and swap tasks.

*Sprint Refinement* happens when the Squad needs to reconsider the construction of a User Story or simply postpone it to the next Sprint. It is the opportunity for the Squad to rethink their planning and make sure they are able to deliver on time.

Finally, at the end of a Sprint, the squad will organize a *Sprint Retrospective*. With the help of an agile coach, the members of the Squad will reflect on how the Sprint was handled in terms of the agile methodology and mindset.

However, agile ceremonies are adapted on a daily basis by Squads according to their own projects and work arrangements. For instance, Squad members who work closely with one another will not necessarily organize a Daily Stand-up every day, but will rather talk directly to one another when a problem arises. In practice, ceremonies encourage the Squads to take time to focus on what they will work on and what the obstacles or opportunities are and reflect on their way of working or whether what they are doing is relevant for stakeholders.

*Integration of the Client*

Selecta's Agile implies the integration of external clients into the bank's back office work along Agile ceremonies. Front office workers (cashiers, call center, etc.) were historically the ones with direct relationships with clients. This was not the case with the back office workers studied—CJEs. With the exception of some experts, most back office workers often only had an abstract understanding of their clients—via some marketing studies, at the very least. Management translated demands from clients into work orders into the organization.

Agile transforms the working process by introducing a third party, making the work process trilateral. Common to front-line workers in the service industry, this is described in the industrial relation literature as a triangular employment relationship (Bélanger & Edwards, 2013). Clients play a significant role in the way the work process is organized. Agility (see Fig. 10.2) brings the client further inside the firm. Back office workers are given direct feedback from clients and may adapt the bank products to keep up with their clients' needs.

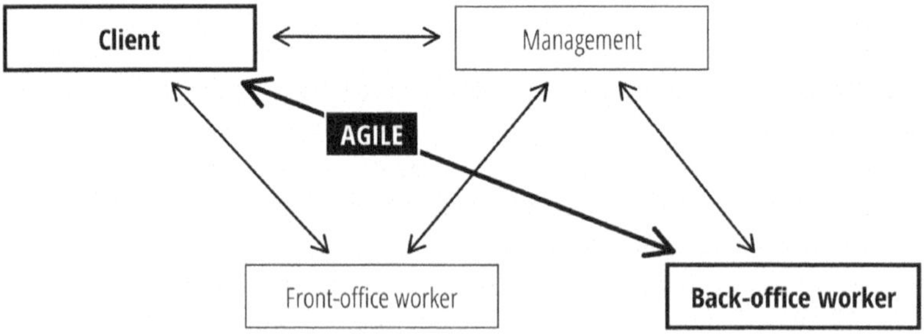


**Fig. 10.2** Agility and the triangular employment relationship

Agile thus introduces an important change: the information from the clients is no longer mediated by management. Workers decode and react directly to the clients' expectations, as illustrated by the "agile" arrow in Fig. 10.2. Of course, as mentioned above, management still participates in the discussion at Sprint Reviews and clients are often "internal clients", i.e. other Squads, etc. As a matter of consequence, agile permeates the clients inside the office, challenging the managers' sole authority over the clients' demands and the conception of products.

## Developing the Capability for Democratic Self-Government of Work

Agility does not challenge the nature of employment relationships, but we have reasons to believe it opens some interesting possibilities for workers. The capability approach highlights the importance of different conditions that allow people to live the life they value. Interviews and close observation of back-office workers—specifically business-oriented workers such as Customer Journey Experts (CJE)—showed how Agility can contribute to the development of a capability for democratic self-government of work: by contributing to the development of a professional self-awareness and by contributing to the institutionalization of collective autonomy.

### *The Development of Professional Self-Awareness*

The first result concerns the development of what we call professional self-awareness. As we will discuss in relation to the fieldwork, this idea of professional self-awareness is twofold. It concerns workers' awareness that what they create has value for someone and the awareness that they are competent in doing what they do. This, we believe, is an important resource in the development of a capability for democratic self-government of work.

#### *Becoming Useful*

At Selecta Bank, part of the workers' satisfaction with Agile is linked to the extensive control of the productive process and the integration of the client into the productive process. As this worker explains:

> I have always appreciated the creative part of my job and the satisfaction of delivering something to the final user. When you work on a project where you are involved from the beginning, you can participate in every step until the end and deliver. When the final user is happy with the new app you delivered, because what took him all day to do he can now do in two hours, this is pleasant! (CJE 14)

Our interpretation is that this satisfaction results, to use Marxian terminology, from the increased concreteness of work (Marx, 1982). As Marx suggests, work makes sense when it is done to satisfy my own or someone else's need. But when the information about people's needs is processed by management, it is formulated back to workers as injunctions. Work, deprived of its meaning as a means to satisfy someone else's need, is reduced to an abstract exchange: obeying injunctions for a salary.[6] In a triangular employment relationship, as explained above, workers regain awareness of making use of value, of producing something that is valued by someone (Bélanger & Edwards, 2013). In the workers' own words, they develop a tangible connection with their clients that allows them to grasp the utility of their work:

> Well, it's nice to see, especially when it is visible for the client, where you can see, right now, it is useful for something. That gives me satisfaction. [...] What makes me really willing to work? It's actually when there are concrete deliverables. Concrete, visible or useful, [...] if I know that it would not be for nothing, you tell yourself, "Is it really useful? Must it really be done?' But now, I must say that there are fewer with Agile than before. (CJE06)

> So, we see that I do my job, and I have a form of recognition from my client. (CJE04)

In the former scheme of work organization at Selecta Bank, work appeared more abstract for workers because management acted as an intermediary between the client and the workers' work. Workers were

[6] This is of course, a textbook understanding of Marx's concrete/abstract distinction. Its use is interesting for heuristic reasons, but should not be taken literally as describing what happens at Selecta or in many workplaces in the twenty-first century. In real life, this abstraction is resisted by workers who, even though they may be stuck in this kind of transactional relationship, find and impose meaning in and around their work (see Ferreras, 2007, 2017; Vendramin & Méda, 2013).

certainly less aware of how their work would satisfy their clients' needs. Clients make their work real and provide a sense of recognition.

### *Being a Professional in the Open*

Working with Agile changes things because workers are allowed to collectively use their creativity, intelligence and skills in an open environment, instead of doing it clandestinely (Dejours, 1993; Linhart, 1991). Organized around the periodic delivery of User Stories, squads have frequent interactions where they address the progress, and adjustments are negotiated with the clients. These demands are refined—in Sprint refinement ceremonies—by the squad in order to break them down into tasks to be accomplished. Agile ceremonies, such as Sprint Retrospectives, allow workers to think back to the last Sprint and reflect on the obstacles they face and how to solve them. Following Dejours (1993), it relieves workers, because they are now allowed to activate their intimate knowledge of work in order to problem-solve:

> FS: What do you like in your work?
>
> CJE03: To use my brain and to have interaction with others. That I'm not my alone on my island reflecting, but that we can really debate on how to do things, the better way to implement this... (CJE 03)

Applying Taylorism, many workplaces like Selecta Bank deprived workers of the possibility to act on the conceptualization of work—for it was a prerogative of management. Agility challenges this separation, allowing workers to express their knowledge, but also to use it in order to problem-solve. By soliciting everyone to participate in the ceremonies like *refinement* and *retrospective*, workers also get to learn from each other. Moreover, this opportunity and the encouragement to participate in the many Agile ceremonies allows some workers to become aware of their own competencies. As one worker explains:

> I think that it gives self-confidence. It's motivating because you become aware that you are able to do things that we would not have imagined being able to do before. It pushes you forward. (CJE 13)

The point we wanted to stress with these excerpts is that in the workers' narrative, the introduction of Agility appears to be a turning point in the awareness they develop about their usefulness, their competencies and the horizon in which they may contribute within their work.

Analyzed in light of the capability approach, we argue that workers changed the perception of themselves as capable professionals who can use their skills to produce something valuable for a client. Deprived of a sense of competency and professional recognition, workers would lack the self-awareness that their work may be valuable for someone other than the firm's shareholders. Instead, reinforcing this self-awareness enfranchises workers as equal members of the working community who should have an equal say in how work should be governed.

We believe professional self-awareness could constitute a prerequisite for a capability for democratic self-government of work. Self-aware professionals value their judgement and reject illegitimate influence on the way they should work.

### *Institutionalization of Collective Autonomy*

A second result concerns the development of practice of collective self-government which (re-)institutes a work collective. We understand the concept of institutions as an intersubjective symbolic order which makes sense for actors subjected to and within them (Castoriadis, 1998; Searle, 1995, 2005). We show that Agility, as a self-government coordination methodology, changes the nature of workers' autonomy and institutes something along the lines of a collective.

### *The Changing Nature of Autonomy*

Workers at Selecta Bank, like most workers in the banking industry, enjoyed important autonomy at work (Courpasson, 2000). As a matter of fact, Agility may have changed not so much the level of autonomy workers had before, but its nature. As one worker explains:

> Now, personally, I thought we were already autonomous. But it's probably because I had my managers' trust, not so much because of a specific methodology. I don't feel an enormous difference. But we could be more autonomous as a team. [...] Today, we are in a situation where we decide everything autonomously in the Squad. (CJE 02)

Before the implementation of Agile, management was individualizing. Proximity managers entrusted workers with a defined perimeter of responsibilities and workers were held individually accountable for them. Workers were autonomous, but with regard to lesser issues —being experts and go-to people for a small number of products.

Interestingly, some workers declare they have lost autonomy since the transition to Agile. But why is this? Conversations with workers are revealing:

> At first, I was under the impression I could not initiate anything. I have always been autonomous and really independent [...]. Now, you find yourself in Daily Stand-up saying, "There, you must do this... You have this many points for this, etc." Then you say to yourself, "What is my degree of latitude?" (CJE 08)

> Before, a lot of product managers were responsible for one or two products. They had all the autonomy possible; they were going their own way. They were experts: 'I'm specialized in that product.' Now, we push [those who were single-product experts] into Squads with a PO over their head, limiting their work to certain tasks. A restriction compared to before. These guys must be frustrated... I would be. (CJE 09)

Both testify to the loss of individual freedom. Instead of having a small perimeter where workers are individually responsible in front of their manager, workers are collectively in charge of a wider perimeter. Because the Squad assumes a collective responsibility, individual workers no longer work for themselves and their individually negotiated priorities, but have to follow collective rules on priorities and workload attribution. As one worker puts it:

> We have to organize a certain workload and it can create pressure. Before, this responsibility was in the hands of different layers of management, layers that are now integrated into teams. (CJE 07)

What has been lost in individual power over a small perimeter has translated to the squad over a wider perimeter. Squad members now collectively endorse the coordination, prioritization and allocation of work to their collective perimeter.

*Instituting the Collective*

But squads are not left to organize on their own terms. Their coordination routine is prescribed by Sprints and punctuated by Agile ceremonies. Ceremonies, as we have seen, are collective tools for planning work, distributing responsibility, making decision and reviewing product/service issues noticed in previous Sprints. Workers describe these ceremonies as a key element in their autonomy:

> I am really autonomous. Outside of validations [with the Tribe Lead], I find that autonomy is well practised inside our Squad because we have ceremonies. We have Refinements, Sprint Planning [...]: it's all us... There is a planning, we know where we go, but we decide: "This Sprint, I think it would be good to work on...". It is well applied autonomy-wise. (CJE 04)

Ceremonies, with their rules and periodicity, institute the collective as a source of decision power. As one worker summarizes it: "Sprints and other ceremonies are a form of governance" (CJE 08). Managerial authority is replaced by the collective authority of the Squads. Where managers used discretionary power to divide and delegate work, workers now use the practices of Agile.

Workers get used to working as a collective to make their own decisions. It even seems to reconfigure the bank's attitude to the work and their collective. As one worker explains:

> I think the introduction of Agile allows you to create affiliation at a more granular level, tightly linked to the activity, to the production, to what you do on a daily basis. It bonds people to what makes them directly productive, to their trade, to the group they work with. (CJE 12)

A performative feature of working in Agile Squads appears to reinforce the understanding of work as a collective endeavour, something that was weakened by the previous, individualizing management practices. Moreover, as this worker explains, it seems to emerge on the basis of work and not the organization per se.

This, we believe, could constitute a condition for the development of a capability for democratic self-government of work. Having a sense of working together and forming a work collective should be interpreted as an emerging constitution of the *demos* on which to base democratic self-government. In the case of Agile, ceremonies allow the development of collective awareness that is necessary to envision complex work without shareholder interest as the sole organizing principle.

Additionally, self-government requires habits and coordination skills that have to be learned somewhere. Democratic self-government, in which participants are deemed equal, differs from top-down management, which Selecta's workers were used to hitherto. Agility, with its structured features and its rules, also fosters the development of a capability of democratic self-government by allowing workers to learn collective coordination techniques.

That being said, the case demonstrates that the methodology lacks some important democratic features. For instance, it does not envision a way to designate product owners. Product owners are still designated by the organization and thus owe their designation to the hierarchy. Being pseudo-managers rather than *prima inter pares*, POs embody the company's authority, a potential threat to workers. However, we have not been able to assess whether this hinders the development of the capability.

## Conclusion

This chapter has argued for critical pessimism about the contribution of Agility, as a management doctrine, to the democratization of the working experience. The capability approach has been used to highlight how workers may still gain something interesting considering the broader range of factors that are in fact needed to foster a capability for democratic self-government of work. Agility, promoting decentralized autonomous teamwork with short and iterative work sequences, involving some level of end-user feedback throughout the development process fosters, among other things, what we have called professional self-awareness and the institution of collective autonomy.

Of course, Agility is neither a necessary nor a sufficient condition for the development of professional self-awareness or the institution of collective autonomy. There are many other ways in which capability for democratic self-government of work may be reinforced, so why wait for benevolent managers and good-willed shareholders? For instance, we could reinforce in-firm institutional check and balance powers for workers with bicameralism (Ferreras, 2017) or strengthen workers' adhesion to democracy through education (Dewey, 1916).

There is room to be critical about Agile and its implementation at Selecta Bank. Among other things, the perimeter of responsibility is very restricted: workers have power only over what they are allowed to do by the remnants of managerial authority. As Johann Chapoutot (2020) puts it perfectly, workers in these kinds of design are "free to obey". Squads are not autonomous in the choice of missions, products they want to develop or clients they want to work with. Therefore, as outlined above, workers may only decide on the means, not on the ends of their work as a collective.

A practical implication of this chapter is to insist on the idea that doctrines such as Agility should not be resisted merely on the grounds that they do not challenge subordination. Neither should they be encouraged without carefully rethinking numerous features. Further research should thoroughly define the necessary conditions for achieving a capability for self-government of work and should also keep a critical eye on how these practices may eventually hinder this capability.

## References


Anderson, E. (2017). *Private governments: How employers rule our lives (and why we don't talk about it)*. Princeton University Press.

Archer, R. (1996). The philosophical case for economic democracy. In U. Pagano & R. Rowthorn (Eds.), *Democracy and efficiency in the economic enterprise* (pp. 13–31). Routledge.

Arnstein, S. R. (1969). A ladder of citizen participation. *Journal of the American Planning Association, 35*(4), 216–224.

Beck, K., Beedle, M., Bennekum A. v., Cockburn A., Cunningham W., Fowler, M., et al. (2001). *Manifesto for agile software development*. http://agilemanifesto.org. Accessed 24 June 2020.

Bélanger, J., & Edwards, P. (2013). The nature of front-line service work: Distinctive features and continuity in the employment relationship. *Work, Employment & Society, 27*(3), 433–450.

Bonvin, J.-M. (2012). Individual working lives and collective action: An introduction to capability for work and capability for voice. *Transfer: European Review of Labour and Research, 18*(1), 9–18.

Cameron, J., & Eyeson, A. (2012). Connecting developments in corporate human management thinking to the capability approach as used in international development research. *Management Review, 23*(2), 173–190.

Castoriadis, C. (1998). *The imaginary institution of society* (K. Blamey, Trans.). MIT Press.

Chapoutot, J. (2020). *Libre d'obéir: Le management du nazisme à aujourd'hui*. Gallimard.

Charbonnier-Voirin, A. (2011). Développement et test partiel des propriétés psychométriques d'une échelle de mesure de l'agilité organisationnelle. *M@n@gement, 14*(2), 119.

Charles, J., & Ferreras, I. (2017). La citoyenneté au travail: Enjeu pour les organisations et la sociologie. In M. de Nanteuil & L. Merla (Eds.), *Travail et Care comme expériences politiques* (pp. 165–178). Presses universitaires de Louvain.

Charles, J., Ferreras, I., Lamine, A., Casterman, L., & Cravatte, T. (2018). *Pratiques et organisation du travail démocratique chez Smart.*

Chassagnon, V. (2013). Contrôle et manipulation au cœur de la firme-monde? *Revue de La Régulation, 14,* 0–14.

Clegg, S., Harris, H., & Hopfl, H. (2011). *Managing modernity: Beyond bureaucracy.* Oxford University Press.

Corbin, J., & Strauss, A. (2008). *Basics of qualitative research: Techniques and procedures for developing grounded theory.* Sage.

Courpasson, D. (2000). Managerial strategies of domination: Power in soft bureaucracies. *Organization Studies, 21*(1), 141–161.

Coutrot, T. (2018). *Libérer le travail.* Seuil.

Dahl, R. (1985). *A preface to economic democracy.* Polity Press.

De Munck, J., & Ferreras, I. (2013). Restructuring processes and capability for voice: Case study of Volkswagen, Brussels. *International Journal of Manpower, 34*(4), 397–412.

Dejours, C. (1993). *Travail et usure mentale: Essai de psychopathologie du travail* (2nd ed.). Bayard.

Dewey, J. (1916). *Democracy and education.* Macmillan.

Dyer, L., & Shafer, R. A. (2003). *Dynamic organizations: Achieving marketplace and organizational agility with people* (CAHRS Working Paper). Ithaca, NY.

Ellerman, D. (1992). *Property & contract in economics: The case for economic democracy.* Blackwell.

Ellerman, D. (1999). The democratic firm: An argument based on ordinary jurisprudence. *Journal of Business Ethics, 21*(2/3), 111–124.

Ferreras, I. (2007). *Critique politique du travail: Travailler à l'heure de la société des services.* Presses de SciencesPo.

Ferreras, I. (2017). *Firms as political entities: Saving democracy through economic bicameralism.* Cambridge University Press.

Habermas, J. (1971). *Knowledge and human interest* (J. J. Shapiro, Trans.). Beacon Press.

Hart, O. (1995). *Firms, contracts and financial structure.* Clarendon Press.

Hirschman, A. O. (1970). *Exit, voice, and loyalty.* Harvard University Press.

Hodgson, D., & Briand, L. (2013). Controlling the uncontrollable: 'Agile' teams and illusions of autonomy in creative work. *Work, Employment & Society, 27*(2), 308–325.

Hudson, & Vlerick Business School. (2019). *Baromètre RH 2019.* Bruxelles.

Kuchinke, K. P. (2014). Perspectives on the concept of development for HRD. In N. E. Chalofsky, T. S. Rocco, & M. L. Morris (Eds.), *Handbook of human resource development* (pp. 112–124). Wiley. https://doi.org/10.1002/9781118839881.ch7.

Le Texier, T. (2016). *Le maniement des hommes. Essai sur la rationalité managériale*. La Découverte.

Linhart, D. (1991). *Le torticolis de l'autruche*. Seuil.

Marx, K. (1982). Les manuscrits parisiens de 1844. In *Œuvres complètes* (Vol. 3, pp. 76–141). Gallimard.

Nagel, R. N., & Dove, R. (1991). *21st Century manufacturing enterprise strategy*.

Olak, A., & Szopa, A. (2018). Agile behaviors in organizations. *Archives of Business Research, 6*(4), 77–83. https://doi.org/10.14738/abr.64.4345.

Reichertz, J. (2007). Abduction: The logic of discovery of grounded theory. In A. Bryant & K. Charmaz (Eds.), *The Sage handbook of grounded theory* (pp. 214–228). Sage.

Robeyns, I. (2017). *Wellbeing, freedom and social justice: The capability approach re-examined*. Open Book Publishers.

Searle, J. R. (1995). *The construction of social reality*. The Free Press.

Searle, J. R. (2005). What is an institution? *Journal of Institutional Economics, 1*(1), 1–22.

Sen, A. (1999). *Development as freedom*. Anchor Books.

Sherehiy, B., Karwowski, W., & Layer, J. K. (2007). A review of enterprise agility: Concepts, frameworks, and attributes. *International Journal of Industrial Ergonomics, 37*(5), 445–460.

Subramanian, D., & Zimmermann, B. (2013). Training and capabilities in French firms: How work and organisational governance matter. *International Journal of Manpower, 34*(4), 326–344. https://doi.org/10.1108/IJM-05-2013-0093.

Vendramin, P., & Méda, D. (2013). *Réinventer le travail*. Presses universitaires de France.

Willmott, H. (1993). Strength is ignorance, slavery is freedom: Managing culture in modern organizations. *Journal of Management Studies, 30*(4), 515–552.

CHAPTER 11

# Agility of Affect in the Quantified Workplace

*Phoebe V. Moore*

## Introduction[1]

In the early twentieth century, when Taylor sought to identify the precision of the work of a 'first-class man' and the Gilbreths looked for the 'one best way' to lay bricks, trade unions became very suspicious. Unions perceived scientific management as a method of speeding up and as giving too much authority to machines (Nadworny, 1955). Today, work design methods accept the supremacy of machines in their apparent capacity to measure work, normalize the risks of continuous workplace transformations in 'agile' management systems and use increasingly invasive tracking and surveillance technologies to decipher measurement of more types of labour, including affective labour, not to pay for it, but to identify to what extent workers can cope with accelerations of change in digitalized workplaces.

[1] A version of this chapter is published as Moore, Phoebe V. (2018) Tracking Affective Labour for Agility in the Quantified Workplace. *Body & Society* 24(3): 39–67.

P. V. Moore (✉)
University of Leicester School of Business, Leicester, England
e-mail: pm358@leicester.ac.uk

 
S. Pfeiffer et al. (eds.), *The Agile Imperative*, Dynamics of Virtual Work,
https://doi.org/10.1007/978-3-030-73994-2_11

This chapter first outlines the Quantified Work school, where body studies meets research on quantification, claiming that what this literature has not yet done is to provide a comprehensive examination of specific *management practices* and work design approaches that have begun to attempt to quantify affective and emotional labour (which I argue elsewhere is inherently unachievable). To contribute to the emerging Quantified Work literature, which sits within 'quantified self' and body studies debates, and to address the gaps, the current chapter focuses on worker self-management and self-discipline for agility in digitalized working environments. It demonstrates management recognition of the qualified aspects of labour that operate on the level of the unseen, the 'affective' level, and, as observed in the case study presented, through wearable and tracking devices, attempt to capture data about it and to therefore turn it into something measurable, tangible and otherwise identifiable. In many data-driven human resource practices, however, some form of remuneration might be available. The findings in this case study demonstrate that the drive towards agility, paired with the quantification of workers' affective labour required for agile practices to be fully realized, is not a move to fully recognize or remunerate this form of unseen labour. Rather, it is a method for identifying purely what the quantified self movement attempts to discover: how much stress or other autonomic drivers are experienced. The difference between the 'quantified self' and the 'quantified worker' is of course that the 'worker' is not a 'free agent', in the sense of the notions of 'self' coming out of the Silicon Valley movement. The worker is subject to an employment relationship, which introduces significant complexity.

The trend in workplace quantification for agility builds on the recent post-Marxist feminist work of Dewart-McEwen (2017) and Jarrett (2016), who look at the ways in which labour outside the formal employment relationship is exploited in digitalized environments, and are committed to feminist arguments in which work is considered to be invisibilized via technologies (Cherry, 2016; Crain et al., 2016). While the history of work design also almost entirely invisibilizes affective and emotional labour, a new work design model has become increasingly popular since its inception in 2001, the *agile (self-)management system*, which serves to expose previously unseen aspects of work. Agile inverts the relationship between the machine and the body, in which, because technology changes, workers are told to expect constant workplace transformation and to thus constantly self-manage the effects of incessant change and to become subjectively 'agile' in line with the work design model they are expected to adopt. The second section makes suggestions for theorizing how agile self-management requires intensified affective labour, which is tied to self-tracking experiences of such changes and data creation for (potentially) intensified management processes with which the impact of workplace change can be assessed.

The final section then presents a case study highlighting worker responses and resistance to participation in a corporate-led worker tracking experiment locally known as the Quantified Workplace, in Rotterdam, Netherlands, where tracking technologies were implemented to manage corporate change towards a merger with a larger company alongside an 'agile' work design model. The case study demonstrates accelerated attempts to quantify affective labour under conditions of continual transformations of digitalized workplaces and of raising expectations of productivity and wellness. The case study provides a precise example of digitalized management methods (Moore & Joyce, 2020) in which systems and devices were introduced to track and measure affective and emotional labour for agility. These forms of personalized change management methods quickly revealed the tensions inherent to these methods, as workers became increasingly aware both of personal experiences of affective and emotional labour, but also became sensitized to the possible impacts and implications of these activities. Of particular interest is the high level of disengagement and resistance to the Quantified Workplace experiment, demonstrating the issues of alienation and control surrounding such corporate initiatives in change management, as well as performance management, when bound up with new workplace surveillance technologies.

## Quantified Work

Here, I outline the literature to which this paper contributes and the surrounding social context. While interest in self-tracking and self-archiving has a longer history (see Moore, 2018a), the term 'quantified self' was popularized from 2008 (Lupton, 2013: 26) and refers to the interest in optimization through intensified personalized tracking practices with the use of technologies first introduced in medical and fitness circles. The term the *quantified self* became increasingly widespread throughout the media because of a range of Quantified Self events starting in Silicon Valley, driven by WIRED founding editor Kevin Kelly and journalist Gary Wolf in 2012/13. From that point, quantified self literature emerged, advanced by Deborah Lupton (2012) and including the work of Crawford et al. (2015), Nafus (2016), Pantzar and Ruckenstein (2015), Ruckenstein (2014), and Schüll (2016). This literature addresses important questions of identity, self-governance, knowledge, optimization, control, regulation and reflection and implications for social interaction, as big data are gleaned from bodies in ways only hinted at when items such as the weight scale (Crawford et al., 2015), stethoscope, stopwatch and Taylor's own michronometer were first invented.

The quantified self literature contributes to body studies and research on affect in that it looks closely at how bodies are measured using increasingly intimate practices with ever more precise measuring technologies, often in the pursuit of idealized self-knowledge or what I have called the 'autonomic self', which could be understood in the quantified self-context as a 'self 'that would otherwise not be knowable' except with the help of new technologies that aid in biometric and physiological analyses (Moore, 2018a). Body-studies debates are outlined in Blackmann's special issue on *Affect* (2010: 1) in the journal *Body & Society*, in which a cross-disciplinary set of concepts emerging from feminism, sociology, anthropology, cultural history and philosophy are calibrated to identify more recent themes of objects and practices in studies of technologies and labour. As stated, Lupton has led the debates on the quantified self and thus body studies, most recently warning about the function creep of dataveillance as it pervades ever-increasing spheres of life, including the body and social experiences. Lupton throws light on cases of self-tracking 'where the choice to participate may be limited' (2016b: 3). Here, I intend to build upon Lupton's argument, arguing that beyond self-improvement pursuits, self- and other-tracking is being incorporated into workplaces in increasingly all-consuming ways, the nature of the employment relationship and management practices transforming rapidly.

To address the latest trends in quantification and body measurement studies, I identify a substratum of these debates in quantified self and body studies which I call *quantified work*. This mostly critical literature focuses on the rise in the use of metrics in subordinating the (supposed) body to the (supposed) mind, whereby calculation is inherently cognitive (Moore & Robinson, 2016), surplus value is captured (Till, 2014), privacy is at stake (Ajana, 2017; Moore & Piwek, 2017), the risks of psychosocial and physical violence are on the rise (Akhtar & Moore, 2016; Moore, 2018b), working time is unpaid (Hayes & Moore, 2016), power is deployed through metrics (Beer, 2016), control is enacted within the labour process via tracking technologies (Thompson & Briken, 2017; Moore & Joyce, 2020), reputations are constantly at stake (Gandini, 2016), and worker quantification facilitates the social reproduction of capitalism (Jarrett, 2016), invisibilizes labour in digital environments (Silberman & Irani, 2016) and intentionally masks 'unseen' labour (Moore, 2018a; see also Fuchs, 2014). Self-tracking for health and wellbeing can be placed in the context of emerging trends in self-optimization and the political economy of anxiety, couched in the rollback of the welfare state and the rise of austerity, where, within neoliberal social relations, nothing is too precious for commodification and control. Management practices to suit such an environment are sometimes called 'gamification' if they are designed to become a pleasurable aspect of work and are part of a wellness 'syndrome' (Cederström & Spicer, 2015) promoted by corporate productivity and benefit packages.

Quantified work research would further benefit from exploring the ways in which measurement and quantification are theorized, as seen for instance in Engster's research on the technique of measurement in Engster (2017) and the entanglement of measurement, quantification and time (Engster, 2014), Elden's work on Heidegger and the politics of time and space (2005), and Porter (1996) on the perceived objectivity in numbers and on the ways algorithms are increasingly used for decision-making or are substituted for adequate human intervention (O'Neil, 2016; Pasquale, 2015). So, to begin this debate and to contribute to this trajectory of thinking, in particular contributing to feminist body studies and the emerging quantified work literature, the present chapter highlights new entanglements in labour processes in which techniques for quantifying affect and emotional labour begin to penetrate subjectivities and bodies.

## Responding Effectively: Affective Labour for Agility

In 2001, 17 software developers, disillusioned with bureaucracy and obstacles to technological development, wrote the *Agility Manifesto* (The Agile Movement, 2008):

> We are uncovering better ways of developing

software by doing it and helping others do it.

Through this work we have come to value:

Individuals and interactions over processes and tools

Working software over comprehensive documentation

Customer collaboration over contract negotiation

*Responding to change* over following a plan [my italics]

That is, while there is value in the items on

the right, we value the items on the left more.

This manifesto reflected the sentiment of other IT workers, who felt the standard waterfall system used in factories was ineffectual for software development (Agile Movement, 2008). Agile approaches 'help teams respond to unpredictability through incremental, iterative work cadences and empirical feedback. Agilists propose alternatives to waterfall, or traditional sequential development' (The Agile Movement, 2008).

After its birth in 2001, companies in many industries began to adopt an agile system in which both workers and management were to have the 'ability over time to respond quickly and effectively to rapid change and high uncertainty' (Joroff et al., 2003: 294). Agile is a 'co-evolution of workplace and work'; an adaptation of ***kaizen***, or 'continuous improvement' (Danford et al., 2008); 'neither top-down nor bottom-up: it is outside-in' (Denning, 2015), relying on the conscious co-evolution and improvement of work which happens through 'experimentation, integration and disseminated learning' (Joroff et al., 2003: 294). 'Agile' has been appropriated into mainstream management terminology and job descriptions, even though it is unpopular with workers precisely because it breeds uncertainty, as the Chartered Institute for Personnel (CIPD) indicates in *Getting Smart About Agile Working* (2014).

While this set of management practices is heralded as a highly normative, horizontal system, its initiators made several assumptions and overlooked specific features of its operations that have and will have ongoing implications for workers. The Agile Manifesto inverts the hierarchy between humans and machines in which humans must be continuously transformative because technology is apparently continuously transforming. In the agile method, humans are expected not only to become subject to rapid technological change and to self-manage these processes through affective labour but to actually emulate machines, which are expected to continuously develop and change, and to embrace constant subjective transformations. Meanwhile, workers are subject to increasingly intimate tracking and monitoring, with their every move surveilled. Agile workers are prepared for constant change, happy to make personal changes, always on the move, always trackable.

The opening scroll for the film *Bladerunner* introduces the Nexus 6 replicants as being 'superior in strength and agility [to humans], and at least equal in intelligence'. Robots are perceived to be agile and we are competing directly with them at this stage in labour history. Agility pushes calculation practices into the affective realm through the quantification and measurement of people's abilities to withstand incessant transformation of work/life as dictated by machinic transformation. Personal investment in self-managing agility requires constant social reproduction of a company's image by workers aligning themselves with the identities and preferences proffered by the company (Land & Taylor, 2010). Workers cannot log out or switch off (Gregg, 2011) and 'struggle to be left alone rather than to be included, a type of refusal that would have looked strange to their Fordist predecessors' (Fleming, 2015: 83). Humans have long used machines as tools, but now, devices identify our activities and aid management judgements at ever more intimate levels, as though we are the tools, playing a role in almost accidentally restructuring the parameters in which we work, behind the smoke and mirrors of inevitability. Lefebvre warns that 'the worker, instead of manipulating a tool, now serves a machine' (1991: 344).

Affective and emotional labour are part of the social reproductive labour that facilitates the processes of agile, where unseen work serves to allow the continuation of capitalist labour relations and the reproduction of capitalist subjectivities (Dalla Costa & James, 1972; Dowling, 2016;

Fortunati & Fleming, 1995; Haider & Mohandesi, 2015; Hoskyns & Rai, 2007; Jarrett, 2015; Kofman, 2012; Kofman & Raghuram, 2015; Weeks, 2011), forms of labour that become a 'moral' obligation imposed by corporate power, where subjectivities are required to be resilient to instability and where subjects take responsibility for personal wellness rather than associating stress and illness with poor working conditions. This moves worker resilience into the realm of a 'necessary part of social and ecological assemblages, which passes through the unconscious field' (Firth, 2016: 131).

Affective labour refers to 'forms of labour that produce and circulate states of being, feelings of well-being, desire, ease and passion' (Read, 2003: 128), which occur at a pre-visceral stage of experience. While affective labour is usually expected of women, it:

> [...] does not refer to gender specific forms of work although at times [it is] defined as 'women's work'. AL refers to the interactive character of work, to its capacity to promote flows of communication, thus it is polyvalent with regard to the activities associated with it. (Federici, 2011: 63)

Affective labour reaches below, behind and above the corporeal. Measuring it is a form of management control by means of the 'modulation of affect' (Bogard, 2010) by recording bodily capabilities, as in the study outlined below, by providing self-tracking devices, and thus potentially controlling resistance.

Not identical to affective labour, the term 'emotional labour' was first coined by Hochschild (2012 [1983]) in 1983, illustrating self-management of emotion at work, be it by suppressing anger or frustration with customers or co-workers, or by providing entertainment and producing joy. Hochschild outlined such labour required of cabin crew and in debt collection work. Brook lists the work of 'nurses, Disneyland workers, retail and childcare workers, schoolteachers, psychotherapists, holiday representatives, call-centre workers, bar staff, waiters and many others' (2009: 8) as requiring emotional labour. Firth states that emotion 'usually refers to an individuated physical feeling (not mental or intellectual) that is passive (not active) and has a more-or-less irrational relationship to the world and outer life'. Altomonte (2015) notes that Hochschild focuses on corporate control over emotional and affective labour through explicit commodification.

Limited to the corporeal, agile labourers do not engage in creative production using their own affective and emotional capacities. They are engaged in a type of repression by which the subordinate performances required corrode their own psychosomatic and bodily wellbeing; people are compelled to self-manage the impacts of seemingly inevitable workplace change through affective labour. Management attempts to externally regulate and modulate all areas of labour and to externalize any costs that are part of this process. In the case of the Quantified Workplace project outlined below, workers became conscious of their own affective and emotional labour, which are classified here as falling within the areas of stress, subjective productivity and wellbeing, again, in the context of a corporate merger and a move towards agile systems. While affect is, by definition, innumerable and outputs are potentially only seen as 'disembodied exhaust' (Smith, 2016) or contrived data proxies, it has historically been invisibilized and all socially reproductive labour has been excluded from payment systems. However, the pursuit of including affective labour in management systems is no longer carried out in order to pay for it, but because worker disengagement, resistance or collapse could reduce the company's 'bottom line'.

Emphasizing empowerment, Hardt and Negri (2000) illustrate affect and immaterial labour from a post-Fordist perspective as providing opportunities for resistance, collective subjectivities and the formation of communities. Debates have been dominated by these authors' English-language publications despite myriad other publications in German, French, Portuguese, Italian and Spanish-speaking spheres (Atzert et al., 2002; Atzert & Müller, 2004; Birkner & Foltin, 2006; Lazzarato et al., 1998; Piper et al., 2007; Corsani et al., 1996; Brumaria, Issue 7 2006; Blondeau et al., 2004; Borio et al., 2002; Lazzarato, 1997, cited in Dowling et al., 2007: 1, 2). The emphasis on affect in management strategies can be seen, on the other hand, as being tied up with labour control and social reproduction of capitalist subjectivity and relations of masked coercion (Hartmann, 1976; Hochschild, 2012 [1983]; Jarrett, 2016). While affect enables or disables our power to act through the body and its power lies in its singularity and universality (Negri, 1999: 85),[2] attempted

[2] The philosophers Merleau-Ponty, Irigaray, Foucault, Deleuze and Guattari are responsible for reviving and continuing affect research, which began with Spinoza's postulation on affect in Ethics Part III def 3. Clough illustrates the 'turn' to affect (2007, 2008), and Gregg and Seigworth (2010) note that interest was further piqued in 1995 with two

corporate colonization of affective labour has become endemic in post-Fordist management and post-bureaucratic techniques precisely because the worker solidarity that becomes possible via the effect humans can have on one another, inspiring empathy and collectivity, would lead to the most difficult form of resistance to stop, since affect ***already infiltrates all of life***.

While affective labour can involve a project that is productive of communities or 'constituting a form of life' (Hardt, 1999: 99), affective labour also involves negotiation of the penetration of capitalist management, now enhanced with a range of technologies outlined in the case study below. In this sense, affect, which as Weeks argues is a feature of reproductive labour, is not separable from capitalism (2007, 2011) but involves preparatory and even defensive labour. So, in this sense, management systems have begun to seek to capture and control affective labour in part so that management can predict worker collapse under the paradoxical weight of agility, but also because when workers become conscious of affect, or their power to act, they also become conscious of their ability to impact one another and to potentially collectively challenge abuses at work (Moore, 2018a). Rather than providing a buffer against the strains of work, new initiatives place unprecedented pressures on workers to cope with popular agile systems which accept the inevitability of constant transformation, a key tenet in Western modernity (Featherstone, 2010: 200) that is now being accelerated.

pieces, Massumi's 'The Autonomy of Affect' (1995) and Sedgwick and Frank's 'Shame in the Cybernetic Fold: Reading Silvan Tomkins'. Blackman (2010) edited the special issue *Affect*, placing research in the field of body studies, with possibility and without image, emphasizing collective intelligence and affective engagement where it emerges. Blackman led discussions in feminist and queer studies perspectives, touching on relations of entanglement and the prowess of intersubjectivity and relationality (2008a, 2008b, 2011, 2012). Colman identified the affective feminist self (2010) and later, Wetherell (2015) critically outlined affect research, calling for a better ontological programme in which questions of emotion, pre-physiological experience and affective transmission and potentials are less bewildered. A by no means exhaustive list of further research includes Clough (2008), Colman (2008, 2010), Gill and Pratt (2008), Coleman (2012), Thrift (2004), Berlant (2011), Haider and Mohandesi (2015) and the edited collection by Karatzogianni and Kuntsman (2012). Two recent issues in 2016 and 2017 on *Affective Capitalism* for ephemera and *Thinking Critically About Affect in Organizational Studies* in organization demonstrate studies on affect continue to be cross-disciplinary. This research, however, does not address the areas of affective labour and quantification systems addressed in this chapter.

The process whereby affective and emotional labour are quantified involves attempts to capture 'invisible labour', which in feminist literature refers to work that goes unrecognized and overlooked (Crain et al., 2016). Through agile systems, then, capital attempts to turn the use-value in affective labour into an exchange, turning the concrete into divisibilities and abstractions, thus commodifying affect and circumventing resistance. Affective labour, however, is not invisibilized without intention. Invisibility has the potential for revelation, but regulations for its viewing are already authored within specific parameters, dictating what is permissible, what is 'seen' and thus what is measured, which is a basic premise for the theory of working time (Hayes & Moore, 2016).

However, what is not counted in workplaces is as important as, if not more important than, what is counted (Cherry, 2016). Processes to monitor and track work using more intimate tracking methods as seen in the Quantified Workplace project may bring working time to the fore, may render it 'seen', but will not necessarily result in remuneration. Heidegger's point that 'calculation refuses to let anything appear except what is countable' (1998: 235) is relevant here, where numeration associated with work may be revealed, but only for a limited purpose. Instead, the hitherto externally invisible aspects of labour are revealed, but increasingly under the microscope of responsibilization and potentially in the context of 'digital nihilism' (Gregg, 2015), where constant productivity tracking in accordance with the mantra of 'Getting Things Done' hyper-individualizes workers. Indeed, Gregg (2010) outlines active blockages to affective communication through pseudo office intimacy created by such activities as Secret Santas. In cases of 'gig work', both online and offline (Moore & Joyce, 2020), individual workers become accountable for reputations that are recounted by algorithm (Gandini et al., 2016); leaving little room for qualitative depiction of visibilized selfhood or non-competitive communities.

Some have equated self-tracking with forms of Taylorization (Morozov, 2013), whereby Taylorism is a 'rationalization of body-machine-management relations' (Von Osten, 2011: 135). In the 1980s, the increasing use of computer technologies in various industries and services was 'not merely to displace traditional skills' but 'also to monitor and hence discipline the remaining workforce' (Hyman, 1987: 37). The selection of, and now imminent resignation to, technology and its predictable unpredictability, is 'a social and political and not merely technical question' (Hyman, 1987: 37). Hyman cites Murray (1985), stating that: ‘computer programmes that are written to control the new systems of production are geared to control labour rather than to emancipate it’ (Hyman, 1987: 37). However, contemporary digitalized wellness tracking practices at work could also be rooted in the Human Relations school, where Mayo and his followers investigated wellness and fatigue as linked to early measurement techniques in the Harvard Fatigue Lab (O’Neil, 2017; Moore, 2018a).

Preparation for the agile workplace extends beyond the types of training and visibilizing of affective labour and requires specific management methods to gain insights about its value and thus to exploit it, rather than to exclusively identify how successfully workers please clients noted in customer feedback systems. Take waitressing for example, where a training manual tells servers to be:

> [...] concerned and dependable and maybe a little provocative. I am myself, the self I most want to be. I am committed to you and I will delight you. This is how we co-produce the product of my labour: your dining experience. (Dowling, 2012: 111)

Feedback is also disseminated by virtue of affective and immaterial relations; a customer may recommend a restaurant at no extra cost to the restaurant owner (Nunes, 2007: 189). Cognitive behavioural therapy and related psychology highlight emotional and affect regulation for stress management entitled Affect Regulation (Psychology Tools, 2016). Indeed, affect ‘shadows every event’, Ducey indicates, and events in care work necessitate affective labour, where the ‘power to act’ is reduced through widespread underappreciation of this type of work. Ducey looks at how health worker training incorporated a discourse and methods designed to aid in people’s affect, or their power to act, given endemic obstacles of institutional and emotional difficulties in this work (Ducey, 2007).

The agility system is a new frontier for prescribing externalized quantification of labour and ascribing (under)value to affective labour, depleting possibilities for subjects to pursue what Deleuze and Guattari call *becoming minoritarian* in the sense of a universal figure of consciousness, leading to real ‘autonomy’ (1987: 106). However, humans do not possess ‘authentic’ selves existing outside of capitalism along the lines Hochschild considered. Rather, the sheer possibility of there being an ‘authentic’ self is commodified by wellness tracking management methods. Arruzza notes that the 'the social management of affects is not an invention of capitalism' whereby emotions are intentionally 'detached from us and constructed as interchangeable and measurable things that can be exchanged on the market or as skills that add to our labour power' (2014: n. p.). Some radical studies of the laws of value postulate that there *is* an 'outside' of capital that cannot be quantified (Negri transl Hardt, 1999: 86). Federici argues there is no longer a conceivable 'outside' as long as we live in a capitalist hegemony (2004). Indeed, digitalized control practices surrounding agile management systems complement a range of neoliberal norms in working life which serve to subsume all aspects of everyday life to capital in which workers are permanently alienated from their product, from one another and from themselves. Along these lines, new technologies are instrumental for subsumption and alienation, monitoring technologies quantifyng the qualitative and revealing previously unmeasured aspects of the labour process, like mood, fatigue, psychological wellbeing, subjective self-awareness, sensitivity to privacy, stress and, in the study below, further forms of affective and emotional labour.

Agility and new forms of worker tracking make workers permanently visible to management and render the sites of everyday resistance facilitated by worker-to-worker communication penetrable by management, meaning it is increasingly difficult to identify *any* outside to digitalized capitalism. New management methods, with influences from both Taylorist and Human Relations disciplines, exceed the study of physical movements seen in scientific management. Concrete labour, or work that the labourer herself explicitly enjoys the proceeds of, is subject to abstraction, and workers to alienation, in agile conditions. So, while measuring and monitoring work is not completely new, it has reached unprecedented levels in attempts to measure and commodify affect, whereby.

> [...] even if the measurement of this new productive reality is impossible, because affect is not measurable, nonetheless in this very productive context, so rich in productive subjectivity, *affect must be controlled*. (Negri, 1999: 87)

Hence quantification recognizes affective and emotional labour as productive, not as an exchange worthy of consistent reward (Jarrett, 2016), but to locate profit for capital.

The following section outlines fieldwork results from the author's study of one quantified corporate wellness initiative which the company entitled the Quantified Workplace. Project participants were, of course, not *explicitly* asked to self-track 'affective and emotional labour' by management in the experiment, but our findings show that via their tracking for 'stress', 'subjective productivity' and 'wellbeing', alongside physical movement, heart rate and sleep, this is what occurred. Framing affective and emotional labour as facilitative of change management at a personal level, and taking place in the midst of a corporate transformation of both a merger and a management shift to an agile system, the project reveals a feature of the quantified worker trend in which less-explored terrain in worker measurement becomes, potentially, an arena for management control.

## The Quantified Workplace

The Quantified Workplace project was run by a single company over a period of 12 months from 2015–2016 in the Netherlands, whereby the company distributed Fitbit Charge HR Activity Trackers devices to 30 employees and installed Rescuetime tracking software on their work computers. The company provided individualized dashboards as well as a shared dashboard where all data from these tracking activities was stored and made visible to all other participants. Participants also received workday lifelog emails asking them to rate their *stress*, *subjective productivity* and *wellbeing* on a Likert scale from 1–5 for each item.

The project took place during a period of change management as one multinational real estate company absorbed a smaller company of mostly work design consultants. The smaller company suggested and led the Quantified Workplace, as part of their way of indicating innovation and good practice to the larger company into which they were being merged. Funded by the British Academy/Leverhulme small grant scheme, the current author's role was to conduct independent academic research on the study via surveys and interviews. My co-investigators and I were also provided limited access to quantified and self-report data (where participants consented).

The Quantified Workplace project manager indicated that her/his intentions were to help workers adapt to an agile and mobile working environment and to see to what extent employees' self-awareness, stress, wellbeing and 'wellbilling' (which s/he described as the amount of revenue an employee generates for the company) would be impacted during the period of transition. The company was interested in comparing subjectively and objectively measured productivity, as linked to health and activity tracking and 'billability' (interview with Moore 05/10/15).

Research collected over the course of the year this project ran reveals that workers were expected to self-manage any emotional or physical impacts of the change, and self-report via daily lifelog emails representing a year's worth of data on this process. Workers reported increased workloads and increased expectations for travel resulting from the corporate merger. While the present study did not link specific change expectations to specific forms of affective and emotional labour, there was a notable rise in areas of personalized change management expectations, as became clear via results from data gathering exercises both by the company itself and in our own surveys and interviews. For example, the workday lifelog email about stress, subjective productivity and wellbeing, provided management with ways to cross-check productivity scores across individuals' perceptions and what we indicate involves affective and emotional labour, while also increasing workloads and responsibilities.

Interviewees readily shared their own experiences of the impact of corporate merger, noting heightened awareness of waning privacy, given the new tracking practices being rolled out, stress resulting from increased workloads and expectations for travel and mobility of work expected, feelings about individual autonomy, and greater sensitization to physical and psychological wellness. Findings based on surveys and interviews showed that the highest increases in participants' expressions about the rise in affective and emotional labour, from the first set of surveys and interviews at the beginning of the Quantified Workplace project, and the final surveys and interviews, conducted in the final weeks of the project, related to feelings of increased autonomy, concern for privacy and a sense of the need for support and coaching.

The data we obtained on people's views on privacy are related to affective labour, because, for example, awareness of desire for privacy is generated from a pre-visceral sense that becomes labour when it becomes a defence mechanism against changing management practices such as corporate merger and the introduction of self-tracking at work.

'Autonomy' is typically defined as the level of control workers have over work tasks, schedules and decisions (Wheatley, 2017), which differs from the autonomist school readings, where autonomy is linked to subjectivity and emancipation. Interviewees were asked about their 'feelings of autonomy', which can be seen as a moderator of emotional and affective labour (see Johnson & Spector, 2007) because it demonstrates an arena of intimately personalized change management in which workers, despite experiencing increased workloads during the period of merger, gained feelings of independence and acted upon them. The improvement of feelings of autonomy coheres with assumptions about the capabilities of electronic devices to empower and automate specific aspects of work that were perhaps once 'ana-logged'. While the increases in autonomy could be perceived as a step towards worker resistance, sitting alongside positive feelings of autonomy, the second highest increase in the category of affective labour was participants' sensitivity to privacy.[3]

Workers' responses in interviews showed some individual increases in awareness of activities that fall outside traditional work parameters we classify as falling into the categories of affective and emotional labour. This is seen in such responses as:

> I see when I'm frustrated my heartbeat is higher.

> [Participation in Quantified Workplace makes me] more conscious of activity, heart rates and wellbeing.

> I learned about my feeling of productivity, so productivity has nothing to do with invoices we can send to our clients and before I was thinking, okay, productivity is like just hours I'm working for my clients, but sometimes I feel very productive, just the internal things, so therefore it helps, the way I think about productivity.

[3] In the first interviews, three comments indicate concern about what personal data management had access to, increasing to 21 in the final interviews. More than half of participants in a separate ADP survey expressed concern about the amount of personal data that employers can access via wearable technology (ADP, 2015). Attitudes towards privacy vary across countries, with 60% of German and a high number of British workers expressing reservations, while only 36% of Dutch employees have reservations about personal privacy at work (ADP, 2015). Based on that study, Quantified Workplace participants' concern for privacy was above average for the Netherlands, and interestingly, participation intensified sensitivity. In some cases, workers tend to feel devices 'spy' on them (*The Week*, 2015).

> I'm more aware of the productivity, I think that's it. It's not that I directly improve my productivity, but I'm more aware of at what moments I'm productive, yeah, but that's the next step, to base some actions on that.

> I'm sure it makes you aware of things you do.

One participant indicated that s/he became more aware of her/his physical body via participation in the project:

> I think awareness is even more key than completely changing behaviour, but that you are more aware of your body and what the problems for it are and that you address that and start to organize your agenda around it.

There was a high dropout rate among participants, 75% leaving before the end of the project. There was also a high rate of increase in people indicating they had stopped using the technologies continuously, some 73%. Research results demonstrate both passive resistance, based on interview discussions, and active resistance, based on active withdrawal. While it was not possible to interview those participants who had dropped out of the project by the time the second set of interviews were held, the survey and some interviews demonstrated difficulties in using the technology as well as high levels of uncertainty about the validity and usefulness of the project, which may have applied to others who stopped participating in the project:

> A big question for me and for a few others as well, is uh, how reliable the FitBit is.

> [...] this thing [FitBit] might be more intelligent than just recording my data.

One respondent in the second interviews indicated frustration:

> I don't get any answers, I just fill in my things, but I don't get an answer as to whether it's good or not, I just want to know if I was good and just start working.

For those who stayed with the project, responses to the question 'How/have your thoughts about the Quantified Workplace project changed?' in the second stage of interviews showed further resistance, including statements such as:

> I still have doubts about the project. And I don't wear the Fitbit very often. And when I do wear it, it is for myself and to see how active I am.

> It confirmed the thoughts I had in the beginning. It is better to change your behaviour based on your feelings rather than a device.

> After monitoring my workplace behaviour over a couple of months I found out that it didn't change a lot.

> I didn't learn very much from it.

It became clear that the Quantified Workplace project was implemented to help employees self-manage the impact of corporate changes and produce data about these processes of what I have identified to be emotional and affective labour, which are areas of work that have historically been ignored by management. Data-driven technology acquired information about workers' experiences of workplace changes. Given quantification allows for seemingly 'objective reason and disinterested rationality' (Beer, 2016: 49), the very real possibility is that this kind of practice masks the intensification of performance management. New tracking technologies and their applications neutralize actions taken on the basis of big data accumulated and facilitate the new arena of human resource management known as 'personal analytics'. Tracking technologies are the measure, and workers' collapse is the risk.

## Conclusion

New uses of technologies in the quantified workplace are part of an emerging form of updated Taylorism, that is, processes of subordination in which quantification of new areas of work through tracking technologies may help corporations keep up with cut-throat competition. In the long term, this approach may subsume life to capital to an unsustainable degree, destroying any possibility of a qualitative outside to capitalism, which both provides the basis for capitalist relations (as use-value, labour-power, desire) and is likely to trigger continued resistance and worker struggle. At the least, we can speak of declining welfare for workers and the associated regime of total mobilization and surveillance as they corrode workers' health and safety and create anxiety, burnout and overwork. Neoliberalism continues to portray such problems as workers' failures to adapt, personal psychological shortcomings or educational deficits. They are, rather, systematic effects of a particular labour process (Moore & Joyce, 2020).

Capital is tempted to invest in new technology not because it may improve the public good, regardless of the rhetoric of wellness that informs current wellbeing initiatives for workers, but rather because it can increase its profit ratios: and this chapter has outlined the most recent innovations in doing so. But quantification of affective and emotional labour assumes that all performers start at an equal level of competence to play such a game of survival and to thrive. Existing skills, working time capacity and/or access to social capital are ignored. These assumptions can easily result in unequal judgements and appraisals or are seen as inducing extra stress and leading to work intensification and speed-up. Indeed, management did not reveal their subsequent use of data from the Quantified Workplace project to the current author (nor, it seems to the participants), but the possibilities are clear. The General Data Protection Regulation (GDPR), rolled out in May 2018, will deal with some of the risks that new forms of data gathering in workplaces introduce, by requiring transparency and consent as well as human intervention into any decision-making using automated and algorithmic data collection (Moore, 2017).

Power relations in capitalist reproduction reflect Marx's critiques, but now more than ever before machines are the symbols for 'the ordering of life itself' (Merchant, 1990: 227), accelerating the labour process and dragging workers with them. Workers' responses and explicit disengagement with the case study outlined above demonstrate awareness to the tensions surrounding new control mechanisms, ongoing struggles in the contemporary labour process, in which agile is a key meme, and the urgency of reviewing of all-of-life management strategies. Workers are required to carry out further forms of affective and emotional labour to self-manage transformations and to become agile subjects under a perpetual state of alienation. The corporate project reported here demonstrates that agile systems rely on workers' affective labour to self-manage external transformation because, as the *Agile Manifesto* makes clear, technology inevitably transforms, meaning workers must inevitably transform too, but only according to some set and quantified criteria. While the power reversal between humans and machines is assumed, agility as a system does not fully crystallize what is at stake for workers: the (im)possibility of a life outside of capitalism and beyond externalized parameters for data acquisition about working lives, encroaching alienation and subsumption as the surpluses of affective and emotional labour are perpetually abstracted, and the acceleration of the calculation of everyday lives within neoliberal capitalism, where people are increasingly told to 'measure your way out of misery' (Cain, 2017). Indeed, significant worker resistance to the Quantified Workplace project indicates that new digitalized management practices are not a *fait accompli*. Future research must focus on how alienated workers respond to such methods of measurement in workplaces and identify the emerging psychosocial and even physical risks that workers face in newly quantified workplaces (Moore, 2018b).

## References

Ajana, B. (2017). Digital health and the biopolitics of the quantified self. *Digital Health, 3*, 1–18.

Akhtar, P., & Moore, P. (2016). The psycho-social impacts of technological change in contemporary workplaces and trade union responses. *International Journal of Labour Research, 8*(1–2), 102–131.

Altomonte, G. (2015, August 8). Affective labour in the post-fordist transformation. *Public Seminar*. http://www.publicseminar.org/2015/05/affective-labor-in-the-post-fordist-transformation/. Accessed 9 April 2018.

Arruzza, C. (2014, August 14). The capitalism of affects. *Public Seminar*. http://www.publicseminar.org/2014/08/the-capitalism-of-affects/. Accessed 9 April 2018.

Automatic Data Processing (ADP). (2015). Tools and technology: Europe at a glance. http://www.adp.co.uk/adp-news/latest-pressreleases/enm/33537/1/putting-wearables-to-work-new-technology-could-revolutionise-the-workplace. Accessed 9 April 2018.

Beer, D. (2016). *Metric power*. Palgrave Macmillan.

Blackman, L. (2008a). The body: The key concepts. Oxford, New York: Berg.

———. (2008b). Affect, relationality and the problem of personality. *Theory, Culture & Society, 25*(1), 27–51.

———. (2010). Affect, special issue. *Body & Society, 16*(1).

———. (2011). Affect, performance and queer subjectivities. *Cultural Studies, 25*(2), 183–199.

———. (2012). *Immaterial bodies: Affect, embodiment, mediation*. London and New York: Sage.

Bogard, W. (2010). Digital resisto(e)rs. *CTheory*, 4–21.

Brook, P. (2009). The alienated heart: Hochschild's emotional labour thesis and the anti-capitalist politics of alienation. *Capital and Class, 33*(2), 7–31.

Cain, R. (2017, September 18). *Measure your own misery self-quantification and the techno-recovery imperative in mental health 'mHealth' discourse*. Presentation, International Initiatives in Promoting Political Economy (IIPPE), Berlin.

Cederström, C., & Spicer, A. (2015). *The wellness syndrome*. Polity Press.

Chartered Institute for Personnel Development (CIPD). (2014). *Getting smart about Agile working*. https://www.cipd.co.uk/knowledge/strategy/change/agile-working-report. Accessed 9 April 2018.

Cherry, M. A. (2016). People analytics and invisible labor. *Saint Louis University Law Journal, 61*(1), 1–16.

Colman, F. (2010). Affective self: Feminist thinking and feminist actions. *Contemporary French and Francophone Studies, 14*(5), 543–552.

Crain, M., Poster, W., & Cherry, M. (2016). *Invisible labour: Hidden work in the contemporary world*. University of California Press.

Crawford, K., Lingen, J., & Karpii, T. (2015). Our metrics, ourselves: A hundred years of self-tracking from the weight scale to the wrist wearable device. *European Journal of Cultural Studies, 18*(4–5), 479–496.

Dalla Costa, M., & James, S. (1972). *The power of women and the subversion of community* (England First edition). Butler and Tanner Ltd.

Danford, A., Richardson, M., Stewart, P., Tailby, S., & Upchurch, M. (2008). Partnership high performance work systems and quality of working life. *New Technology Work and Employment, 23*(3), 151–166.

Deleuze, G., & Guattari, F. (1987). *A thousand plateaus: Capitalism and Schizophrenia*. University of Minnesota Press.

Denning, S. (2015, July 22). How to make the whole organisation agile. *Forbes*. https://www.forbes.com/sites/stevedenning/#60fa15e41b2d. Accessed 9 April 2018.

Dewart McEwen, K. (2017). Self-tracking practices and digital (re)productive labour. *Philosophy and Technology, 31*, 235–251. https://doi.org/10.1007/s13347-017-0282-2.

Dowling, E. (2012). The waitress: On affect method and (re)presentation. *Cultural Studies—Critical Methodologies, 12*(2), 109–117.

Dowling, E. (2016). Valorised but not valued: Affective remuneration, social reproduction and feminist politics beyond the crisis. *British Politics, 11*(4), 452–468.

Dowling, E., Nunes, R., & Trott, B. (2007). Immaterial and affective labour: Explored. *Ephemera, 7*(1), 1–7.

Ducey, A. (2007). More than a job: Meaning affect and training health care workers. In P. Clough & J. Halley (Eds.), *The affective turn: Theorising the social* (pp. 187–208). Duke University Press.

Elden, S. (2005). *Speaking against number: Heidegger, language and the politics of calculation*. Edinburgh University Press.

Engster, F. (2014). *Das Geld als Maß, Mittel und Methode: Das Rechnen mit der Identität der Zeit*. Neofelis Verlag.

Engster, F. (2017). Geist, Logik, Kapital und die Technik des Maßes, in Russel, E-J, Engster, F. Dead Dogs Never Die. *Revista Opinião Filosófica, 7*(1), 137–205.

Featherstone, M. (2010). Body image and affect in consumer culture. *Body & Society, 16*(1), 193–221.

Federici, S. (2004). *Caliban and the witch: Women the body and primitive accumulation*. Autonomedia.

Federici, S. (2011). On affective labour. In M. A. Peters, & E. Bulut (Eds.), *Cognitive capitalism: Education and digital labour*. Peter Lang.

Firth, R. (2016). Somatic pedagogies: Critiquing and resisting the affective discourse of the neoliberal state from an embodied anarchist perspective. *Ephemera, 16*(4), 121–142.

Fleming, P. (2015). *Resisting work: The corporatisation of life and is discontents*. University Press.

Fortunati, L., & Fleming, J. (1995). *The arcane of reproduction: Housework prostitution labour and capital*. Autonomedia.

Fuchs, C. (2014). *Digital labour and Karl Marx*. Routledge.

Gandini, A. (2016). *The reputation economy understanding knowledge work in digital society*. Palgrave Macmillan.

Gandini, A., Pais, I., & Beraldo, D. (2016). Reputation and trust on online labour markets: The reputation economy of Lance. *Work Organisation, Labour and Globalisation, 10*(1), 27–43.

Gregg, M. (2010). On Friday night drinks: Workplace affects in the age of the cubicle. In M. Gregg & G. J. Seigworth (Eds.), *The Affect theory reader* (pp. 250–268). Duke University Press.

Gregg, M. (2011). *Work's intimacy*. Wylie.

Gregg, M. (2015). Getting things done: Productivity self-management and the order of things. In M. Petit, S. Paasonen, & K. Hillis (Eds.), *Networked affect* (pp. 187–202). MIT Press.

Haider, A., & Mohandesi, S. (2015). *Social reproduction* (special issue). *Viewpoint Magazine*, 5.

Hardt, M. (1999). Affective labour (A. Negri, Trans.). *Boundary 2*, 26(2), 89–100.

Hardt, M., & Negri, A. (2000). *Empire*. Harvard University Press.

Hartmann, H. (1976). Capitalism, patriarchy, and job segregation by sex. *Signs: Journal of Women in Culture and Society, 1*(3, Part 2), 137–169.

Hayes, L. J. B., & Moore, S. (2016). Care in a time of austerity: The electronic monitoring of homecare workers' time. *Gender, Work and Organisation, 24*(4), 329–344. https://doi.org/10.1111/gwao.12164.

Heidegger, M. (1998). Postscript to 'What is Metaphysics?' (W. McNeill). *Martin Heidegger: Pathmarks*. Cambridge University Press.

Hochschild, A. R. (2012 [1983]). *The managed heart: Commercialisation of human feeling*. University of California Press.

Hoskyns, C., & Rai, S. (2007). Recasting the global political economy: Counting women's unpaid work. *New Political Economy, 12*(3), 297–317.

Hyman, R. (1987). Strategy or structure? Capital, labour and control. *Work, Employment and Society, 1*(1), 25–55.

Jarrett, K. (2015). Devaluing binaries: Marxist feminism and the values of consumer labour. In C. Fuchs, & E. Fisher (Eds.). *Reconsidering value and labour in the digital age*. Springer.

Jarrett, K. (2016). *Feminism labour and digital media: The digital housewife*. Routledge.

Johnson, H.-A., & Spector, P. E. (2007). Service with a smile: Do emotional intelligence, gender, and autonomy moderate the emotional labor process? *Journal of Occupational Health Psychology, 12*(4), 319–333.

Joroff, M. L., Porter, W. L., Feinberg, B., & Kukla, C. (2003). The Agile workplace. *Journal of Corporate Real Estate, 5*(4), 293–311.

Kofman, E. (2012). Rethinking care through social reproduction: Articulating circuits of migration. *Social Politics, 19*(1), 142–162.

Kofman, E., & Raghuram, P. (2015). *Gendered migrations and global social reproduction*. Palgrave.

Land, C., & Taylor, S. (2010). Surf's up: Work life balance and brand in a new age capitalist organization. *Sociology, 44*(3), 395–413.

Lefebvre, H. (1991). *The production of space*. Wiley-Blackwell.

Lupton, D. (2012). M-health and health promotion: The digital cyborg and surveillance society. *Social Theory & Health, 10*(3), 229–244.

Lupton, D. (2013). Understanding the human machine. *IEEE Technnol. Soc. Mag, 32*, 25–30.

Lupton, D. (2016a). *The quantified self: A sociology of self-tracking*. Polity Press.

Lupton, D. (2016b). The diverse domains of quantified selves: Self-tracking modes and dataveillance, *Economy and Society, 45*. https://doi.org/10.1080/03085147.2016.1143726.

Merchant, C. (1990). *The death of nature: Women Ecology and the scientific revolution*. Bravo Ltd.

Moore, P. (2017, December 7). Work and the GDPR: The future for algorithms and people analytics? *Global Judgements and Ideas* (Blog post). https://phoebevmoore.wordpress.com/2017/11/07/the-gdpr-algorithms-and-people-analytics/. Accessed 9 April 2018.

Moore, P. (2018a). *The quantified self in precarity? Work, technology and what counts*. Routledge.

Moore, P. (2018b). *The threat of physical and psychosocial violence and harassment in digitalized work*. Discussion paper, Work Quality Unit, International Labour Organisation, Geneva.

Moore, P., & Joyce, S. (2020). Black box or hidden abode? The expansion and exposure of platform work managerialism. *Review of International Political Economy, 27*(4), 926–948.

Moore, P., & Piwek, L. (2017). Regulating wellbeing in the brave new quantified workplace. *Employee Relations, 39*(3), 308–316.

Moore, P., & Robinson, A. (2016). The quantified self: What counts in the neoliberal workplace. *New Media & Society, 18*(1), 2774–2792.

Morozov, E. (2013). *To save everything, click here: The folly of technological solutionism*. Public Affairs.

Nadworny, M. J. (1955). *Scientific management and the unions 1900–1932: A historical analysis*. Harvard University Press.

Nafus, D. (2016). *Quantified: Biosensing technologies in everyday life*. MIT Press.

Negri, A. (1999). Value and affect (M Hardt, Trans.). *Boundary 2*, 26(2), 77–88.

Nunes, R. (2007). Forward how? Forward where? I: (Post-) Operaismo beyond the immaterial labour thesis. *Ephemera, 7*(1), 178–202.

O'Neil, C. (2016). *Weapons of math destruction: How Big Data increases inequality and threatens democracy*. Penguin Books.

O'Neil, C. (2017). Taylorism, the European science of work, and the quantified self at work. *Science, Technology and Human Values, 42*(4), 600–621.

Pantzar, M., & Ruckenstein, M. (2015). The heart of everyday analytics: Emotional, material and practical extensions in self-tracking market. *Consumption Markets & Culture, 18*(1), 92–109.

Pasquale, F. (2015). *The Black box society: The secret algorithms that control money and information*. Harvard University Press.

Porter, T. M. (1996). *Trust in numbers: The pursuit of objectivity in science and public life*. Princeton University Press.

Psychology Tools. (2016). *Affect regulation / Emotion regulation*. https://psychologytools.com/technique-affect-regulation.html. Accessed 9 April 2018.

Read, J. (2003). *The micro-politics of capital: Marx and the prehistory of the present*. Suny Press.

Ruckenstein, M. (2014). Visualized and interacted life: Personal analytics and engagements with data doubles. *Societies, 4*(1), 68–84.

Schüll, N. (2016). Data for life: wearable technology and the design of self-care. *BioSocieties, 11*(3), 317–333.

Silberman, S., & Irani, L. (2016). Operating an employer reputation system: Lessons from Turkopticon, 2008–2015. *Comparative Labour Law and Policy Journal, 37*(3), 505–541.

Smith, G. J. D. (2016). Surveillance data and embodiment: On the work of being watched. *Body & Society, 22*(2), 108–139.

The Agile Movement. (2008). *Agile methodology*. http://agilemethodology.org/. Accessed 9 April 2018.

The Week. (2015). *The rise of workplace spying*. Staff Analysis. http://theweek.com/articles/564263/rise-workplace-spying.

Thompson, P., & Briken, K. (2017). Actually existing capitalism: Some digital delusion. In K. Briken, S. Chillas, M. Krzywdzinski, & A. Marks (Eds.), *The new digital workplace: How new technologies revolutionise work* (pp. 241–263). Palgrave.

Till, C. (2014). Exercise as labour: Quantified self and the transformation of exercise into labour. *Societies, 4*(3), 446–462.

Von Osten, M. (2011). Unpredictable outcomes / Unpredictable outcasts: On recent debates over creativity and the creative industries. In G. Raunig, G. Ray, & U. Wuggenig (Eds.), *Critique of creativity: Precarity, subjectivity and resistance in the "creative industries"* (pp. 133–146). MayFly.

Weeks, K. (2007). Life within and against work: Affective labor, feminist critique, and post-fordist politics. *Ephemera, Theory & Politics in Organization, 7*(1), 233–249.

Weeks, K. (2011). *The problem with work: Feminism Marxism antiwork politics and postwork imaginaries*. Duke University Press.

Wetherell, M. (2015). Trends in the turn to affect: A social psychological critique. *Body & Society, 21*(2), 139–166.

Wheatley, D. (2017). Autonomy in paid work and employee subjective well-being. *Work and Occupations, 44*(3), 296–328.

# Index

## A



## B



## C





S. Pfeiffer et al. (eds.), *The Agile Imperative*, Dynamics of Virtual Work, https://doi.org/10.1007/978-3-030-73994-2

The manufacturer's authorised representative in the EU is Springer Nature Customer Service Centre GmbH, Europaplatz 3, 69115 Heidelberg, Germany. If you have any concerns regarding our products, please contact ProductSafety@springernature.com

Printed and bound by CPI Group (UK) Ltd, Croydon, CR0 4YY
30/09/2026
02225698-0009